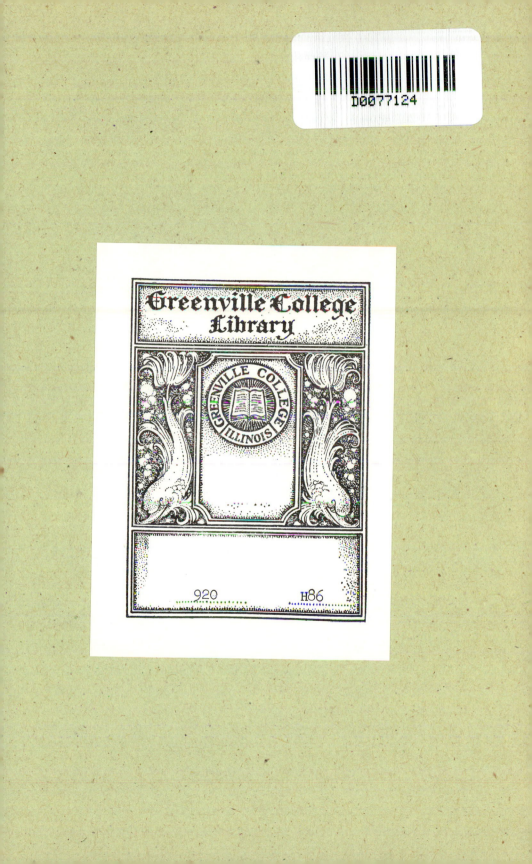

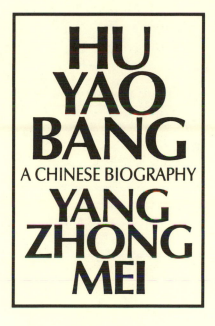

HU YAO BANG

A CHINESE BIOGRAPHY

YANG ZHONG MEI

HU YAO BANG

A CHINESE BIOGRAPHY

YANG ZHONG MEI

TRANSLATED BY WILLIAM A. WYCOFF
EDITED BY TIMOTHY CHEEK

WITH A FOREWORD BY
RUDOLF G. WAGNER

An East Gate Book

M. E. SHARPE, INC.
ARMONK, NEW YORK
LONDON, ENGLAND

An East Gate Book

Copyright © 1988 by M. E. Sharpe, Inc.

Available in the United Kingdom and Europe from M. E. Sharpe,
Publishers, 3 Henrietta Street, London WC2E 8LU.

Library of Congress Cataloging-in-Publication Data

Yang, Zhongmei.
    Hu Yaobang : a chinese biography.

    Bibliography: p.
    Includes index.
    1. Hu, Yao-pang. 2. Statesmen—China—Biography.
I. Cheek, Timothy. II. Title.
DS779.29.H79Y36   1988   951.05′092′4   [B]   88-4518
ISBN 0-87332-457-9

Printed in the United States of America

Despair is as absurd as hope!

—Petöfi Sandor, 1847[1]

Contents

RUDOLF G. WAGNER

Foreword

Hu Yaobang is perhaps the most important and certainly the most controversial animator of the Chinese reforms of the last decade. Yang Zhongmei's biography of this man presents a well-documented record of Hu Yaobang's life and thus greatly enhances our knowledge and understanding of the personalities in the Chinese leadership who were willing, skillful, and powerful enough to opt for this course of radical change although all of them had long records of supporting or initiating orthodox policies along Leninist and Maoist lines.

At the same time, Yang Zhongmei's study presents us with a particular way of writing history and biography, which goes back to older Chinese and to more recent Communist traditions, both of which make for some difference with writings by Western-trained scholars on similar topics.

Yang Zhongmei comes from a well-to-do ("capitalist") family in Shanghai. He was born before the founding of the People's Republic, and his parents at the time expressed their hopes for China's future through their son's given name Zhong-mei, which means "Sino-American." Such a background, and such a name, would have excluded him in other cities from the potential ranks of Red Guards when the Great Proletarian Cultural Revolution started in 1966; not so in Shanghai, where there was a sizable group of people with such "difficult" backgrounds in the schools. Many of them played an active part in this upheaval. Yang Zhongmei had good writing skills and was recruited, as had been many other intellectuals during this period, to become a writer of speeches, articles, and pamphlets for a powerful Shanghai political faction. He worked for a while under Wang Hongwen, the young worker from Shanghai who later rose to become the single "proletarian" member of the much denounced "Gang of Four" around Mao Zedong's wife Jiang Qing. Yang eventually left China for Japan; he now works at Rikkyo University in Tokyo, where he completed his Ph.D. dissertation.

Chinese historiographical tradition is marked by two elements, both of which have survived in the Communist period. First, there is great emphasis on facts. Dates and places are checked and verified, documents ascertained, a factual and chronological historical record established. The appreciation of the scholarly nature of a work is substantially determined by the quality of factual investigation. A mistake in this realm, even if seemingly irrelevant to the character of the person or the event described, will lead to harsh judgments about the scholarly quality of the work. A very large part of research energy is thus invested in verifying the record of the things described.

Second, the basic thrust of historical writing is evaluative. Was it a good man or a bad man? Was the policy good or bad? Was it a progressive action or a reactionary action? These are questions which might seem judgmental, irrelevant, or even unscholarly to Western researchers who are more interested in the inner logic of events; but both in traditional and in modern China, these questions are all-important. As there can be little scholarly discussion about this second aspect where so much depends on value judgments and political beliefs, discussion among scholars focuses on the first aspect, where there is meaningful ground for contention.

Scholars are not beyond politics, however, and it is the rule rather than the exception that the prime motive for some work of historical research is to interfere in some discussion about present politics. Political leaders are well aware of these implications and therefore have time and again intervened with authoritative decisions to change the evaluation on certain historical figures, events, and periods in the context of their own latest policies. When radical anti-imperialism is the order of the day as it was during the first decades of the People's Republic, the antiforeign Boxer rebellion was officially considered "progressive." Once relations with the United States and Europe improved and foreign capital was invited to China as happened during recent years, the Boxers were consigned for the time being to the dust-bin of history as a retrograde and reactionary movement. The pressure of the present upon the past increases dramatically when "revolutionary history," that is, history of the recent past, is treated, and becomes paramount when the past of still active leaders becomes the subject as is the case in Yang Zhongmei's work.

Yang Zhongmei has grown up in this historiographic environment, and his study evinces the influence from and the stress of this tradition. He has gone through an extraordinarily large and diverse body of

materials to establish the factual record of Hu Yaobang's life, and it is
in this realm that Western scholars will find his work most gratifying.
From the memoirs of journalists who earlier had worked under Hu
Yaobang to interviews with his relatives published in a specialized
journal for old people, from strictly internal documents to the vast
published record, Yang Zhongmei has with painstaking care established a rich and detailed record of Hu Yaobang's life and labors which
will become an important source for studies on modern Chinese history, the history of the Chinese Communist Party, the socio-political and
personal elements going into the various alliances within the party and
into their changes, as well as the types of personalities who make up the
leadership of this largest political organization in the world.

Yang Zhongmei's study is at the same time, and quite explicitly so, a
personal statement. To him, Hu Yaobang, despite some mistakes,
represents the hope of China. Hu Yaobang is a good man and merits
support. The biography shows that Hu Yaobang's qualities have
grown and matured over the years, some drawbacks notwithstanding,
and are not cheap publicity. The study was written during a time of
much political strife concerning the reforms and the make-up of the
new leadership. In this context Yang is perfectly right in his assertion
that a biography of one of the most important leaders could not have
been written by a Chinese in China, or, were it written, the work would
have suffered from much governmental interference and would not
have been able to present a balanced portrait. When, after the completion of the draft of the biography, Hu Yaobang was deposed as head of
the party in January 1987, Yang appended a sad note to his text. It
seemed to him that with Hu Yaobang's demotion, China's hopes were
crushed. As it seems now, this might have been premature. In one of the
sudden turns in Chinese politics, which have often surprised, shocked,
or delighted but always frustrated scholars, the Thirteenth Party Congress in October 1987 grandly maintained the reform course, the threat
of a major purge of Hu Yaobang's associates in the Center and the
provinces subsided for the time being, and Hu's most vocal critics
suddenly found their names erased from the list of Central Committee
members. Hu Yaobang is still in the Politburo, although not in its
Standing Committee, and his direct associates are said to make up
about 10 percent of the new Central Committee. We might not have
seen the last of him.

We are not entirely without biographies of top Chinese Communist
leaders. Mao Zedong himself narrated his life to Edgar Snow, Jiang

Qing tried the same with Roxane Witke, Agnes Smedley wrote a life of the military commander Zhu De. Although not written by these leaders themselves, these texts were strongly dominated by their own self-depiction. The authors were sympathetic to their views or at least felt that the documentary value of these statements merited their unadorned reproduction. We have, on the other end, some biographies from the PRC itself which intend to demolish the image of a former high Communist leader. The best recent example might be Zhong Kan's *Kang Sheng pingzhuan* (Biography of Kang Sheng), about the friend of Mao Zedong and powerful head of the internal security machinery of the party, who was expelled from the party posthumously in 1978. This and similar texts operate from a strictly hostile perspective. Both types of biographies share a common concern for factual accuracy and differ widely and freely in their evaluative judgments. In recent years, biographies of Mao Zedong, Zhou Enlai, Deng Xiaoping, and Jiang Qing have appeared from the hands of Western researchers and scholars, most of them taking a more analytical and less evaluative approach. These studies certainly are more evenhanded in their approach and use much ''outside'' material that has been neglected by the insiders. On the other hand, the materials at the disposal of these researchers are often no match to those used in studies that had access to internal Chinese archives and participants in the historical events themselves.

There is one other kind of study which attempts to combine the best of both worlds. The most famous example is Deutscher's biography *Stalin*. Deutscher himself had been a political activist in Stalin's Russia. This gave him a first advantage, namely, a thorough familiarity with the ideology on which the debates and power struggles were drawing for legitimacy. Deutscher had been associated with the Trotskyist opposition to Stalin. This slightly hostile perspective gave him a certain distance from the object of his study and opened his view to the more complex motives, attitudes, and facts underlying many of these debates. In Stalin's own depiction, these struggles were but attempts by the class enemy to undermine the revolution through ideological diversion, while in many studies done by Western scholars, ideology only ranks as a post factum justification of decisions made on the basis of purely political power calculations. Deutscher left the Soviet Union and wrote his book in the context of Western scholarship, a change which matured his political viewpoint into a scholarly distance and eliminated the strongly evaluative purpose of such a study in favor of an analytical approach. This gave him a second advantage. Having grown up amidst the bitter ideological/factional struggles of the Cultural Revolution, and writing now in a context removed from the direct pressures of internal Chinese debates, Yang to an extent shares both of Deutscher's advantages.

To study the top leader of a Communist state, however, is easy, particularly in cases like Stalin and Mao Zedong, both of whom had a very strong personal standing. It is much more difficult in the case of the second- or third-level leaders. The Communist Party as a social and political body presents a strong environment with its particular laws and dynamics. While it might be possible to write a biography in the narrow sense of the strong top leader because he is in fact the only person able to develop his personality and live it, the environmental pressure on the inhabitants of the lower echelons is so much stronger that the largest part of their thinking, sayings, and doings, that is, most of the evidence a historian might have at his or her disposal, seems to be more determined by environmental pressure and adaptation to it than by their innate desire to think, speak, or act in this way. What might already on the level of the top leader appear as a system of recondite and elusive communication might turn to ever more abstruse forms of indirect communication among the lower orders so that the biographer will at times wonder whether or not his object of study indeed has any thoughts of his own at all.

The Communist Party is a self-perpetuating elite body with no outside checks. Standards for admission into the party vary from time to time, but at any given time they are rather rigorous and unified. This makes for a fairly unified type of personality in each of the subsequent cohorts of party members. In the case of the Chinese party, the first generation of leaders were social rebels who threw themselves into the revolution. Although still a young boy when he joined the revolution, Hu Yaobang is of this type. By the time of the Anti-Japanese war, the Communist Party operated as something like a government. The majority of cadres recruited corresponded to essential military virtues of obedience and devotion to the cause. The Yan'an Rectification Movement tried to instill the same new virtues into the recent crop of social rebels from among the students and intellectuals. The long years of the war made military command structures the basic operating model of the party. The idea of military subordination structured the hierarchy.

After the founding of the PRC, the rationale for this military structure radically changed. It now became an instrument of control for the former military and now civilian leaders. They could use it to ward off the challenge from better qualified younger people, and they fortified their own position by recruiting their own replicas into the party. The core recruitment quality for a substantial body of the Party members who entered in the first years after 1949 was thus defined as *laolao shishi fucong dang de lingdao,* honestly and obediently following the leadership of the party. This made for a fairly uniform type of personality within the party. As insiders recruit the newcomers, they tend to recruit their replicas and to exclude people whose character traits are incompatible with their attitude, namely, people who would dare to speak out, keep to their own counsel, suggest innovations, and the like.

Quickly, the middle-level leadership of the party consisted of yesmen as well, and the former rebels at the top were confronted with a dilemma, namely, that their own policies produced the opposite of what they wanted. In effect, the rebels were recruiting the yes-men. These leaders are perhaps best described as authoritarian personalities in the sense that they were willing to follow authority and vest all their skills into this process, until they were themselves in a position of authority. Then they would expect the same submissiveness from their underlings. Thus we see a particular type of personality making it to the top in such an organization. Yang Zhongmei's important discovery that a substantial part of the revolutionary leaders not only of pre-Communist but also of Communist China are of Hakka background seems to suggest that the particular personality traits fostered by Hakka socialization fit especially well the career requirements in tightly structured organizations like the Communist Party.

To a biographer, this type of personality presents a great challenge. He has to come to grips with the fact that time and again a leader from the second level comes out on top and espouses the most encompassing reforms with a radicalism only matched by the radicalism with which he formerly supported the system he is now reforming, to witness Khrushchev, Kadar, Deng Xiaoping, or Hu Yaobang. Have these leaders hidden their true opinions for decades, calmly toeing the line and waiting for the opportunity to come out into the open as Milosz suggested decades ago in his *The Captive Mind* with his notion of *Ketman*? Are they only politicians who set up a reform program to have good reasons for bringing in their own retainers and attack the old guard as a roadblock to history? Or how else is their mind operating?

Every historical actor climbs to his or her place of prominence, which usually makes them an object of biographical inquiry in the first place, in a particular historical environment. These environments are not all structured in the same way, and the social laws and dynamics that are at play within them and act on the fate of the person to be studied vary greatly. For the biographer of a second-level Communist leader, a thorough familiarity with the laws operating in the given environment is essential. Having grown up amidst the harshest fights between the different factions in the PRC, Yang Zhongmei has this familiarity. Although many methodological points are not explicitly made in his text, they will be noticed by the conscientious reader. One will notice, as an example, how most people associated with Hu Yaobang were recruited by him into the party or had worked under him; inversely, Hu Yaobang has strong links of loyalty to people under whom he worked himself, such as Deng Xiaoping. In a framework where all links outside official organizational relationships reek of factional activity or bourgeois life style, silent links of this kind seem to operate as a guarantee of loyalty even if the persons involved have not seen each other for a decade, and even if they are in opposing camps in a given period. The biography thus provides ample material for the sociological study of inner-party social relations.

Hu Yaobang is one of the few important Chinese Communist leaders who was throughout his career involved in recruitment. First, he recruited "little red devils"; then in Yan'an, officers; after this, young intelligentsia as the head of the Youth League; and finally he became head of the party itself, where he built up the "third echelon" of future younger leaders. He was one of the very few top leaders of the older generation who pondered the question of the type of personality the Party would need to manage the development of the country, and who acted on his insights. Tactically speaking, these recruitment activities created a vast network of loyalties. As his earlier recruits gained in age, seniority, and rank, Hu Yaobang's own power "naturally" grew with them. The middle-aged and young cadres running the reforms have strong ties to him.

When Hu Yaobang took over the Youth League leadership in the 1950s, the ideal personality for recruitment into both the Youth League and the party was the *laolao shishi* type, who made no problems and was obedient. Mandatory reading for Youth League members was Ostrovskij's *How the Steel Was Tempered*, and youths were supposed to learn from the hero Pavel, who wholeheartedly devotes his life to revolution, losing most of his limbs in the process, and using his remaining powers at the end of his short life to write his memoirs. The country was no longer at war, however, and the military virtues of self-effacement, which might have had their value before 1949, were not necessarily optimal for the development of a modern economy, which required a more innovative and daring type. This type, however, was ostracized as "rash," "immature," and "risk-prone" by those who had made it into the lower party levels. In the midst of a reckless campaign against "bourgeois liberalism" which ended in a campaign to "purge the counterrevolutionaries" in 1955, Hu Yaobang and his Youth League used the small leeway provided by some statements of Mao Zedong in the summer of 1955 to create a niche for the very types attacked during this period. The most outspoken and daring characters among the young intellectuals of the time, people like the journalist Liu Binyan or the student of journalism Lin Xiling, found a place in this niche and could use it to challenge the dominant personality type, life style, and behavior in the public sphere with their articles and talks long before there was a "Hundred Flowers" policy. Hu Yaobang himself does not appear to be such a buoyant personality, but one might consider it his greatest contribution at this crucial time to have protected such innovative characters, and to have given to these people the minimal chance to develop in a political culture with such tremendous pressure for homogeneity. In this niche they could develop long enough to influence the ideals of a part of the educated younger generation before they went down in the Antirightist campaign in mid-1957. Although their time and their framework of action were limited, these "new personalities" among the writers, journalists, and young leading cadres, who Hu Yaobang grouped around himself, would become an important recruitment pool for daring and innovative people after the Third Plenum in December 1978, when the Chinese clocks were set back to 1957, and the reform leadership (which indeed had been the leadership in 1955–57) went back to the tracks laid out by the Eighth Party Congress in 1956.

While it would be immediately satisfying to describe Hu Yaobang as this primordial reformer who had the patience and the wit to bide his time, and while there is much material to support such a contention, in particular if other than strictly biographical sources are adduced, the historical record laid out by Yang Zhongmei forces on us the authoritarian ideals of this man. It was indeed Hu Yaobang who supported some of the most refreshing characters of modern China, but Hu Yaobang is also the inventor of Lei Feng shushu, Uncle Lei Feng, the early sixties' reincarnation of the *laolao shishi* ideal of obedient and self-effacing

Pavel Korchagin, which has been held up for emulation to Chinese youths by an ageing leadership. Furthermore, it had been Hu Yaobang himself, then head of party propaganda, who in 1981 banned six film scripts and plays, among them Bai Hua's *Kulian*.

In this context, the official documents relating to the dismissal of Liu Binyan from the party and of Hu Yaobang from the party chairmanship deserve closer attention. Hu was dismissed because he failed to suppress the student demonstrations of December 1986. He was even accused of encouraging them. It was held that if a leader were to encourage spontaneous protest from the lower orders, the threat of a new Cultural Revolution would quickly emerge. The clamors by the students were directed against ever stronger attempts by leaders around the then head of the National People's Congress, Peng Zhen, to curtail the fairly free public debates on many issues of the time. The old cadres feared that they were in for another round of attacks and used the reference to the Cultural Revolution to denounce Hu Yaobang's nonintervention as politically irresponsible. It seems that Hu Yaobang acted much in the same pattern as in 1955–57. His own speeches at the time were patently orthodox, mouthing the latest dispensations. But he did not interfere when his subordinates said other things. This willingness to tolerate a certain diversity even when one has the authority to impose homogeneity marks an important and even vital feature of Hu Yaobang's personality, and in the extreme concentration of discretionary powers in the hands of the top leaders characteristic of the PRC, this personal feature is even of national importance.

Liu Binyan was dismissed, among other, and factional, reasons, for having publicly attacked the "Learning from Lei Feng" propaganda dispensed to Chinese youths. Against this "slave" obedience to each and every word from "the party," Liu Binyan had claimed that a "second kind of loyalty" was called for, namely, a loyalty to the long-term ideals of the party, which might on occasion mean to put oneself in opposition to the dominant party line. It seems that the split between these two ideals of elite personalities expressed in Lei Feng's loyalty and in what Liu Binyan calls the "second kind of loyalty" goes right through Hu Yaobang himself.

The University of Heidelberg   Rudolf G. Wagner
April 1988

Preface
to the English Edition

Hu Yaobang, former general secretary of the Central Committee of the Chinese Communist Party, some fifty years ago was part of an ordinary peasant family in a mountain village of Liuyang county, Hunan province. After more than half a century of struggle, he became the most active leader of the reform group within the Chinese Communist Party.

In response to the student democratic movement of December 1986, a group of the old guard conservatives engineered the coup d'etat of January 16, 1987, that forced Hu to resign as general secretary. At the same time, three of China's most respected intellectuals, Liu Binyan, Fang Lizhi, and Wang Ruowang, were stripped of their party membership.

At the time, having just completed my research at Harvard University, I was visiting New York. As a Chinese scholar studying abroad, it was of course impossible to be indifferent to this momentous political event that shook China and reverberated throughout the world. It was for this reason that I participated in the two discussion meetings on "China's Future" of December 30, 1986, and January 17, 1987, sponsored by Chinese students studying in the United States and held at Columbia University. As Hu Yaobang's biographer, I was asked to speak at these two meetings. In these talks, I expressed my support for the students' democratic movement in China and also indicated my support for Hu as the representative of the reform group within the Chinese Communist Party, and for the three intellectuals, Liu Binyan, Fang Lizhi, and Wang Ruowang.

It makes me very happy to see Chinese intellectuals begin to stand up courageously and express their political views. Many of the Chinese students studying in the United States have expressed views similar to mine. More than two thousand Chinese students in the United States signed their names to a public letter to the Central Committee of the Chinese Communist Party expressing their support for Hu Yaobang and the others. This is the first time in the history of the Chinese Communist Party that Chinese intellectuals, the Chinese people, have publicly defended a leader who had fallen from power. This demonstrates the extent of their respect for Hu Yaobang. As the representative of the reform group within the Chinese Communist Party, Hu Yaobang also represents the forces and the direction of progress in China today.

In the Chinese edition of my *Biography of Hu Yaobang*, I wrote, "My original intent was to study Hu Yaobang as a representative of his generation of Communists, as representative of the leadership of the contemporary reform group. I wanted to examine how such men first became involved in the Chinese Communist revolution, their later role in the historically unprecedented Cultural Revolution, and finally their obvious rejection of Mao Zedong's style of socialism and the gradual opening to the world of that window that had been senselessly closed for so long, and the determined rush toward the intelligent path of reform."

Ever since the monumental *Records of History* of Sima Qian, written two thousand years ago, Chinese historians have continued the tradition of using biographical writing, of studying selected individuals to study the history of the nation. This is because, beginning with the establishment of a centralized authoritarian power structure in the Qin and Han dynasties, the concentration of authority in China has remained historically unchanged. Chinese historical development revolved around individual leaders and heroes, and it is they who continue to be the leading actors on the political stage, the mirrors of history.

Looking back on the history of China, it was men like Liu Bang of the Han dynasty and Zhu Yuanzhang of the Ming dynasty, who came from peasant backgrounds and carried the torch of peasant uprisings, who became the founding emperors of new dynasties. In more recent times, revolutionary leaders like Hong Xiuquan, Sun Yat-sen, and Mao Zedong also came from humble peasant origins. It was their ideals and actions that in large measure opened up new vistas in the development of modern Chinese history and influenced the forward progress of modern East Asia and the world. And Hu Yaobang is the natural historical extension of this type of great leader.

Hu Yaobang is one of the foremost leaders of the Chinese Communist Party, the most creative political leader in the reform movement. He understands fully that China must move away from emphasizing political revolution and class struggle and turn toward democratic reform of both the political and economic systems, that China must be more open to the rest of the world, that this is the only way for the country to move forward from its present position as a developing nation and become an advanced modern nation.

It is for this reason that Hu Yaobang and the reform group, the core of which is the Communist Youth League group, proposed the five changes in the structure of the party's cadre system (to bring in more intellectuals, more professionals, and more younger people, to make it more revolutionary, and to set a fixed age for retirement). Addressing the desire of the intellectuals for greater freedom and democracy, he has also implemented more lenient and liberal policies. All of this shows that Hu Yaobang wants to bid farewell to the traditional Chinese political structure of autocratic rule. But the political conservatives within the party, to protect the autocratic powers they were losing, joined together in the Beijing coup d'état of January 1987 to crush the reforms in the political system that Hu Yaobang was instituting.

The resignation of Hu Yaobang has cut short the "Chinese-style socialist" modernization program originally proposed by Deng Xiaoping. Without democratic reforms in the political system and without the support and cooperation of intellectuals, China's modernization cannot possibly succeed. The conservative faction of the party of which Peng Zhen is the representative, in attacking bourgeois liberalization and demanding adherence to their four cardinal principles, is taking every opportunity to prepare to strangle Deng Xiaoping's present emphasis on economic reform.

China's only option, however, is to implement fully democratic reforms in both the political and economic systems. China's modernization has been the fervent hope of its people for more than a hundred years now. It is not just wishful thinking to assert that, when Deng Xiaoping's modernization fails, Hu Yaobang and those within the Chinese Communist Party who have promoted reform will inevitably be swept back into political power again, with the support of the people and China's intellectuals.

I hope that this American edition not only will help the reader know more about the details of Hu Yaobang's life and the changes in his thought from the time he first joined the revolution through the recent reforms, but will also make it possible to understand better this important period in the history of modern China and the Chinese Communist Party, and also the possible future direction of political change in China under the reform forces that Hu Yaobang represents.

Finally, I would like to express my sincere thanks to the following persons who lent their assistance to the publication of this English-language edition. The publication would not have been possible without Professor Roderick MacFarquhar of Harvard University, who first approached M. E. Sharpe, Inc., and the thoughtful decision of Douglas Merwin to undertake this project. To Professor Rudolf G. Wagner, who spent a great deal of time checking through the Chinese manuscript and wrote the foreword to this edition; to William A. Wycoff, who provided the excellent translation; to Timothy Cheek, who worked on behalf of the publication of this edition; to Anita O'Brien for her careful copy editing; and to Nancy Hearst for her warm enthusiasm and beautiful smile, I offer my lasting gratitude.

The publication of this book in the United States is for me, as my personal name implies (Zhongmei means "China and America"), a symbol of cultural exchange and ties between China and the United States. I hope American readers will like this work, and that they will not hesitate to instruct me further.

May 28, 1987
Tokyo, Japan

Preface
to the Chinese Edition

Three years ago, I started making preparations to write a biography of Hu Yaobang. With this in mind, I made a special trip to his hometown in Liuyang county in northeastern Hunan, and to other places where he had participated in revolutionary activities. I also interviewed some of his close friends who were familiar with his past, and I collected as many relevant source materials as possible.

I have had no presumptions about being able to write the definitive biography of Hu Yaobang. The reason is quite simple. The reform movement that Hu Yaobang is leading is still in progress. His work and his thought are still developing. Furthermore, some of the events that have taken place within the inner chambers of the Forbidden City are still inaccessible to outsiders. There are many historical materials that will not be released to the public for many years. A definitive biography requires a definitive biographer, who will most certainly bring his skill to bear on this subject some day in the future.

In writing this biography of Hu Yaobang, my original intent was to study Hu Yaobang as a representative of his generation of Communists, as representative of the leadership of the contemporary reform group. I wanted to examine how such men first became involved in the Chinese Communist revolution, their later role in the historically unprecedented Cultural Revolution, and finally their obvious rejection of Mao Zedong's style of socialism and the gradual opening to the world of that window that had been senselessly closed for so long, and the determined rush toward the intelligent path of reform.

This indeed was not an easy task. Aside from the fact that I still had not finished my studies, even more important was the fact that as an ordinary citizen bearing the passport of the People's Republic of China, a student wandering off to Japan, I had both real and psychological burdens to overcome.

If one looks back, Mao Zedong talked earnestly with Edgar Snow of his personal life; the dictatorial Jiang Qing flattered Roxane Witke and revealed her secret story; Agnes Smedley gave us a very true biography of General Zhu De; as for Jiang Nan, who wrote that famous biography of Jiang Jingguo in Taiwan, even though he had an American passport he died of an assassin's bullet in a foreign land. This would seem to tell us that in this land called China, unless granted an imperial commission by the emperor himself, people are not allowed to write biographies or critiques of "leading figures"; this task can only be undertaken by foreign scholars of political science. I find this very strange.

But this historical anomaly is finally, if belatedly, being recognized. At the Fourth Congress of the Chinese Writers Association [December 1984], Hu Yaobang asked Hu Qili to convey his greetings in these words: "Socialist literature is a truly free literature." This made me finally believe that Chinese history is indeed going forward. If the steps have been halting and tortuous, they are simply the starting point for even greater strides forward. The people long for freedom, for democracy. The people hope for progress and reforms. This tide of history cannot be held back by anyone, no matter how he may try.

It is for this reason that I have chosen to write on this historical theme, a *Biography of Hu Yaobang*, to plough the first exploratory furrow in this as yet unexplored virgin territory in China, to advance the people's rights to freedom, with a free and critical assessment of a "leading figure."

I only hope that I may sow the seeds of the dragon, and that the harvest will not be fleas!

August 1985
Kōrakurō, Tokyo, Japan

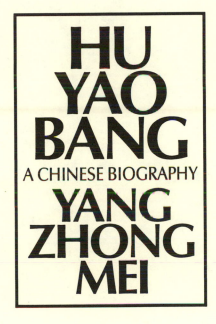

HU YAO BANG

A CHINESE BIOGRAPHY

YANG ZHONG MEI

1
Birthplace
and Family Origins

Above the ruins of the shattered imperial rule of Mao Zedong's dictatorship, a red star now shines brightly. This red star is Hu Yaobang. From patriotic youngster under the banner of Mao Zedong, after more than half a century of turbulent storms, he stands at the forefront of the times, directing China's great reforms. The development of such an outstanding man and the changes of his thought, his belief in and hope for reform, his attitudes toward people, events, and the world, and his own personal interests and character are all subjects worthy of serious research.

Birthplace

Hu Yaobang comes from Liuyang county in Hunan province, the native place of Tan Sitong, the first person in modern China to sacrifice his life for constitutional reform. This is recorded in the biographical sketches distributed by the Chinese Communist Party introducing Hu Yaobang.

In February 1980, at the Fifth Plenum of the Eleventh Congress of the Chinese Communist Party (CCP), Hu Yaobang was elected secretary-general of the Central Committee of the CCP. On March 2, 1980, the *People's Daily*, in a "Biographical Sketch of Comrade Hu Yaobang," noted that he was "from Liuyang county in Hunan, born of a poor peasant family in 1915."

In a talk on May 10, 1985, Hu Yaobang revealed that he was from South township [Nanxiang] in Liuyang county. The Liuyang Gazetteer has the following entry: "The Liu district is 329 *li* long by 200 *li* wide [110 by 70 miles], reaching to Liling in the south, to Xiangtan in the southwest."[1] As the crow flies, the Liuyang county town is less than forty-five miles from Liling, the hometown of the famous early leader of the Communist Party, Li Lisan, and only fifty miles from Xiangtan, the birthplace of Mao Zedong.[2]

The clear, fast waters of the Liuyang River, from its source on Dawei Mountain in East township, flow from one end of the county to the other, over 300 li. In modern Chinese history the Liuyang River has nurtured a number of heroes, martyrs, and men of talent, beginning with Tan Sitong of the 1898 Reform Movement; the brothers Liu Daoyi and Liu Kuiyi and Tang Caichang, who promoted Sun Yat-sen's revolutionary activities for many years; Qiao Dafeng, who gave his life raising the first banner of the 1911 Revolution in Hunan; to the untold numbers of even greater heroes who rose from the back hills to take up the cause of the Chinese Communist revolution. Wang Zhen, one of the original veterans of the Chinese Communist Party, came from North township in Liuyang county. The only woman general of the Chinese Communist Party, Li Zhen, came from East township. Yang Yong is from the same township as Hu Yaobang. The first CCP governor of Hunan province, Wang Shoudao, and Li Xin, gunnery adviser to the Chinese People's Liberation Army, both grew up along the banks of the Liuyang River.

Date of Birth

In 1984, announcing the joint venture between the *Chinese Encyclopedia* and the U.S. *Encyclopedia Britannica* in the publication of the *Abridged Encyclopedia Britannica*, Liaoning's *Gongchandang yuan* (Communist Party Member) published part of the entry on Hu Yaobang that was being prepared for publication. It read: "Hu Yaobang, born November 20, 1915, in Liuyang county, Hunan province, of a poor peasant family."[3] Thus the birthdate of the secretary-general of the Central Committee of the Chinese Communist Party became known to the world via the circuitous route of a joint Chinese-American project.

When I was visiting the hometown of Hu Yaobang, I was told by a number of people of the older generation that Hu was born around midnight on a night when the moon was bright and there were few stars.

Class Background

All official CCP biographical sketches and documents made available to the public to date insist that Hu Yaobang was "born of a poor peasant family." Actually, among the widespread mountain villages of Hunan, Hu Yaobang's parents were quite ordinary peasants. Among the thirty or so peasant families of Zhonghe village, their standard of living was that of the average family. Hu's family had a nine-room, one-story house of clay tiles. They had arable fields of five or six *mu* [about one acre], the average yearly yield of which was nearly twenty *dan* [1.1 tons] of rice or wheat. In the South, China's peasants have a saying, "Ten mu of land and a three-room house are hard to come by in this world." These were the standard of middle-class comfort that peasants sought. Although the family into which Hu Yaobang was born did not have ten mu of land, they had more than half that, and they had a very spacious house, larger by far than that owned by the average peasant family.

Hu Yaobang's family lived frugally and worked hard to maintain a modest life, comfortable, warmly clothed, and well fed. The family worked together growing and preparing flax for Hu's mother to weave into Liuyang "summer cloth," a local specialty. The money earned from the sale of this cloth added to the family income or paid the tuition for Hu Yaobang's schooling. Hu's father, who had had a few years schooling himself and could basically read and write, put a great deal of emphasis on the children's education and, pooling the family's resources, was able to provide Hu Yaobang with an education seldom attained by the average peasant child.

Using Mao Zedong's definition of class divisions in China, one might classify Hu Yaobang as coming from a "middle-class peasant" background. A family with a nine-room house of clay tiles, five or six mu of arable land with a yearly harvest of nearly twenty dan, a man to till the fields, and a woman to weave would be financially self-sufficient and comfortable, able to send the son to the county middle school, and definitely not a poor peasant family.

The general view of the peasants from Hu Yaobang's hometown was that he came from a middle-class peasant family. At the time, first-year tuition at the Liuyang County Middle School was more than ten silver dollars. Room and board was one silver dollar a month, and the price of one dan of rice was two silver dollars. A poor peasant family did not have enough to keep itself warm or fed and could not possibly have spent thirty silver dollars a year to send one of its sons to the county middle school to study.

Family and Clan

Hu Yaobang's parents were still alive when Liberation came. His father died in the early 1950s, having heard only that after the success of the revolution his son had become a high official in Sichuan. In the late 1950s, Hu's mother made one trip to Beijing and stayed in the residence of her son, now a first secretary of the Central Committee, saw her grandson and granddaughter, and was frequently accompanied by her son and his wife by car to see the sights, or for a leisurely stroll through the former imperial gardens. But after a short while she returned to Zhonghe village, where she died in the early 1960s, having gone through the upheavals of the Great Leap Forward.

Hu Yaobang has one brother, four years older than himself, named Hu Yaofu. He is still in good health today. In the third issue of 1983, *Ba xiaoshi yiwai* (After Work) published an article, "Stories from the Banks of the Liuyang River," by the well-known writer Tian Shuang, which included a report on his interview with Hu Yaofu. This article quotes Hu Yaofu as saying,

> "It was probably 1981. One of the leading cadres of Yueyang county wanted to have Dezi [Hu Yaofu's second son, Hu Dezi] transferred over there to take a high government position. By chance Hu Yaobang heard about it and got real angry. Had Dezi sent back. In April of the same year I went to Beijing and saw Yaobang. I mentioned this and he blew up. 'I told you a long time ago that [the children] De'an and Dezi should be content to stay at home and farm. You refuse to listen, and go ahead and tell Dezi to become a national official. What do you mean by this!' When he said this, I didn't know what to say, because I didn't know a thing about Dezi being transferred over there before it actually happened. So I asked him to explain. I don't know anything about politics, and I certainly never asked anyone to help me use any back doors. He didn't seem to believe me and criticized me pretty severely. 'If nobody is willing to stay on the farm and everybody wants to go become a high official, who's going to do the planting? What are one billion people going to eat?' At this point I was getting upset too, and I shouted back at him, 'Look, other people's kids can be high officials, why not mine? Dezi has graduated from junior high school. I say he should take the job!' 'To be an official you have to start at the bottom. Why does he want use his connections and go over to Yueyang?' 'You get nowhere at the bottom!' 'If you're afraid of getting nowhere then be a farmer! Stay at home quietly and be a good farmer!' Seeing that neither of us was about to budge, my sister-in-law advised Yaobang, 'First of all, you shouldn't blame your older brother. Find out

what really happened. Then you can talk about it.' We parted, still mad at each other. Last year I made another trip to Beijing hoping to clear up that misunderstanding. I told him that Dezi had already resigned that position and returned home to farm again. Yaobang had also thought about his attitude and said that it was clear to him now that it was not my fault. He also advised his nephew to be content to stay home and farm, that he hoped he would do well, and that when he became a model worker he should come to Beijing again to see him.''

Hu Yaobang also has a paternal cousin (female) who was married some years ago and lives in Shanzaotan village in East township. Even today Hu Yaobang's son still goes there frequently to visit his relatives.

Hu Yaobang joined the revolution early and in 1941 married Li Zhao, a student from the Chinese Women's College in Yan'an. At the time Hu Yaobang was twenty-seven and Li Zhao was twenty-one. The two were very much in love, and to show their deep respect for each other gave their daughter the mother's surname, Li, and their son the father's surname, Hu. This was also very much a mark of the equality between the sexes that prevailed during the Yan'an period. However, there has been very little public information about the members of Hu Yaobang's family. The first official introduction to the public came on March 24, 1984, when Hu Yaobang entertained Japanese Prime Minister Nakasone and his wife for lunch at his home in the Zhongnanhai residential area. The New China News Agency reported this as follows:

> When Nakasone arrived by car at Zhongnanhai at 11:30 a.m., Hu Yaobang, his wife, and son and daughter welcomed the guests at the door of the reception hall. Hu Yaobang introduced his wife, Li Zhao, the sixty-two-year-old member of the Beijing Advisory Committee of the Chinese Communist Party, his son, Liu Hu, who works for the Ministry of Foreign Trade, his daughter, Li Heng, editor of the magazine *Zhonghua neike* (Chinese Internal Medicine), and his ten-year-old granddaughter, Hu Zhizhi (in the fifth grade), to Prime Minister Nakasone and his wife.[4]

In addition to those mentioned by the New China News Agency, Hu Yaobang also has an elder son, Hu Deping, and a third son, Hu Dehua, a college teacher. Hu Deping graduated from Beijing University's history department in 1967. In early 1967, Deng Xiaoping and Hu Yaobang were branded as reactionary capitalist roaders by the Red Guards of Mao Zedong. Deng Xiaoping's son, Deng Pufang, and Hu Yaobang's son, Hu Deping, were also dubbed children of reactionaries. They were investigated and slandered on the orders of the Red Guard

Revolutionary Committee of Beijing University, which supported the Nie Yuanzi faction.[5] After the Cultural Revolution, Hu Deping passed the exam for the master's degree program in the department of Chinese intellectual history under Hou Wailu at the Chinese Academy of Social Sciences and has since become a devoté of *hong xue* [i.e., the textual and historical study of the classical novel *Dream of the Red Chamber*]. He served as assistant director of the Chinese Museum of History and is now chairman of the United Front Department of the CCP Central Committee. His wife, An Li, is the daughter of An Ziwen, who before the Cultural Revolution was director of the Organization Department of the Central Committee.

Hu Yaobang's second son, Liu Hu, was born in 1946 just at the time the civil war between the Nationalists and Communists exploded again. Because the situation was very tense, Liu Hu was sent to live with Liu Shichang, who was then a local cadre in northern Shaanxi province and assistant director of the South district production cooperative. Hu Yaobang and Liu Shichang together agreed on the name Liu Hu. In 1962, Liu Shichang sent Liu Hu back to live with Hu Yaobang. In 1964, Liu Hu entered the chemical engineering department of Qinghua University in Beijing. He is now assistant director of the Technology Import-Export Office of the Chinese Ministry of Foreign Trade. His wife is the daughter of the veteran Communist and diplomat Wang Youping. In 1984, Liu Hu visited the United States for a brief investigation tour of the U.S. mining industry.

By today's standards Hu Yaobang has a large family, with three sons and one daughter, all of whom have had a good education. All are married, giving Hu Yaobang a total of five grandchildren. The two branches of the family, the old family rooted in the mountain village in Liuyang county and the new family in the Zhongnanhai residences in Beijing, have close ties.

2
Student Days

To date, none of the party resumés introducing Hu Yaobang or other biographical sketches have mentioned anything about his student background. They say simply that he "left home at age fourteen to go to the red base area to join the revolution." They say absolutely nothing about his education and studies.

However, an article in the *People's Daily* on May 26, 1983, by the well-known writer Zhang Zhenguo entitled "The Source of the River" shed some light on this subject, revealing for the first time that when this youth of fourteen left home he had already attended the first year of the Liuyang County Middle School. Also in 1983, in an article published in *Zhongguo laoren* (China's Elderly), Zhang Zhenguo provided some further detail on this topic. These two reports contained a letter of January 29, 1981, written by Hu Yaobang to his junior high school teacher, Yu Keying, in which he says, "I have not forgotten you, nor the other teachers I had in elementary school and junior high school. The proper and upright attitude of these teachers, never tiring of teaching others, has already given me a great deal of strength." Hu went on to invite Yu Keying to Beijing, and on July 7, 1982, the teacher and student who had not seen each other for more than half a century met at Hu's home in Zhongnanhai. Hu Yaobang was reported to have said, "Comrade Yang Yong was also your student, do you remember? Unfortunately, he is not in Beijing just now. Otherwise, he would certainly come see you!" His teacher replied, "You are very busy, I know. I must not take any more of your precious time." "My dear old teacher!" Hu responded. "I have been looking for my old elementary and junior high school teachers for quite some time now. You are the only one I have been able to find!"[1]

These two articles indicate that Hu Yaobang "was one of the

school's talented students.''[2] It is also interesting to note that one of the generals most respected by Deng Xiaoping, Yang Yong, who once was a member of the high command of the Chinese People's Volunteer Corps in Korea, was a schoolmate of Hu Yaobang. But neither of these two articles tells us anything concrete or specific about the studies or politics of this fourteen-year-old student about to leave home. We must continue to search for footprints left behind from Hu Yaobang's student days.

From Village Tutorials to Liwen Higher Elementary School

Before formally entering elementary school, Hu Yaobang had already been tutored for more than two years in the informal village school of Zhonghe village. This school was jointly sponsored by the Hu clan and other families in the village. The room, board, and salary of the Zhonghe village tutor were shared by the families of children attending the school. Both Hu Yaobang and his older brother, Hu Yaofu, took classes with the village tutor.

The textbooks and content selected by the tutor usually followed the old custom, the *Hundred Family Surnames*, the *Thousand Character Classic*, matching simple couplets, calligraphy copy books, memorizing Tang poetry, and a little later the *Mencius*, the *Analects* of Confucius, and so forth. Hu Yaobang had a good memory and quick reactions, and he was diligent in his studies. Consequently, he matched couplets quickly and aptly, his characters were well written, and it was hard to beat his recitation of the memorization lessons. He was better at his studies than his older brother, and he often received a few words of praise from the old men of the village. Hu Yaobang's father knew very well how hard farming was, and that only by studying could one get ahead in the world. Thus he was determined to make it possible for his younger son to continue his studies. In the spring of 1926 he sent Hu Yaobang, not yet eleven years old, off to the higher elementary classes of Wenli Elementary School in Wenjia town, some twenty li to the south. This was Hu Yaobang's first venture out into the world beyond the isolated mountain village.

Liwen Elementary—Starting Point of a Revolutionary Career

Liwen Elementary School, named Liren Elementary School today, was then located within the grounds of the Literary Temple [Wen Miao] of Wenjia town. It was a complete elementary school, having both a junior elementary school and a higher elementary school. Wenjia town, about twenty li north of Pingxiang county in Jiangxi province, was the major town of Liuyang county.

When Hu Yaobang began classes at Liwen Elementary School, he would make the roundtrip of forty li between his home and the school on foot every day. It was this daily trek on the mountain path from which he developed the habit of walking fast and forged his sense of determination. Later on, Hu completed all ten thousand li of the Long March on foot even when wounded, and today he still maintains the habit of walking ten thousand paces every day to keep in shape.

The curriculum of Liwen Elementary School included Chinese, mathematics, geography, history, physical education, and music. In 1927 a course in the "Three People's Principles" of Sun Yat-sen was added. Virtually none of these had been taught by the village tutor in Zhonghe.

This peaceful life of studies was soon to be disrupted by the Northern Expedition and the rolling tide of the Nationalist Revolution. The year 1926, when Hu Yaobang entered Liwen Elementary School, was the time of cooperation between Communists and Nationalists. The brave winds of the New Thought Movement, of ousting the foreign powers from Chinese soil, of the National Revolution that would wrest for China its independence, spread rapidly from the coastal centers up the great rivers far inland, soon to engulf the entire nation.

That spring, Hunanese students from the Peasant Training Institute in Guangzhou, in line with the growing Nationalist Revolution and acting as specially appointed members of the peasant movement under the Hunan branch of the Nationalist Party, were actively speaking and organizing throughout Hunan province. Using their positions as middle and elementary school teachers, they spread the message of revolution among their students. In many places they organized Communist youth groups, children's groups, and peasant associations.

Gan Sizao, one of the teachers at Liwen Elementary School, was a member of the Communist Party. He taught the students that if the peasants were to stand up they would have to struggle, and they would have to participate in the propaganda training and education sessions of the national revolutionary movement. He and his colleagues developed the Communist Youth League, a secret branch of which Hu's fellow students Yang Yong (originally named Yang Shijun) and Zhang Qingyi joined. Hu Yaobang, who was three years younger than Yang Yong, was another of the "seedlings" painstakingly cultivated by Gan Sizao. Gan frequently had them read some of the new fiction and publications such as *Zhongguo qingnian* (China Youth), and he talked to them of the exploitation of the peasants by the landlords.

On July 9, 1926, Chiang Kai-shek became commander-in-chief of the National Revolutionary Army and its 100,000 troops, which started out from Guangdong province on the Northern Expedition. The march reached Hunan very quickly. At the same time, thirty-six Hunanese Communist Party members from the Sixth Peasant Movement Institute, which was led by Mao Zedong, arrived one by one back in Hunan, and under Mao's leadership they began to organize peasant associations to agitate for lower rents, lower interest rates, and lower deposits, and, in more extreme cases, to kill local tyrants, run out large landlords, divide the land, and create an atmosphere of red terror. The peasants of Liuyang rose up to overthrow tradition with fury and determination. According to the membership records of the All-Hunan Peasant Association, Liuyang county had 21 district peasant associations and 586 village peasant associations, with a total membership of 9,190 people. Liuyang county ranked third among the fifty-nine counties of Hunan in the number of village peasant associations and membership.

In the second half of 1926, Hu Yaobang joined the Children's Corps and became one of its activists, propagandizing against superstition and gambling, teaching songs, and writing such slogans as "Throw out the foreign powers!" "Defeat imperialism!" "Overthrow the landlord gentry!" Fond of wielding the brush, Hu Yaobang wrote not only on paper but also on walls.

But the situation quickly turned against them. In Shanghai on April 12, 1927, Chiang Kai-shek openly declared his policy of liquidating the Communists. On May 21, Nationalist troops under Xu Kexiang began the "Day of the Horse Incident," a movement to suppress "ruffians." Then on July 25, Wang Jingwei announced in Wuhan a "peaceful splitting with the Communists." The first small light of cooperation between the Nationalists and Communists was totally snuffed out in the ensuing bloodbath of the white terror.

In Liuyang county the red terror had been severe, but the revenge of the landlords and the Nationalist troops in the white terror against the village organizations was truly horrible. Every day leading members of the peasant associations were murdered. Yang Yong and Gan Sizao, hearing that they had been named as instigators, fled. Hu Yaobang, just a child, and not that much of an activist, went unnoticed, so he was able to continue his forty-li hike to and from school every day.

On August 7, 1927, the CCP Central Committee held an emergency meeting, electing Qu Qiubai as its new leader and dismissing Chen Duxiu, who was considered a ''rightist'' by the Communist International. This meeting also decided to carry out the land revolution and armed uprisings in pursuit of a Communist revolution in China. After the ''August 7'' meeting, Mao Zedong was designated a special delegate of the Central Committee with responsibility for the Hunan Autumn Harvest Uprising.

The crowd of workers and peasants hastily assembled for the uprising, however, were in the end no match for the trained army of Tang Shengzhi. Although the rebels did attack and take the Liuyang county town on September 16, they were badly defeated and forced to retreat when Tang Shengzhi's new Eighth Army counterattacked. On September 19, the troops of the Third Route Army regrouped in Wenjia town, where the astute Mao Zedong decided to abandon the plan to attack Changsha and to retreat instead into the peasant villages of Jiangxi. On September 20, on the athletic field of Liwen Elementary School where Hu Yaobang was studying, Mao Zedong convened a conference of the Workers and Peasants Revolutionary Army and announced the plans for retreat. From there he led this regiment of troops up into Jinggang Mountain, where he established the first Chinese Communist military base.

Hu Yaobang witnessed all of this with his own eyes. He experienced personally the rise and fall of the Hunan peasants' revolutionary movement. He witnessed a truly momentous upheaval of mankind. As the son of a peasant family, he was already nourishing the ambition to join the path of the peasant revolution. Thus he spent two years of higher elementary school half in study, half in revolution.

Passing the ''Xiuzai'' Examination

In the spring of 1928, Li Zongren and Bai Zhongxi took command of the Western Pacification Army under Chiang Kai-shek's general command and defeated the army of Tang Shengzhi, who was allied with the Hunan warlord in Wuhan. With this the Nationalist government in Nanjing gained control of Hunan province. That spring, as the situation in Hunan stabilized, Hu Jixian, a native of Liuyang, returned home from studying in Japan to found Liuyang County Junior High School.

He himself took the position of school principal. Most of the teachers he hired were bright graduates of Wuhan University, although some were promising young people from Liuyang county who had graduated from other universities and were committed to teaching in their hometown. For example, the teacher to whom Hu Yaobang's letter was written, Yu Keying, a native of North township in Liuyang county, had graduated from Beijing Agricultural College. The new junior school had over twenty teachers, who were paid according to the number of hours they taught at the rate of half a silver dollar per hour of classes.

The school's curriculum included English, algebra, physics, chemistry, geography, history, art, music (primarily Chinese), physical education, and morals.[3] The school also had faculty and student dormitories, an athletic field, and a dining hall. Students were recruited through an entrance examination in five parts—mathematics, Chinese, geography, history, and the Three People's Principles of Sun Yat-sen. On a scale of 100, 60 was passing. It was a three-year system, and the first class of fifty students began in the spring of 1928.

The location of Liuyang County Junior High School in the county town made it convenient for young people from Liuyang and neighboring counties. Before this, those who had graduated from higher elementary school and wanted to continue their education had to go to Changsha, the provincial capital. The timing was perfect for Hu Yaobang: the opening of the modern-style school coincided exactly with his graduation from elementary school. That very summer examinations were announced to recruit one hundred students for the fall term. When Hu heard the news he was very excited, and he talked with his parents about taking the examination. They of course agreed. Hu threw himself into reviewing his lessons day and night; he was determined to pass the exam on the first try.

There were ten or so graduates of Liwen Elementary School who decided to take the examination. Yang Yong, who had gone away to escape the earlier counterrevolutionary backlash and had been staying with relatives in Wanzai county, Jiangxi, now returned to his home in Wenjia, where he arranged to go with friends to take the examination.

Hu Yaobang's grade on the examination put him among the top ten. Yang Yong also passed. The Liuyang county town was at least eighty li from Hu's home, but when he found out that he had passed he hurried all the way back to the village without stopping. His parents and relatives were delighted; this was considered a great event for the little mountain village.

In the eyes of his fellow villagers, who had planted the fields for generations, becoming a student in the county junior high school was considered the equivalent of having passed the *xiuzai* degree under the former Qing dynasty. Hu was now a recognized scholar. His father and mother now had to find a way to scrape together the money for his tuition and expenses. Since the school was so far away it would be impossible for him to travel back and forth every day. His room and board would be two silver dollars a month, plus more than ten silver dollars a year for tuition; he would need at least thirty silver dollars a year. For a local farming family this was not easy, but Hu's parents finally got enough money together to make it possible for their son to enter Liuyang County Junior High School.

A "Youthful Sense of Burden"

In the autumn of 1928, Liuyang County Junior High School accepted one hundred new students, fifty of whom were put in section 1, and the others divided between sections 2 and 3. Being older and taller than some, Yang Yong was placed in section 2. Being younger and shorter, Hu Yaobang was placed in section 3. Sharing the same desk with Hu Yaobang was a student named Yang Yougen, who had graduated from Liuyang County Chengguan Elementary School, the principal of which was Song Shaobin, who had studied in France before returning to China to found the school in the county city. Many of its students came from wealthy families. Most of the students who passed the examination for the county junior high school had graduated from the well-equipped and staffed Chengguan Elementary School. Some of these looked down on students from the smaller towns and villages and frequently picked fights with them. But Hu Yaobang and his deskmate Yang Yougen got along very well together and became good friends.

According to his classmates' recollections, Hu Yaobang was very diligent in his studies, liked to read and to ask questions, and was always among the top few students in his grades—a real "honor student." Hu could be very stubborn. Given the chance, he liked to argue with others over right and wrong. He spoke very well and had quick responses. Before long the other students learned that they had better not underestimate this boy from South township, even though he was almost the shortest in the class. They all feared their active classmate with the sharp piercing eyes and slightly buck teeth, who was good at arguing and possessed a "youthful sense of burden, fearless and calculating.''

Hu Yaobang and Yang Yong, with some of their other close friends, were very active after class, often playing the game of ''close the window and catch the sparrow'' in the dining hall. Every time an unlucky sparrow flew into the dining hall and was trapped it became a meal, their ''unexpected flying gourmet delicacy.'' Hu also became the drummer in the school band. At school or in the town, for ceremonies and holiday parades, he would beat a drum, marching at the head of the ranks.

There were several teachers who liked this very responsive, quick-witted student—Yu Keying, who taught English and chemistry; Zhou Naijin, who taught Chinese; and Li Gucun, who taught physical education. Hu's classmates still remember the time one teacher told Hu to recite from memory the introduction to ''Entering the King's Palace.'' He recited it flawlessly, without missing a single word. His written essays also frequently came back from the teachers with the comment ''very well written.''

But there were also some teachers who did not like Hu Yaobang and some of the other, more active ''troublemakers.'' Senior morals teacher He Zhenwu, for example, a member of the county branch of the Nationalist Party and later Liuyang county chief, could not avoid inserting into his discussion of the Three People's Principles various criticisms of these students. One time, he made the statement that, because the national revolution had already been successfully completed and the three provinces of the Northeast had come over, it was important for the students to study, to calm down, and to discipline themselves. After they graduated and were working for the nation, then they could struggle for their own personal futures. Later, when Hu's classmates were talking together, one of them said, ''Mr. He is right. The national revolution of the Nationalist Party has been successful. Now we should study hard, and in the future, depending on our own abilities we will raise our heads in society.'' Hu Yaobang, however, retorted, ''Although the three provinces of the Northeast have come over, the Japanese troops are still stationed there. On the Yangzi River, foreign gunboats still carry their flags back and forth. Our Hunan province keeps changing warlords, one after the other. When Tang Shengzhi was defeated, Cheng Qian took over. Now we have Lu Diping. Who knows who will come next to be the new chairman of Hunan. It seems to me that the world still hasn't found peace. The foreign powers still haven't been defeated. The warlords still haven't been defeated. We students have to study, but we also have to be concerned about our country. Has it not been said in the past, 'The fate of the nation is everyone's responsibility!'" This great truth rendered his classmates speechless. Silently, they just stared at him. The school principal, Hu Jixian, had overheard this speech and praised Hu highly. The next day, he commended him before the whole school.

The world was indeed as unsettled as Hu Yaobang had said, and this was especially true in Hunan. In February 1929, Lu Diping was forcibly ousted from Hunan by He Jian, who was personally loyal to Chiang Kai-shek. He Jian became the new chairman of the Hunan provincial government on March 2. Li Zongren's Guangxi Clique, attempting to challenge Chiang Kai-shek, finally took the Hunan question as their firing line, precipitating open war. The two armies battled each other for over a year with no decision.

Peng Dehuai, who had come to the CCP's Jiangxi Soviet after participating in the Pingjian county uprising, now led the Red Army into Hunan. In April 1930, Peng "occupied Wanzai and Tonggu [in Jiangxi, near the Hunan border]. In the middle of the month, he attacked Dongmen and Wenjia in Liuyang, killing 200 of the enemy troops." However, by the end of April Peng's forces had to retire back to Jiangxi.[4] At this time, the central plains war in the North between Feng Yuxiang and Chiang Kai-shek had again broken out.

Under these unstable conditions of in-fighting and treachery among the warlords and the contest between the red [CCP] and white [KMT] forces, the Liuyang county town, located in the very center of the devastating battles, was in chaos, which meant that Liuyang Junior High School was in chaos too. Some of the students were for the red forces, some capitulated to the white. Yang Yong, for example, in February, "with an introduction from the county committee, [had] gone to Huangjintong to join the school of the Fifth Army and the Chinese Workers and Peasants Red Army."[5] Other students and teachers fled to escape the troubles. The principal, Hu Jixian, had no choice but to announce the temporary closing of the school. Having just entered his second year of junior high school, Hu Yaobang, too, said good-bye to his student days and started out on a new road.

3
In the
Red Soviet District

In October 1929, the economic panic that started with the crash of the stock market in the United States threw the entire capitalist world into the depths of the cyclical economic crisis predicted earlier by Marx. The Chinese civil war among the warlords old and new continued unabated, scorching the central plains.

This appearance of monumental chaos in the world made Stalin, head of the Communist International, dance with joy. On December 29, 1929, *Pravda* published a "Letter from the Administrative Committee of the Communist International to the Central Committee of the Chinese Communist Party," which proclaimed that "The period of profound national crisis that China has already entered" and capitalism's "worsening economic crisis" were "indicators of the approaching high tide of revolution." Thus the Comintern gave final warning that if the Chinese Communist Party "does not overcome all petty bourgeois vacillation within its own ranks, it will not be able to play a role in starting, organizing, or leading the new revolutionary tide."[1]

This appearance of great chaos in the world and the strongly worded letter from the Comintern made CCP members, who were already in the midst of a bitter struggle, sense that an historical turning point was fast approaching. On January 5, 1930, Mao Zedong sent a letter to Lin Biao criticizing his defeatist pessimism and optimistically claiming that "The high tide of the Chinese revolution is rapidly approaching."[2] Mao firmly believed that the success of the plan to "take Jiangxi province in one year" was virtually guaranteed.

At that time, Li Lisan, who held the reins of authority within the Central Committee, was even more optimistic and enthusiastic than either Stalin or Mao Zedong about the signs of the coming high tide of revolution. On June 11, 1930, the Central Committee's Politburo, under Li's leadership, passed his draft resolution of June 9, "The New Revolutionary Tide and Achieving the Victory First in One or Several Provinces." This resolution proclaimed that "The Chinese revolution will explode first, making possible the great world revolution, the final and decisive world war." Therefore, "to prepare for the first victory in one or several provinces and to set up a political organ of the national revolution are the overall strategic plan of the party today."[3]

To welcome this "approaching new Chinese revolution," Li Lisan issued a slogan to all China's red armies, the party and its branches, and workers' organizations: "Move out, burst out, explode!" "Attack, attack, boldly attack the central cities." "Achieve the victory of the final decisive battle of steel and blood." "Defeat Changsha, take Nanchang, conquer Wuhan, water your horses at the Yangzi [Yangtze] River."

In accordance with the Central Committee directive, on July 27, 1930, Peng Dehuai led the Third Red Army Corps in an attack on Changsha, and on July 30 the establishment of the "Hunan Workers, Peasants, and Soldiers Soviet Government" was pronounced, with Li Lisan as chairman and Yang Youlin as vice-chairman (Li was not in Hunan at the time, so Wang Yifen and Wang Shoudao acted as temporary representatives). However, Peng's troops were soon surrounded by the superior forces of the Nationalist Army and had no option but to leave Changsha on August 5, turning the war back to the area of the Pingjiang-Liuyang Soviet District.

As this was taking place, Zhu De and Mao Zedong, on orders from Li Lisan, hastily organized the First Army Corps, came down from Jinggang Mountain, and advanced from Jiangxi into Hunan, preparing to join with the Third Army Corps and reinforce this victory. In the dawn of August 20, the First Red Army Corps of Zhu and Mao arrived at Wenjia town and, after several brief though violent skirmishes, totally wiped out the contingent of He Jian's troops commanded by Dai Douyuan in a campaign known as "The Great Victory of Wenjia."

The First and Third Army Corps subsequently joined in Liuyang to form the First Front Red Army. Mao Zedong was made secretary of the Political Committee and of the Front Committee, and Zhu De was named commander-in-chief. The entire army, comprising over 30,000 persons, started out for the second attack on Changsha. In the meantime, the Pingjiang-Liuyang Soviet District was dividing the land among the peasants, holding struggle meetings with bad landlords, organizing peasant associations, and establishing soviet governments at all levels, spreading out to form one large soviet district along the border regions of Hunan, Jiangsi, and Hubei provinces.

In this rapidly expanding revolutionary situation, fourteen-year-old Hu Yaobang had become a member of the Communist Youth League, and as chairman of the Wenjia Children's Corps he was very active in the Pingjiang-Liuyang Soviet. Baptized in the great 1927 Hunan peasant revolution, Hu Yaobang was already an experienced leader of the Children's Corps. In the campaigns to take Wenjia and Changsha, Hu participated in Red Army maneuvers as a messenger and scout and also helped with such tasks as serving water and food and writing slogans and political propaganda.

Because he could read and write, Hu also helped with teaching at the Red Elementary School. According to the accounts of the Soviet Cultural Committee of Liuyang county, "Said county has four Lenin Schools with 211 students, 144 male and 67 female. There are 116 Red Elementary Schools with 4,237 students, 2,983 male, 1,254 female."[4] Having attended high school, Hu Yaobang was well suited to teaching beginning students.

The second Changsha campaign dragged out for more than a month because of the stubborn resistance of He Jian ensconced behind the high walls and heavy barricades of the city. The Red Army leaders were in difficulty and were losing troops. Faced with the grave threat of being caught in a pincer attack by Chiang Kai-shek's army, they had no choice but to retreat to southern Jiangxi.

In the meantime, the Li Lisan line of wildly aggressive attacks was being rejected by the Comintern. Under the direction of Stalin, the Comintern had originally intended to push Lenin's Asian agrarian land revolution to achieve the strategy of protecting the Soviet Union in order to establish socialism in one country. Then it received the first open challenge of the Chinese Communist Party's spirit of nationalism from its representative Li Lisan. Borrowing the hallowed vocabulary of "the Communist International" and "world revolution" sung so loudly by Stalin, Li Lisan asked him to risk war with Japan and the world powers so that the victory of the Chinese revolution might be ensured. Stalin was not at all pleased at having his own words and schemes turned against him, so he immediately ordered Qu Qiubai and Zhou Enlai, who were in the Soviet Union, to return home and put an end to the Li Lisan line.

On September 24, Qu Quibai and Zhou Enlai in Shanghai convened the Sixth Plenum of the Third Congress of the CCP to terminate the policy of organizing general uprisings throughout the entire country and concentrating all the red armies in attacks on central cities. They announced the return to independent organization and normal work of all branch parties, armies, and workers associations. Li Lisan was stripped of his positions. With the end of the Li Lisan line, the high tide of the Chinese red revolution rippled a few times and then receded again.

Then the white wave rolled in. On the orders of He Jian, Liu Jianxu, commanding three divisions of troops, followed the retreating army of Zhu De, Mao Zedong, and Peng Dehuai, organized an Office for the Pacification of Pingjiang and Liuyang Counties, issued ten proclamations of those to be killed, and began a massive attack on the Pingjiang-Liuyang Soviet. In every district and village landlords replaced the village committees and raised the cry of revenge: "Even the rocks will be put to the sword." The Pingjiang-Liuyang Soviet grew smaller by the day.

In that troubled age of constant turmoil and change, fifteen-year-old Hu Yaobang had already made up his mind to follow the revolutionary road. In the spring of 1931, he said farewells and set out for the Jiangxi Central Soviet base. Before leaving, he said to one of his close friends and schoolmates: How can a boy take care of a few mu of fields and his home? I want to be like Li Lisan and take on the world. I must leave home and make revolution!

During his high school days, Li Lisan had written on the back of a photograph of himself and his schoolmate Luo Zhanglung, "You and I may be the only true heroes in this world. Even if we don't achieve it, we cannot help striving for it. Not out of self-conceit, but to really try our hardest." Before graduating from high school and leaving home to go out and challenge the world, Li wrote a poem telling of his dream. "A determination that reaches to the stars, to destroy the nation's foes. Goodbye to poetry and books, I'll throw away my pen and become a warrior."

Influenced by Jiang Guangci's novelette *The Youthful Tramp* and inspired by the heroic spirit of Li Lisan, in 1931 the young Hu Yaobang was determined to move the world, to leave his native village and rush off to the Jiangxi Central Soviet to join the revolution.

In the Jiangxi Central Soviet

On March 2, 1980, the *People's Daily* printed an account of Hu Yaobang's activities in the Central Soviet. "In 1930 he joined the Communist Youth League and in 1933 became a member of the Chinese Communist Party. Leaving home at age fourteen to participate in the revolution in the Red base camp, he moved directly from children's work to being the secretary-general of the Central Committee of the Children's Corps in the Central Soviet."

A 1984 article in the Liaoning *Gongchang dang yuan* (Communist Party Member) said, "In 1930, he joined the Chinese Communist Youth League in his hometown. The next year he went to the central revolutionary base in southern Jiangxi and western Fujian where he successively held the positions of chairman of the Youth Office and Propaganda Office of the Anti-Imperialist General Alliance [Fandi zong tongmeng] and secretary-general of the Soviet Central Bureau of the Chinese Communist Youth League."

Clearly, the account in *Communist Party Member* is more specific than that in *People's Daily* on the positions held by Hu Yaobang in the Jiangxi Central Soviet. At the same time, it corrects the statement in *People's Daily* that has Hu "Leaving home at age fourteen to participate in the revolution in the Red base camp." According to *Communist Party Member*, Hu Yaobang went to the Chinese Communist revolutionary base in Fujian and Jiangxi in 1931, when he was fifteen, not fourteen. The *Communist Party Member* account is historically correct.

Nonetheless, the description of Hu Yaobang's positions is still rather sketchy. Cai Xiaoqian, who was chairman of the Anti-Imperialist Alliance from its inception to its disbanding and later became a member of the Nationalist Party, included some information on Hu Yaobang in his recollections:

> During the two years and four months that I was directing the work of the "Anti-Imperialist Alliance" in the soviet district, some ten persons were delegated to work with me in the alliance at one time or another, including Mao Zedong's third brother, Mao Zetan (who had been a member of the Jiangxi Committee of the CCP); Hu Yaobang, who had held the position of director of the Organization Department of the Central Bureau of the soviet district's Youth League; Chen Dejin (a Korean), who had been a pilot in the Red Air Force flying missions in the area around Xian; Zhang Rong, who had been a ranking cadre in the Chinese Communist Longyan County District [in Fujian]; Ren Zhibin, the intellectual who had just come from the Nationalist area to the soviet district; and others, such as Zhang Xin and He Juesheng. In addition there were also a few who had

been delegated to come here by their local alliance branches, such as Zhong Jiakun, the Youth League cadre from the Xingguo County [Jiangxi] Alliance, and Youth League female cadre Yang Xiuzhen, from the Ruijin County [Jiangxi] Alliance. These people coming from many different places and organizations to work with me can be roughly divided into three types: (1) those who had been struggled with for some kind of "error" and had been sent here temporarily to engage in collective work so that they could examine themselves in real practical work, such as Mao Zetan, Chen Dejin, and He Juesheng; (2) intellectuals who had just slipped in from the Nationalist areas and were first assigned to the alliance to give them some practical experience in mass work, people like Zhang Xin and Ren Zhibin; and (3) Youth League cadres who had been promoted from local organizations to train and strengthen their leadership capabilities.[5]

The recollections of Cai Xiaoqian, who entered the Jiangxi Soviet District in June 1932, are comparatively reliable. However, his reports concerning Hu Yaobang's circumstances prior to June 1932, being based on second-hand knowledge recorded much later, inevitably include some inaccuracies. His statement, for example, that Hu Yaobang "had held the position of director of the Organization Department" does not make sense, nor is it historically factual. Joining the Soviet District Anti-Imperialist Alliance after June 1932, Hu Yaobang was at the time only sixteen years of age and not yet a Communist Party member. He could not have held this important post just before being promoted to secretary-general of the Central Committee of the Youth League. Similarly, recent biographical sketches of Hu Yaobang, written when he was CCP Central Committee secretary, would hardly have overlooked such an important position in the Communist Party.

The Central Bureau of the Chinese Communist Youth League was the leading organ of the Youth League in the Central Soviet District. It had been set up in February 1931. That spring, all of the leading members of the CCP Central Committee, originally located in Shanghai, filed into the Jiangxi Central Soviet. In actuality, the Jiangxi Soviet Central Bureau of the Youth League had already become the de facto Central Bureau of the Youth League for all China. Its first officers entered the Jiangxi Central Soviet District in February 1931, including Gu Zuolin, who had previously been director of the Organization Department of the Central Bureau of the Youth League; Zhang Aiping, who was secretary-general; and Lu Dingyi, director of the Propaganda Department. There are two versions of who was director of the Organization Department. One says that Gu Zuolin held this position; the other says that it was held by Wang Yongji. It definitely was not Hu Yaobang.

From the above one can see that Hu Yaobang was one of the "Youth League cadres who had been promoted from local organizations to train and strengthen their leadership capabilities," sometime after June 1932. At that time he was made director of the Youth Office of the Soviet District Anti-Imperialist Alliance.

Sometime before June 1933, the director of the alliance's Propaganda Department, Zhang Xin, resigned on charges of corruption. Hu Yaobang was then assigned to this post. *Hongse Zhonghua* (Red China), the official organ of the central government of the Jiangxi Soviet, published an article entitled "Get Rid of the High-Level Big Corruption of Bureaucratism," written by Hu Yaobang, chief officer of the Propaganda Department. The article said, "The former director of the Propaganda Department and member of the Standing Committee and teacher of the Workers and Peasants Theatrical Society, Zhang Xin, acted like an arrogant bigshot and was a thoroughly negative slacker whose work style was totally bureaucratic, corrupt, and rotten. Every day he took money from the alliance's till and went to the tavern. The last time he was transferred from the Anti-Imperialist Alliance to go to work at the Theatrical Society he took all of money in the alliance expense fund with him. Only after repeated requests to hand it back did he give back a portion of it."[6]

In April 1933, General Kai Feng of the International Clique, which was headed by Bo Gu (Qin Bangxian), replaced Gu Zuolin as secretary of the Central Bureau of the Youth League. In the fall Zhang Aiping, who had been Central Bureau secretary-general, replaced Wang Rongsheng as director and chief planner of the Central Corps of the Young Pioneers. At the beginning of 1934 Zhang Aiping was made responsible solely for the leadership of the Central Corps of the Young Pioneers. Hu Yaobang, who had come up through the ranks from local cadre and had demonstrated his excellence as director of the Propaganda Department of the Soviet District Anti-Imperialist Alliance, was promoted to the position of secretary-general of the Central Bureau of the Youth League. Mao Zetan was transferred to Hu's former post as director of the Propaganda Department.

From Bugler to Secretary-General of the Youth League

Upon arriving in the Jiangxi Central Soviet from the Pingjiang-Liuyang Soviet, Hu Yaobang began participating fully in the Chinese Workers and Peasants Army. At first the fifteen-year-old Hu Yaobang was appointed to the Red Army as a bugler in a communications corps.

At the time, 80 percent of the Youth League members in the Central Soviet District were illiterate and about 95 percent of the people in general could not recognize even the simplest characters. When Hu Yaobang first arrived in the Central Soviet District, the work of the Children's Brigade, the Young Pioneers, and the Youth League was not making any effective progress. Very soon after he joined the communications corps, his educational background and propaganda and organizational talents were noticed by his superiors. He was promoted to do political ideology and teaching tasks among children for the communications corps and became Youth League leader of the corps.

After Hu rose to the position of secretary of the party's Central Committee in the 1980s, many of the articles on his background tended to give the impression that during his time in the Jiangxi Central Soviet he was a messenger or dispatcher for Mao Zedong, and that this was the reason he later rose with the leadership. In fact, at that time Hu Yaobang "only saw their actions from a great distance."[7]

On June 23, 1932, the first conference of the Soviet District Anti-Imperialism Alliance was held in Ruijin, Jiangxi, chaired by Zhou Enlai and Xiang Ying, who also gave speeches. When the alliance was founded it contained five provincial alliances: Jiangxi, Fujian, Guangdong-Jiangxi, Zhejiang-Jiangxi, and Hunan-Jiangxi. The total membership of the alliance was said to be six million, including 300,000 members of the Red Army Alliance. In actuality, this was a highly inflated number since it included the Soviet District Red Army, the Youth League, Young Pioneers, and the Children's Brigade, whose members could only be considered symbolic members of the alliance. Nonetheless, it is true that it was one of the largest nonparty mass organizations directly under the leadership of the CCP Central Committee at that time.

Soon after Hu Yaobang started working for the alliance, because of his experience, abilities, and achievements, he "was promoted from the local organization to be a Youth League cadre" and made director of the Youth Department of the alliance. As head of the Youth and Propaganda departments he was mainly responsible for providing leadership for the Central Soviet District Children's Brigade, for expanding the organization of the brigade, for the general education and political training of the children, and for expanding their activities in support of the Red Army.

In September 1933, Hu wrote an article entitled "The Lively Activities of the Soviet District Communist Children's Brigade in the Last Three Months Under the Leadership of the Communist Youth League." He signed the article "Yaobang." The following are passages from this article.

> In support of the Red Army, we have established a Young Communist International Brigade in which workers and Pioneers [members of the Young Pioneers] have worked hard to help in mobilization, in such activities as organizing a Propaganda Brigade, organizing a Shock Brigade to help the families of new recruits with the harvest and with collecting firewood, and organizing an Investigation Corps to investigate and urge deserters to return. Especially in Changting, Xingguo, Wantai, Bosheng, Ruijin, and Yongfu [counties], many of the Children's Brigade members have each recruited seven or eight or even ten young persons to join the Red Army. In this way, the Children's Brigade has recruited more than 4,000 members.
>
> In support of the Soviet, in June the Propaganda Brigade participated in the mass movement to save and lend grain, and in July and August it participated in an investigation . . . that discovered a dozen or so rich landlord families who were secretly hoarding. They also uncovered a good deal of hidden gold and silver jewelry. Their participation in the enforcement of the Red martial law demonstrated a spirit of courage.
>
> Reply to doubling the organization: One of the two things that we were instructed to achieve in the September 3 memorandum of the Central Children's Office was to double our membership. To this task some of the Pioneers have responded brilliantly. For example, Ninghua [county] in three months has recruited 5,000 new members. . . . They not only doubled their membership, they clearly went way over that figure. But overall, we have only gained one-seventh of the target. This is due to the fact that some places have not taken this very seriously, have not carried their work down to the grass roots, to the masses of the children.

Hu Yaobang's leadership in children's work for the Soviet District Anti-Imperialist League was outstanding and effective. At the same time, he developed close friendships with Cai Xiaoqian, Zhang Aiping, and with the secretary of the Central Children's Office, Chen Pixian. He became especially good friends with Mao Zedong's younger brother, Mao Zetan.

Cai Xiaoqian's recollections note that

> Mao Zetan was very warm and frank. Although we worked together in the Anti-Imperialist League for only a half year, we had already established a close friendship. He and I, with Hu Yaobang, would often talk until late into the night. When he talked of the time he was on the Jiangxi Party Committee and was accused of implementing the "Luo Ming line," bitter tears would come to his eyes. He was still very angry about that. His health was not very good. Add to that this political blow. Emotionally he was very sensitive, and he said what he thought without any hesitation. Sometimes, Mao Zedong's very pretty young wife, He Zizhen, to show her concern, would send her younger sister, He Yi (Mao Zetan's wife), over with sauteed peppers or eggs for Mao Zetan. Mao Zetan was always very open about the things his wife brought over. Hu Yaobang and I once shared a sumptuous meal with him. Mao Zetan was a very frank and open person. When there was some free time he would always look for Hu Yaobang to play chess with him, or he would read fiction. The works he liked to read the most were the *Romance of the Three Kingdoms* and *The Water Margin*.[8]

Through his close friendship with Mao Zetan formed from common goals and interests, and through the indirect gifts brought by He Yi, Hu Yaobang, who had observed the work of Mao Zedong only from a great distance in the Central Soviet District, was filed away in Mao's memory bank, until one day much later when Mao Zedong would rediscover and decipher that memory once again.

At the end of 1933, having just turned eighteen, Hu Yaobang was admitted to the Chinese Communist Party, undoubtedly one of the great moments in his political career. In early 1934 he was promoted to secretary-general of the Central Committee of the Youth League, succeeding Zhang Aiping. From his former post of leadership in a non-party mass organization, Hu now moved to a position of leadership within the party. From leadership of the Children's Brigade, he rose to leadership of the Youth League.

This was just the moment when a very complex political struggle was developing within the Jiangxi Central Soviet, a struggle between the internationalist faction headed by Bo Gu and the grass-roots faction headed by Mao Zedong. The young Hu Yaobang obviously was not involved in any of the factional struggles. At the same time, the Jiangxi Central Soviet District was being threatened by the blockade and tightening encirclement campaign of Chiang Kai-shek's million-strong army. The supreme command of the Chinese Communists lay in the three-man group of Bo Gu, Zhou Enlai, and Otto Braun (German adviser from the Comintern, Chinese name, Li De). The strategy to break the grip of Chiang Kai-shek's fifth "extermination" campaign depended on the dual policy of military resistance and mobilization of the manpower and matériel of the soviet district in support of the front lines, while at the same time pursuing a hit-and-run war of quick surprise attacks.

But the Jiangxi Central Soviet was by now already in its last days. Hu Yaobang and the Young Pioneers mobilized the Red Youth Brigade and joined the larger movement of the Red Guardians (*chi weidui*). After a month of hit-and-run surprise attacks, only 70 percent of the planned objectives had been attained, and worse, some people were beginning to waver. At the time, *Red China* published an article entitled "Summary of the Past Month's Red Youth Brigade Surprise Attack Movement," which noted: "In some places the bureaucratism of the leadership organs blocked it. In some places the masses just fled into the mountains. . . . The movement to get deserters to return was even more ineffective. In the Bosheng-Yuangu district, of more than three hundred deserters, only four returned. In Changsheng, only a few dozen of over one thousand deserters returned. . . . In some of the border districts the Red Youth Brigade was disrupted by counterrevolutionary activities, such as the public counterrevolutionary propaganda in Guangchang, 'Only hoodlums make revolution, or join the Red Guardian Army.'"9

Meanwhile, in April 1934 at the battle of Guangchang, Bo Gu, Zhou Enlai, and Otto Braun concentrated the crack troops of the First, Third, and Fifth armies and prepared to use "staunch defense and quick surprise attack" tactics to "drive out the enemy." However, thanks to their blockade, control of the air, and heavy fire power, the much better equipped troops of Chiang Kai-shek were able to break into Guangchang, the northern gate of the Jiangxi Central Soviet.

This attempt to pit the brainpower of the Chinese Communist leadership and the manpower and resources of the Central Soviet in a do-or-die contest against the superior army of Chiang Kai-shek resulted in very costly and bloody losses. From this point on, the Jiangxi Central Soviet District diminished in size daily, and the situation became increasingly precarious. In October, to avoid being wiped out completely, the Red Army of the Jiangxi Central Soviet had no choice but to retreat to the west.

At the end of September Hu Yaobang had been notified by the party's Central Organization Office that he should make preparations to retreat west with the Red Army. This concluded Hu's tasks as Youth League secretary-general. However, this was not the end of his association with the Chinese Communist youth movement. Rather, one might say that it was the beginning of a slower Long March.

4
The Long March

After five months of secret preparations, in October 1934 the organization for the Long March of the Central Soviet's Red Army had been
completed. The plan to retreat to the west and join forces with the Sixth
Army Corps led by He Long and Guan Xiangying, active in the border
districts of Hunan, Hubei, Sichuan, and Guizhou, had been secretly
decided upon and implementation begun by the three men of the supreme command, Bo Gu, Zhou Enlai, and Otto Braun, following the
Guangchang defeat of April 1934. With the First Red Army Corps
under Lin Biao leading the right vanguard and the Third Red Army
Corps under Peng Dehuai leading the left vanguard, the central column
was made up of the members of the various bureaus and departments of
the CCP Central Committee, the Central Soviet government, the various departments of the Revolutionary Army, the high command of the
Red Army, various support groups, the cadre corps, the political militia, and security groups, a total of over 15,000 persons divided into the
First Central Military Column and the Second Central Military Column, which together were called the Central Military Column or "Red
Star." Protecting the rear of the Central Military Column was the Fifth
Red Army Corps under Dong Zhentang. The Eighth Red Army Corps
of Zhou Kun and the Ninth Red Army Corps of Luo Binghui protected
its left and right flanks respectively. In all, the army consisted of 85,000
persons, which in round terms was called "100,000." The entire Red
Army took the form of a covered corridor or passageway. Peng Dehuai
said that "The First and Third Army Corps were like two sedan-chair
bearers carrying this sedan-chair of the Central Column." In the early
evening of October 16, 1934, the army started out, moving toward the
banks of the Youdu River.[1]

As a member of the central administration of the Chinese Communist government, Hu Yaobang was assigned to the Central Work Corps of the Military Commission Second Field Column as secretary of the column's general branch party office. He was also made responsible for the leadership of the political ideology of the Youth League members of the Central Work Corps. Like every Red Star fighter, the eighteen-year-old Hu wore the new military outfit, had four hand grenades strapped to his chest, a rifle with bayonet slung from his shoulder, and ten pounds of grain and a knapsack on his back. He wore this full auxiliary military outfit throughout the entire course of the Long March, although just three days after the march began, he was laid up with an attack of malaria that took him about a month to recover from.

Slipping through the blockade and encirclement lines along the Jiangxi, Guangdong, and Hunan borders, though fraught with struggles against rain and frost, was possible because the Chinese Communists had a secret cease-fire agreement with the Guangdong warlord, Chen Jitang, who commanded the Guangdong Army segment of the encirclement campaign. The Red Army reached the banks of the Xiang River by the end of November without any major difficulties. It was there that the first defeat occurred. Chiang Kai-shek had already figured out that the Red Army intended to join up with the Second and Sixth Red Army Corps in the border areas of Sichuan, Guizhou, Hunan, and Hubei. Thus he immediately ordered the dispatch of a 400,000-man army made up of detachments of the Hunan, Guangdong, and Central armies to spread out and form a noose on the east bank of the Xiang River south of Quanxian to annihilate the Red Army.

It was a fierce battle. Covering the river crossing of the "Red Star Column," the First and Third Army Corps fought desperately, heroically. Amidst the earth-shattering cannon fire, the huge, cumbersome column spent nearly a week crossing the river and the Hunan-Guangxi highway. The Red Army lost all its supplies in this terrible defeat. More than six thousand of their transport personnel fled; one of the construction companies of the Eighth Red Army Corps was totally annihilated on the east bank of the river. The 85,000-man army was reduced to 30,000. Murmurs of disaffection were heard throughout the badly depleted ranks of the surviving troops.

Before and After the Zunyi Conference

An intense debate over the direction of the Red Army's flight broke out among the top party leadership. The elimination of the A-B [Anti-

Bolshevik] League, which Mao had pressed for during the last half of the Jiangxi Central Soviet period, and which had been criticized by the International faction led by Bo Gu, was now broadened. Mao Zedong, representing the rich peasant line, and the real power behind the Luo Ming Line, took immediate advantage of the circumstances to split Wang Jiaxiang and Zhang Wentian from the International faction and organize an underground triumvirate.

On December 18, 1934, the CCP Central Committee called a Politburo meeting in Liping, Guizhou. With the support of Wang Jiaxiang and Zhang Wentian, Mao Zedong proposed changing the original plan: meeting up with the Second and Sixth Army Corps, the column should advance toward and occupy the town of Zunyi in northern Guizhou and make it the center of a Sichuan-Guizhou border base. Adroitly perceiving the realities of military power, Zhou Enlai, seeing the changing opportunities, sided with Mao, ensuring the plan's acceptance.

On January 6, 1935, the advance troops of the Red Army attacked and took Zunyi, the main town of northern Guizhou. The Red Army headquarters then established itself in Zunyi, and in a revolt at first led by Wang Jiaxiang, the underground triumvirate headed by Mao Zedong, in liaison with those high officers who were not happy with the leadership of Bo Gu, Otto Braun, and Zhou Enlai, called an enlarged Politburo conference to examine the lessons of the failures since the Fifth Encirclement campaign. The Zunyi Conference met from January 14 to 16.[2] Mao Zedong accused the supreme triumvirate of having been "defensively conservative, offensively adventuristic, and flightist in times of change."[3] Mao's underground group, venting the full anger of the Red Army high officers, "shouted down" the three-man rule of Bo Gu, Otto Braun, and Zhou Enlai and successfully engineered a military coup d'etat. After the conference Mao was elected a member of the Standing Committee of the Politburo and, with Wang Jiaxiang and Zhou Enlai, organized a new supreme triumvirate that then also pushed out Zhang Wentian for being in collusion with Bo Gu. In the process of the continuing Long March they step by step gathered the real political and military power into their own hands.

In the assault on Zunyi, Hu Yaobang served in Peng Xuefeng's Thirteenth Regiment, a tough fighting unit that had become famous throughout the entire Red Army after a battle in the Gaohu'nao campaign in the Jiangxi Soviet period. Not long after Hu had been transferred to the position of party branch secretary in the regiment, he participated in the fierce battle to take Loushan Pass, as part of the second attack on Zunyi. On February 10 the Red Army took Weixin (Zhaxi) in Yunnan. Because the river crossing was blocked, the Thirteenth Regiment, under orders from Peng Dehuai, turned back and recrossed the Zhi River to attack Loushan Pass. But a detachment of Wang Jialie's army got to the pass before the Red Army. On February 15, after a forced march, the Thirteenth Regiment reached the pass. If they could take the pass, the defenseless town of Zunyi would be their prize.

By this time Hu Yaobang had already become a specialist in political propaganda. Before the attack he encouraged the regiment: "Comrades! To capture Zunyi, we must take Loushan Pass!" "Don't forget the past glories of our Thirteenth Brigade! Is Wang Jialie as good as the Nineteenth Route Army? That opium addict Wang Jialie has already been taught one lesson! We have crossed the Xiao River! We crossed the Xiang River! We leaped over the Wu River! We climbed Miao Mountain! Comrades, are we going to be stopped by one Loushan Pass? Do you really think we can't take it? We'll fly up it! We'll trample over it!"[4] The assault on Loushan Pass was a fierce, treacherous battle, but the Thirteenth Regiment finally took the pass at dusk. In this battle, Hu Yaobang built up their morale and also put himself at the head of the troops, risking all dangers, showing that he had the qualities of both an educated cadre and a soldier.

Following the victory of Loushan Pass, on February 27 the Third Red Army Corps fought its way down from the pass in a fierce attack as the First Red Army marched quickly on Zunyi, skirmishing with the enemy all the way. That afternoon Hu and his propaganda team waited not far outside Zunyi for their troops to clear the town so they could return. While they were waiting, fragments from a bomb dropped by a Nationalist airplane struck him, seriously wounding him in the right buttock.

The March of the Wounded to Northern Shaanxi

During the course of the Long March, the Red Army had a policy of protecting its cadres. To its seriously wounded cadres it gave the best medical care it could. Some were even carried on military stretchers with guards to protect them.

After being wounded, Hu Yaobang was carried into Zunyi on a stretcher and taken to the church. There he was treated by Dr. Wang

Bin, whom Hu thought was one of the first-class surgeons of the Red Army. For quite a few days Hu was carried on a stretcher, until he was finally able to ride a horse. The constant jolting was very painful. He rode horseback for eight or nine days and then gave the horse to someone who needed it even more. Thinking back on those days, Hu Yaobang says, "I didn't think once of giving up. There was no other way, just struggle."

Not long after his wounds had begun to heal, Hu Yaobang took on the responsibility of the Welfare Brigade, attached directly to the Third Red Army Corps. He took charge of organizing the wounded and sick, the old and weak, keeping up their fighting spirit, showing them how to take care of each other and overcome danger and obstacles, following along with the army.

The path of the Long March was extremely hazardous, not only because of the hostile terrain it traversed, but because it was always being pursued and attacked by the Nationalist forces. There was also the threat that came from the internal divisions and contest for power within the top party leadership. On or about March 11, 1935, the Red Army reached the area of Yaxi and Gouba, Guizhou province, where Mao Zedong formally took over important leadership powers of the Red Army. The new three-man military directorate—Mao, Zhou Enlai, and Wang Jiaxiang—took the place of Zhou Enlai's Red Army Political Committee. But Mao soon faced a serious challenge.

On June 16, 1935, at Mougong in northern Sichuan, the exhausted 30,000 troops of the First Front Army commanded by Mao Zedong joined forces with the more than 80,000 strong, rested troops of the Fourth Front Army commanded by Zhang Guotao. Zhang had been one of the sponsors and participants in the CCP's First Congress of 1921 and was senior to Mao in the party. His reasoning went, "He who has the troops and is strongest should be the leader." There was a subtle difference between this and Mao's "political power comes out of the barrel of a gun."

On June 25, the CCP Central Committee held an enlarged Politburo conference at Lianghekou, which, upholding Zhang Guotao's argument of superior troop strength and "responding to the current military needs, decided to restore the system of the Workers and Peasants Red Army Political Committee [and] made Zhang Guotao political commissar of the Red Army with responsibilities for the leadership of the National Red Army." At the same time it also added eight people to the Central Committee—Xu Xiangqian of the Fourth Front Army (originally an alternate member), Wang Shusheng, Fu Zhong, Zhou Chunquan, Zeng Chuanliu, Li Xiannian, He Wei, and Otto Braun.[5]

Not long after the Lianghekou conference, on August 6, the Central Committee held another Politburo meeting at Maoerkai. Zhang Guotao insisted on taking the troops south and establishing a revolutionary farming and herding district on the borders of Sichuan and Xizang [Tibet]. Mao Zedong would not budge an inch from his proposal that they should go north in the name of fighting the Japanese and establish a soviet district in the area of Shaanxi and Gansu. The overbearing obstinacy of Zhang Guotao, who had the superior troop strength, aroused the high leadership of the First Front Army to oppose his plan to go south. Even Otto Braun, who had lost much of his influence at the Zunyi Conference, rose to support Mao Zedong's plan to proceed north. The Red Army finally split, Mao Zedong leading the First Front Army as the core of the Right Route Army north into Shaanxi and Gansu, and Zhang Guotao leading the Fourth Front Army, the main body of the Left Route Army, south to Sichuan and Xizang. The town of Baxi was the spot where Mao and Zhang parted company. As the Fourth Front Army was leaving it shouted out: "Comrades of the First Front Army! Don't follow the big nose [Otto Braun]! Hurry back! The road north is only a dead-end! The road south is the only way out!"[6]

Nineteen-year-old Hu Yaobang, in command of the Welfare Corps of sick and wounded, marched forward without so much as a glance backward. The column passed through Naozikou, crossed snow-clad Min Mountain, forded the Wei River, and broke through the last of the Nationalist blockade lines on the Xian-Lanzhou highway, constantly harassed by the mounted troops of Ma Honggui and Ma Hongbin. It was late October 1935 when they finally walked into the town of Wuqi in the Shaanxi-Gansu Soviet District. After one year and 25,000 li [over 8,000 miles], having crossed eleven provinces, the Long March came to an end. Hu Yaobang was one of the 7,200 warriors who survived the Long March. Fifty years later, looking back on that year, he would say with pride, "Although China is today engaged in the Long March of modernization, we can still draw courage, strength, and wisdom from the Long March of the Red Army."[7]

5
Yan'an Years

Not long after the Long March reached northern Shaanxi, where the Central Red Army joined forces with the Fifteenth Red Army Corps led by Xu Haidong and Liu Zhidan, the two armies joined in a battle at Zhiluo village. That battle wiped out the 109th Division of the Northeast 57th Army, which was engaged in its third "annihilation" campaign against the Shaanxi-Gansu Soviet base. Mao Zedong remarked, "The battle of Zhiluo village in which the Central Red Army and the Northwest Red Army joined as brothers to shatter the 'encirclement and suppression' campaign of the traitor Chiang Kai-shek against the Shaanxi-Gansu Border District has laid the foundation for the party's Central Committee to establish a national revolutionary base in the Northwest."[1]

Mao immediately set up the Northwest Revolutionary Military Committee, with himself as chairman and Zhou Enlai and Peng Dehuai as vice-chairmen. But the land and the people of northern Shaanxi were very poor. There were many troops and few civilians, and just the desolate yellow earth stretching out as far as the eye could see. The great army of more than 20,000 troops would surely be "exterminated" by starvation.

In mid-December 1935, the Politburo of the Central Committee convened the Wayaobao Conference to discuss ways to keep the party alive and growing, and to find and take a new place for its members to live. There were many different views raised at the conference. The International faction wanted to go west and make contact with the Soviet Union. Lin Biao wanted to lead guerrilla attacks into southern Shaanxi. Peng Dehuai advocated stabilization and waiting for a good opportunity for action. Mao Zedong cut them all off, deciding that they should cross over to the east of the Yellow River and take the Luliang

Mountain Range as their base of operations, from which they would "expand while consolidating," moving into Shanxi province, responding to the student movement in Beiping and Tianjin, and beginning to construct a new world.

Mao became commander-in-chief of the Chinese Anti-Japanese Vanguard Army with Peng Dehuai as assistant commander-in-chief, Lin Biao and Nie Rongzhen commanding the First Army Corps as the Right Route Army, and the Fifteenth Army Corps of Xu Haidong and the Twenty-eighth Army Corps of Liu Zhidan as the Left Route Army. On February 6, 1936, Mao led the army's general headquarters to Yuanjiakou in Qingjian county on the banks of the Yellow River, preparing to cross over in the next day or so. Unexpectedly a heavy snow fell that night, inspiring Mao's poem "Snow": "Wintry scene in this northern land, a thousand li sealed in ice, ten thousand li of swirling snow. . . . From end to end, the great river's rushing torrent is stilled, and lost." The river crossing had to be delayed, but Mao's poem, after reflecting on China's past heroes, then concludes, "For really great men, we must look to the present."[2]

Because the land in the Shaanxi-Gansu border region was so impoverished, aside from the rations, ammunition, and medicine that the army carried with it, continued warfare depended on capturing supplies from the enemy. Li Fuchun had overall responsibility for the food and supplies of the army's Eastern Campaign. Under him were twelve work brigades providing propaganda, carrying out recruitment, and collecting supplies. Hu Yaobang was the captain of the Shilou county work brigade.

By 10 p.m. on February 20 the snow had stopped. Under dark clouds, with no moon and no stars, Hu Yaobang and his brigade successfully crossed the Yellow River with the Fifteenth Army Corps, with which Mao Zedong was also traveling. The next day they reached Yidie village, less than one day from Shilou county where Hu Yaobang's work brigade was to be stationed.

The poverty of Shilou county was not much different from that of northern Shaanxi. The Qing dynasty *Shilou Gazetteer* notes that, "With towns in the mountain valleys, it is extremely poor. The Fen commandery is the worst. The farmers do not sell any of their grain, and the women do not weave. Life is unbearable." It also says, "In Shilou there is not a single full community or family unit, all because of the marauding of Captain Li [Zicheng], which wasted the entire population."[3] At the time Shilou county had a population of something over ten thousand people. It was one of the poor counties of the Luliang Mountain area. The Fifteenth Army Corps took Shilou very quickly. The First Army Corps also took Xi county easily. Thus, the Shilou and Xi county area became the first temporary Red Army base east of the Yellow River.

The work brigade headed by Hu Yaobang immediately plunged into its tasks of propaganda, recruitment, and collecting supplies. In his former positions in the Jiangxi Soviet as director of the Youth and Propaganda departments of the Anti-Imperialist Alliance and secretary-general of the Youth League Central Committee, Hu Yaobang already had a good deal of experience and a successful record in recruitment and collecting supplies. His work in the Eastern Campaign was thus that of a seasoned veteran.

As head of his work brigade, Hu also had the tasks of mobilizing the people to resist Japan and carry out the Chinese Communist land reform program. The work brigade confiscated the property and houses of some landlords and local bullies, distributing them to the peasants. They also went house to house telling the people that the Red Army was making a revolution for the poor, and exposing the fact that Yan Xishan [the local governor] was in league with the Japanese and was guilty of cheating and oppressing the people. They posted notices of the Chinese People's Red Army Anti-Japanese Vanguard on every house in every village of the county. Hu also organized the members of his work brigade to use musical skits and performances, wall pictures, and big lecture meetings to make their propaganda messages popular and easy to understand, to overcome the language barrier. Though Hu was overworked, exhausted, and sick, his determination helped build the various anti-Japanese organizations, and "Red Army recruitment centers" daily received applications from poor young people who wanted to join the Red Army.

Shilou county quickly became a replenishment and operations base for the Red Army on the east side of the Yellow River. At that time the army's Eastern Campaign was divided into three parts: the Fifteenth Army Corps of Xu Haidong and the Twenty-eighth Army Corps of Liu Zhidan went north to threaten Taiyuan; the First Army Corps of Lin Biao and Nie Rongzhen went south following the watershed of the Fen River; and the Central Route Army made up of special personnel and the espionage corps led by Mao Zedong moved around in western Shanxi to attract and pin down the army of Yan Xishan. According to the recollections of Cao Danhui, one of the special personnel of the

Eastern Campaign, "The route of our movement was changeable. Sometimes we would head north and sometimes south, or again west, moving back and forth generally in the area west of Xiaoyi and Lingshi, south of Zhongyang, and east of Shilou and Xi counties. Then, when the enemy caught up with us we would always head west leading him straight to the banks of the Yellow River. . . . Because the masses loved the Red Army so much and because we emphasized mass work, news of our whereabouts was very well controlled, so that the enemy never really knew where we were."[4]

But the Eastern Campaign strategy of "expanding while consolidating" did not bear fruit because it soon ran into the counterattack of the joint forces of Chiang Kai-shek and Yan Xishan. Yan, who had all along run his own independent kingdom, as he called it, fully realized that the resources of one province were hardly a match for the Red Army. Consequently, he sent an urgent telegram to Chiang Kai-shek asking for help.

Chiang had originally wanted to take over Shanxi province himself, and he now responded immediately to Yan Xishan's plea by sending Tang Enbo's Thirteenth Army and Guan Linzheng's Twenty-fifth Division, which entered Shanxi from Hunan separately via the Qinghai-Gansu and Zhengzhou-Taiyuan railroads. When they reached Taiyuan they set up a "Bandit Suppression General Headquarters" for the four provinces of Shanxi, Shaanxi, Suiyuan, and Ningxia, with Chen Cheng as commander-in-chief. The objective of the Chiang-Yan cooperative effort was to force the Red Army into a narrow strip of territory on the east bank of the Yellow River, set up a new blockade, and then annihilate it.[5]

To avoid being surrounded as had happened in the Jiangxi Soviet District, Mao Zedong immediately recalled his armies. However, during the Eastern Campaign the Red Army had gained more than seven thousand new recruits and brought in some 500,000 yuan. So although the results were not quite as hoped for, the campaign did bring some small benefit to the Gansu-Shaanxi Soviet District.

To summarize the Red Army's experiences for the benefit of future campaigns, after crossing the river Mao called a meeting to discuss developments on the local level during the campaign. It was the recommendation and praise of Li Fuchun that prompted Mao to ask Hu Yaobang for a report.[6] This was the first time that Hu had met Mao. Speaking with a strong Hunanese accent, Hu gave a very orderly and clear presentation of the process of the work brigade's development and its achievements in recruitment and collecting funds. Mao was duly impressed.

A New Youth Movement

The Communist International held its Seventh Congress in Moscow in July and August 1935. In light of Fascist Italy's invasion of Abyssinia and the increased aggression of Japanese militarism against China, the Comintern felt that the Soviet Union was in danger of a pincer attack from the east and the west by Germany and Japan. It therefore called upon all Communist parties to do their utmost to form united fronts against fascism.

In September the International Communist Youth League held its Sixth Congress. In line with the Comintern's decision, the congress decided that national Communist Youth Leagues should effect fundamental changes that would make them "broadly based mass youth groups." At the same time, the International Communist Youth League directed the Chinese Communist Youth League to "cooperate and join with the young people of national liberation organizations and national reform organizations, and cooperate even with young people still under the influence of the Nationalist Party."[7]

The Central Committee of the CCP, which had just come from Jiangxi to the Shaanxi-Gansu border area, was also very dissatisfied with the work of the Communist Youth League. Because of the failure of the attempts to expand the revolution and because of the leftist tendency toward closed-doorism, or exclusivism, the Communist Youth League had long been a small organization of a few scattered families and individuals with no broad-based mass activities in the Nationalist districts. In the Red districts, the Communist Youth League had a tendency to act like an independent second party. It was for this reason that, upon receiving the directives of the Comintern and the International Communist Youth League, the party decided to revamp completely the Communist Youth League. On November 1, 1935, the party announced its "Decision Concerning Youth Work," the main points of which were: (1) to disband the Youth League organizations in areas under Nationalist control; all league members were, in accordance with concrete local circumstances, to join or organize legal, public youth mass organizations; (2) to accept a large number of the Youth League members into the party, while those who were not party members were to become activists in local satellite organizations of the party but were not to set up other branches or cells of the Youth League; local party organizations were to form youth offices or youth work committees and organize youth activities; (3) to stop all "second party" and closed-doorism tendencies, and instead to encourage democratic, flexible, and public youth activities, to expand youth organization membership at all levels.

Edgar Snow, who visited Yan'an in 1936, in his *Random Notes on Red China* lists the names of those who were then members of the Central Committee of the Chinese Comunist Youth League: Kai Feng (secretary), Feng Wenbin (assistant secretary), Guan Xiangying, Bo Gu, Cheng Changhao, Lu Dingyi, Wang Rucheng, Huang Liyi (a student, in prison), Liu Ying (female), Hu Yaobang, Wang Shengping, Chen Shifa, Pan Zhiming, Gao Langshan, and Li Ruishan.[8] Thus, after having made the Long March, Hu Yaobang was promoted from secretary-general of the Central Office of the Jiangxi Soviet Youth League to membership in the Central Office of the Chinese Communist Youth League. He was now one of the bright new talents among the leadership of the league.

After the announcement of the "Decision Concerning Youth Work," Hu became involved in reforming the league. He returned to Shaanxi from the Eastern Campaign to work primarily with organizing the border district National Salvation Youth Association (Qingnian Jiuguohui). This task was basically completed by the winter of 1936. Other than this, Communist Youth League organizations in the white districts had mainly been turned over to the Chinese National Liberation Vanguard. For this reason, on January 1, 1936, the Central Office of the Communist Youth League, of which Hu had been a member, was formally abolished. The reorganization of the Youth League as anti-Japanese National Salvation youth groups opened the door wide and drew in many young people who were enthusiastic about resisting Japan and saving the nation. It greatly strengthened the CCP's influence and vitality among the population as a whole and made it possible to engage openly in youth organization activities in the white districts. In the city of Xi'an, not far from the Shaanxi-Gansu Border District, student activities under the CCP's leadership created a climate of popular opinion favorable to resisting Japan, which was one of the factors that compelled Zhang Xueliang and Yang Hucheng to decide to kidnap Chiang Kai-shek and "force him to resist Japan" in the Xi'an Incident of December 12, 1936.

The united front strategy and the Xi'an Incident gave the Communist

Party some badly needed breathing space following the failure of the Eastern and Western campaigns. After the Xi'an Incident, the Communist and Nationalist parties joined hands for the second time to form a national united front to fight the Japanese.

Responding to the explosive growth of the anti-Japanese movement following the Xi'an Incident, the Chinese Communists hosted the First Northwest National Salvation Conference on April 12–17, 1937, at Yan'an's Lu Xun Arts School. Attending the conference were 312 delegates representing mass youth organizations having a total membership of more than 200,000. Among the Chinese Communist leaders who presented their greetings and talked at the conference were Mao Zedong, Zhou Enlai, Luo Fu, Zhu De, and Bo Gu. Hu Yaobang also attended as a youth delegate.

The conference proposed a draft "All-China National Salvation Youth Program" and passed the "Organizational Articles of the Chinese National Salvation Youth Association." It also decided on establishing a Northeast National Salvation Youth Association that would incorporate the highest leadership organs for National Salvation youth groups from all over China until a national association could be set up. The conference elected fifty-five executive officers who held their first executive meeting on April 18, at which an Executive Standing Committee was elected, with Feng Wenbin as chairman, Bai Zhimin, Gao Langshan, Liu Xiumei, Huang Qingxi, Xu Keren, and Li Ruishan as members, and Hu Yaobang and Liu Xiyuan as alternates.[9]

Less than three months after the conference, on July 7, the Marco Polo Bridge Incident began the full-scale Japanese invasion of China. The Xi'an Conference had helped the Chinese Communists to prepare ideologically and organizationally for developing the youth movement in the long war with Japan that lay ahead. But although Hu Yaobang had been elected as an alternate member of the Standing Committee, he was not devoting full time to the work of the youth movement. Beginning in the Yan'an period, and continuing for many years, the leading actor in Chinese Communist youth work was clearly Feng Wenbin. It was not until September 1952 that Hu replaced him.

Kangda—Resistance University

After the Xi'an Incident, Mao Zedong decided to implement an important plan modeled after the experience of the Huangpu Academy of Sun Yat-sen and Chiang Kai-shek—to train a large group of Chinese Communist military and political cadres who would be politically and militarily qualified, would understand the tactics and strategy of the national united front against Japan, and would be loyal to the political ideology of Mao Zedong.

In the spring of 1937, Mao moved what was originally the Chinese Red Army Anti-Japanese Military and Political College at Baoan to the Red capital at Yan'an and renamed it the Chinese People's Anti-Japanese Military and Political University, known as "Kangda," or "Resistance University," for short. Mao himself took the position of chairman of the the the Academic Committee. Lin Biao was made president of the college, with Luo Ruiqing as vice-president and Liu Yalou as academic dean, all from the highest levels of the CCP. Mao also lectured on his *Problems of Strategy in China's Revolutionary War, Policies, Measures and Perspectives for Resisting the Japanese Invasion, On Contradiction, On Practice,* and *On Protracted War,* which became known as the cornerstones of Mao Zedong Thought. This shows how important the trainees at the college were to Mao.

For the spring term of 1937, the university recruited 2,767 trainees, most of whom were high-ranking cadres from the First, Second, and Fourth Front armies, and from the North Shaanxi Army. A portion of the trainees were young intellectuals from the outside who wanted to fight Japan. Actually this was the school's second term, but it was also called the first united front term. The trainees were divided into eight groups. The first group was made up of division-level officers, the second of company-level officers, and the others, except for the young intellectuals, consisted of officers or cadres from battalion level or higher. As soon as the First Northwest National Salvation Conference was over, Hu Yaobang was immediately transferred to the first group, headed by the famous general Chen Geng. Hu was selected to be branch secretary of the group.

Mao considered the first and second groups to be very important, and they attracted the attention of the whole school, not just because they brought together the high-level officers of the Red Army, but even more because of the "revolt" of the high military officers from the Fourth Front Army who were part of these two groups. This incident shook the party leadership and was to have far-reaching influence.

After the Fourth Front Army commanded by Zhang Guotao had parted company at Baxi with the First Front Army commanded by Mao Zedong, it had set up its own independent Central Committee in the Sichuan-Xizang border region. But after a year of fighting it was badly defeated by a joint campaign of the Sichuan Army and Nationalist Army. A contingent of more than twenty thousand men commanded by Xu Xiangqian and Chen Changhao was also almost entirely wiped out by the cavalry of the Ma family. Thus, Zhang Guotao had no choice but to join the Second Front Army, made up of the Second and Sixth Army Corps of He Long, Ren Bishi, Guan Xiangying, and Xiao Ke, and come north. In early October 1936, after many difficulties and hardships, the First, Second, and Fourth Front armies finally joined up in Gansu.

Zhang Guotao now had no troops of his own, and not only was he not suitable for leadership, Mao Zedong criticized him for representing leftist opportunist and splitist tendencies. After reaching the Shaanxi-Gansu border region, a number of the high officers of the Fourth Front Army were ordered to join the Resistance University's first and second groups for training. These included Wang Weizhou, He Wei, Xu Shiyou, Wang Jian'an, and Wang Bo. Mao thought that the officers, having being tested in this struggle between the two different positions, should criticize the mistakes of Zhang Guotao and at the same time criticize their own errors of misunderstanding. Mao expected that they would thus be won over to the position he represented. The officers of the First Front Army, who had followed the correct position, quite naturally initiated the struggle between the two positions, which then led to hostility and ideological clashes between the officers of the two armies and ultimately erupted into the "revolt" incident.

In his *My Recollections*, Zhang Guotao says defensively:

> The Anti-Japanese Military and Political University [Kangda] was chosen to be the center of the Zhang Guotao struggle. Before anything happened, a secret directive saw to it that the other sections were separated from the Red Army sections so that outsiders would not be able to see what was going on within the ranks of the Red Army itself. All the school's weapons were collected and put away to avoid the possibility of an armed incident breaking out in the course of the struggle. . . . The essentials of Zhang Guotao's "crime" had already been determined, so the main purpose of this struggle became the attempt to get the support of the Fourth Front Army officers. The struggle experts loudly exhorted the officers of the Fourth Front Army to come back under the leadership of the Central Committee of the CCP, to admit their past mistakes and never again be influenced by a certain Mr. Zhang, to renounce their mistakes. But this approach did not have the desired effect, because a great many of the officers proposed that there should be a full and impartial discussion

of mistakes or errors, not just a partial or one-sided discussion. They even said that they wanted to discuss whether or not the Central Committee led by Mao Zedong hadn't made mistakes too. . . . [This] finally aroused a loud outcry of support from most of the students of the school. Ten of the top officers of the Fourth Front Army, including Xu Shiyou and Wang Jian'an, leading four or five hundred of the students, planned to get up and leave [the university] on the spot. . . . Over forty were arrested and turned over to Dong Biwu, chief justice of the Supreme Court, for indictment and sentencing.[10]

The storm then spread to the lower ranks of the Fourth Front Army. For example, in one of their work reports to Mao Zedong several of the comrades said,

> Generally speaking, everybody's consciousness was raised very quickly, but there was also some confusion and misunderstanding.
>
> Mao Zedong encouraged them, saying, "What are you afraid of? Without confusion there cannot be understanding! Don't worry, speak truthfully."
>
> . . . It was like this—one Fourth Front Army brigade officer told the troops, "Think about it, comrades. Who has the greater learning, Mao Zedong or Zhang Guotao?" To which several soldiers replied, "Zhang Guotao!" "Oh? That's pure nonsense . . . the idiot who said that needs to be straightened out!"
>
> Mao Zedong calmly shook his head, "You can't do it that way!" Later he also stated very firmly, "Please go back and make it clear to everyone that you are only to criticize Zhang Guotao's errors. Don't attack the Fourth Front Army officers. They should not be held responsible for the errors of Zhang Guotao's position. And certainly not the soldiers."[11]

During the Yan'an period, Mao Zedong's use of the "divide and conquer" [lit.: one divides into two] strategy was very subtle and flexible. As soon as he saw that the situation might get out of hand he immediately and decisively drew a line between Zhang Guotao and the officers and troops of the Fourth Front Army and focused the attack on Zhang. At the same time, by setting up a Hubei CCP, and with the help of Dong Biwu, who had strong ties with the Fourth Front Army, Mao dealt peacefully with those who had been taken into custody for planning the "revolt." "Most of the comrades were released and a small number were sentenced to short jail terms, the longest of which was three months. All were released early, and all were then sent back to the Resistance University to continue their studies."[12]

As party branch secretary of one of the units at the heart of the incident, Hu Yaobang had firmly maintained that Mao Zedong's policy of going north had been the right one, and that Zhang Guotao's policy of going south and of setting up a separate Central Committee had been wrong. Thus Hu Yaobang, with Xu Shiyou, Wang Jian'an, and others, stood at the front line of those vigorously pushing the progressive view. Thanks to his quick reactions and ironclad arguments, forged in his long experience of political propaganda, simple but honest followers like Xu Shiyou always felt that Hu Yaobang's critical acumen and arguments were hard to resist. Hu's style tended to be one of laying out the facts and basic principles, with very little empty political posturing. Furthermore, in criticism struggles his work demonstrated the flexibility of one who was good at organizing and emphasizing the official ideological changes of the Fourth Front Army. Hu also observed closely the dynamics and attitudes of the trainees, on which he periodically reported. In this close-quarters battle in the Red capital, Hu experienced his first major ideological struggle within the upper ranks of the party. He showed himself to be on the vanguard of the Mao Zedong line.

Clearly, Mao appreciated the loyalty and flexibility that Hu Yaobang demonstrated. Following the Marco Polo Bridge Incident, in response to the needs of the anti-Japanese war, the second-term trainees of the Resistance University graduated in July, somewhat ahead of schedule, and were sent off to the front lines. Of the class of 2,767 trainees, Hu Yaobang was one of 28 selected to stay on at the college and continue with advanced studies.

The head of the advanced studies class was Shao Shiping, who, with Fang Zhimin, was one of the founders of the Northeast Jiangxi Soviet District and the Tenth Red Army. At age twenty-two, Hu Yaobang began his close association with high-ranking leaders such as Chen Geng and Shao Shiping. It was in this period that Hu began calling Shao, in the manner of good friends, "Older Brother Shao," and calling Shao's wife, Hu Delan, "Older Sister Delan." Su Zhenhua, head of the fifth section of the second-term trainees at university, and Yang Dezhi, head of the seventh section, were also classmates who would later become top officers in the military.

It was his studies in the advanced training class of Resistance University that laid the foundation for Hu's later achievements in Marxist-Leninist theory and philosophy. These were the classes where Mao Zedong lectured on the finest products of his thinking, *On Practice* and

On Contradiction. It was here that Hu mastered the weapon of critical thought that in later years would lead to his own sense of self-confidence and to his success as a top party leader.

School "Administrator"

Following the Marco Polo Bridge Incident, many young people burning with the desire to fight Japan and save the nation poured into Yan'an from all parts of China. The third term of Resistance University enrolled 1,272 trainees, some of whom were Eighth Route Army officers, but most of whom were young intellectuals from the outside. In the autumn of 1937, after graduating from the advanced studies class, Hu Yaobang was kept at the school at Mao Zedong's personal suggestion, to be party general branch secretary of the university.

In an article commemorating Mao Zedong entitled "My Best Memories," Hu Yaobang wrote, "He taught me that to do the work of a general branch of the party well, we must first publish a good school paper. When he saw the first issue of this school paper, he criticized us for not having written anything ourselves, and himself courageously wrote that famous public call to battle, 'Combat Liberalism.'"[13] Resistance University's paper was called *Sixiang zhanxian* (Ideological Battleline). It was printed on a mimeograph machine. Mao's article was printed on September 7, 1937. Under Mao's urging and instruction, Hu Yaobang then wrote an article entitled "On Liberalism and Antiliberalism," which was published in the next issue. In it he addressed the appearance of various kinds of liberal carelessness and sloppiness among the trainees at the university.

It is interesting to note that publication of Hu's mimeographed newspaper was paralleled by that of Deng Xiaoping, who the same year, while studying in Paris, published *Shaonian bao* (Youth Report) and became known as "Dr. Mimeograph." Both were one-man operations. Hu Yaobang did everything on *Ideological Battleline*, from the rough draft, through setting up columns and writing headlines, to making the masters, running the mimeograph machine, and distributing the product.

At the beginning of 1938, Hu was promoted to the position of assistant director of the Political Department of Resistance University, responsible mainly for "actively and carefully developing party members" among the young intellectuals arriving from the outside. At the time, the party's Central Committee wanted the University Committee to work with the young trainees from the outside, to give them "politically a thorough grasp of the party's basic teachings so they will understand its main principles, to teach him (or her) the political strategy of the United Front, to give him (or her) an unshakeable political direction, to raise him (or her) to the level of a Communist Party member with the high ideals and selflessness of a professional revolutionary, and furthermore to induct into the party as many as possible of the outstanding ones."[14]

For Hu Yaobang this was a new task, because the old methods for recruiting party members were not usable here. One could no longer just ask, "Where are you from? How many are there in your family? What jobs have you had in the past? Would you like to join the Communist Party?" It was now necessary to propagandize among the trainees. "The Chinese Communist Party initiated the anti-Japanese national united front. Today the strengthening and expansion of any party strengthens and expands the anti-Japanese battleline, strengthens and expands the anti-Japanese forces. The teachings, political program, organizational principles, and regulations of the party must make him (or her) understand that this is why the party is expanding, why it is accepting many outstanding people into the party."[15] Hu busied himself in this work.

Reviewing the applications for party membership and the trainees' background reports was very time-consuming. The historical circumstances and social relationships that appeared in the background essays of the young intellectual trainees were often several thousand characters long and were much more complex than those of party members from peasant backgrounds. Hu not only examined each case himself, he asked other cadres in the Organization Division (Zuzhi ke) to look through the materials and then raise questions, after which he would talk with the applicants individually. Then, knowing the true facts about the applicant, a decision would be made quickly. During Hu Yaobang's time as assistant director of the Political Department of the university, more than 70 percent of the third-term trainees were recruited as new party members. The trainees that Hu sponsored for party membership that year are even today one source of his political power.

A Model of the United Front

In April 1938, Hu moved from the position of assistant director of the Political Department to that of political officer of the first section of the university's fourth-term trainees. The section leader was Su Zhenhua, Hu's classmate in the second term.

By this time the anti-Japanese war had already spread from China's coastal cities into the hinterland. The Chinese Communist policy had turned from "Force Chiang Kai-shek to resist Japan" to "Help Chiang Kai-shek resist Japan." The battle cries of the united front were already beginning to be heard, bringing large numbers of young intellectuals to Yan'an. This was the golden age of Resistance University's growth.

The fourth-term trainees at the university numbered 5,562 persons, the great majority of them young intellectuals from the outside, including a number of prorevolution young women (organized as the school's Section 8). Most of the Section 1 trainees for whom Hu Yaobang was political officer were "seedlings" who had a relatively high level of schooling and some revolutionary experience.

Because of the war, Resistance University was split into four units. The school administration and sections 2, 3, 4, and 8 were stationed in Yan'an. Section 5, headed by He Changgong, was sent to Qingyang in Gansu province. Section 6, headed by Wei Guoqing, was located in Luochuan; Section 7, under Xu Decao, was at Panlong; and Section 1, under Xu Zhenhua with Hu Yaobang as political officer, moved into Wayaobao in May 1938.

At the time, Wayaobao was part of the Suide Special District of Anding county (later named Zichang county) in northern Shaanxi. Wayaobao was a very lovely village, a rarity for Shaanxi province, a beautiful flower on the impoverished yellow plateau. The buildings all looked like matching brick kilns, neat and clean, with a smooth, straight street of stone slabs and a protective town wall. Almost anywhere around Wayaobao one can find coal that lights easily and burns without smoke, and because heating resources are so cheap, the peasants all build brick kilns. The difference in life style between rich and poor in the Wayaobao area was not very great. On the average, landlord families had 5.78 *shang* of fields (1 shang is about 5 mu, or something less than an acre), rich peasants had 5.66 shang per family, middle peasants had 3.9 shang, and poor peasants had 2.38 shang. Even hired farm laborers had an average of 1.72 shang per family. Wayaobao may be described as a reasonably prosperous area of self-sufficient peasant life on the north Shaanxi plateau. When Mao Zedong led the Central Red Army on the Long March into northern Shaanxi, it had been the temporary "capital."

From the beginning of the anti-Japanese united front in 1937 to the first serious outbreak of friction in 1940, this second period of cooperation between the Nationalists and Communists saw the establishment of both Nationalist and Communist organs in the Shaanxi-Gansu-Ningxia Border Region, including Yan'an. During this period the Nationalists maintained rather large forces in the border region, such as those of the Nationalist special deputy He Shaonan in the Suide Special District, those of Tian Jiesheng, magistrate of Anding county and the Nationalist special deputy for Longdong Special District, and those of County Magistrate Fang in Ning county. The Chinese Communists felt that all of these men were specialists in creating friction and were extremely difficult to deal with. The districts under their supervision were especially sensitive and prone to friction. For this reason, the struggle to secure these prosperous districts and their peoples became a special battle between the Nationalists and Communists. At the beginning of May 1938, Hu Yaobang and Su Zhenhua led Resistance University's fourth-term Section 1 students, about three hundred in all, into Wayaobao. There they created an outstanding model for expanding the influence of the CCP. Even Nationalist Party journals in Taiwan today recognize this:

> Hu Yaobang has long experience not only in military and party work, he was unusually effective in United Front work. It was after the Marco Polo Bridge Incident, some 100 li east of Yan'an in the county town of Suide County [Wayaobao], which was administered by a [Nationalist] government-appointed county magistrate and protected by a county defense corps. This was an important government base within Communist-controlled northern Shaanxi district. Although the 359th Brigade of the Eighth Route Army's 120th Division commanded by Chen Bojun and Wang Zhen was stationed outside the county town, they did not dare occupy it by force. Then, Hu Yaobang, head of the Political Department of this branch school of the "Anti-Japanese Political and Military University" [i.e., Kangda], brought two to three hundred trainees from said school into the Suide county town, ostensibly for "joint resistance against Japan." They took over the campus of the Suide Teachers School which they turned into a "Resistance University Branch School." Then, using "united front" tactics and talking big about the great principles of the "Anti-Japanese united front," Hu Yaobang asked the county magistrate voluntarily to turn over the town to them. At the same time, mobilizing the "Resistance University" trainees to act like they were "making friends," they mounted broad psychological warfare on the defense corps personnel to create political dissension in their ranks. At the same time he maintained constant contact with the 359th Brigade stationed outside of

town to discuss strategy for the use of force. Thus, by Hu Yaobang's use of the "united front tactics" of "both unity and struggle" at the same time, the Chinese Communists took the Suide County town without wasting a single bullet. Later on, Hu Yaobang's united front experience with "both unity and struggle" became an important part of Mao Zedong's "united front" theory and strategy. The "united front tale" spread widely among the Chinese Communist cadres and was to have a profound influence.[16]

This shows that Hu's "united front tale" was not just romantic fiction, but was indeed based on fact.

The Section 1 trainees led by Hu Yaobang and Su Zhenhua, using the Normal School as their base, in addition to their rigorous and disciplined military and political training, were also mobilized to go out into the countryside to spread propaganda in accordance with the "Ten Articles for Resisting Japan and Saving the Nation." They especially emphasized article 7 on the reduction of rents and interest rates. In this way the trainees gained practical experience in the united front, which developed their leadership talents, while at the same time actually bringing the Communist Party's policies and style of working with and for the people to the inhabitants of Suide county.

At the beginning of 1939, the Nationalist county magistrate of Suide county, Tian Jiesheng, detained the county magistrate for the Communist side, Xue Lanbin, over questions of recruitment and authority. As soon as he heard the news, Hu Yaobang immediately initiated two actions. On the one hand he led the school's trainees to intercept Tian Jiesheng and let him know the seriousness of his act and the principles underlying it and to propose a reasonable solution, and, on the other hand, he sent an emergency message asking Wang Zhen to put the 359th Brigade on alert to provide support. Finding himself in an untenable position, lacking both sufficient reasons and adequate force, Tian Jiesheng had no choice but to release Xue.

In March 1939, Liu Zhong's fifth-term Section 5 from Resistance University was sent to Wayaobao to take over for Hu Yaobang's Section 1. The trainees and teachers of Section 1 returned to Yan'an. During Hu's stay in Wayaobao, in spite of continuous friction between the Nationalists and Communists there, not a single shot had been fired. In the course of the clashes between the two sides, Hu had clearly dominated over Tian Jiesheng. His model experience of "both unity and struggle" in Wayaobao was adopted as a permanent guideline for the Chinese Communist united front strategy, as presented in Mao

Zedong's articles "On the Question of Political Power in the Anti-Japanese Base Areas," "Current Problems of Tactics in the Anti-Japanese United Front," and "On Policy."

A Lovely Spring Breeze

After returning to Yan'an, Hu Yaobang was first assigned as political officer of the Central Committee's Security Force (*jingwei tuan*) (of which Wang Dongxing was then assistant chief of staff). Before long, at Mao Zedong's personal suggestion, he was appointed director of the Organization Department of the Military Commission's General Political Bureau. Of Hu Yaobang's tenure in this position and relations with others there have been a number of different, conflicting accounts, none of which is very reliable. Let us turn rather to Hu's own account. In his preface to *Remembrances of Wang Jiaxiang*, Hu writes, "I have an unusually profound impression of comrade Wang Jiaxiang. This is not just because I worked directly under him from 1939 to 1944, and learned much from him during these years. More importantly, at a key time in the history of our party, he made a very important contribution."[17]

This refers to the period of the Long March when Wang Jiaxiang very early split with the International faction to support and cooperate with Mao Zedong, bringing down the triumvirate headed by Bo Gu. This began the consolidation of Mao's position of leadership of the Chinese Communist Party, both militarily and politically. In late June 1937, after the Long March reached northern Shaanxi, because he was so severely wounded Wang was sent to the Soviet Union for treatment. In August 1938, he returned to Yan'an and was immediately appointed vice-chairman of the Central Committee's Military Commission and chairman of the General Political Bureau. When Wang first took these positions, Tan Zheng was director of the General Political Bureau's Organization Department. Tan Zheng was also from Liuyang county, another hometown neighbor of Hu Yaobang, one of the three sons of Sanwan [county], Jiangxi, to follow Mao Zedong up into Jinggang Mountain after the Autumn Harvest Uprising. Mao placed great faith in Tan Zheng not just because the characters for their names in both cases contained a total of twenty-eight strokes, but because he had once been Mao's secretary on Jinggang Mountain, and Mao felt they shared a common Communist destiny.[18] The fact that Mao Zedong personally proposed that Hu Yaobang succeed to Tan Zheng's position as director of the Organization Department shows that Mao thought Hu was a responsible young man of promise.

At the time the personnel of the General Political Bureau of the Military Commission of the Central Committee were as follows:

Wang Jiaxiang, chairman
Tan Zheng and Fu Zhong, vice-chairmen
Tao Zhu, general political secretary
Hu Yaobang, director, Organization Department
Xiao Xiangrong, director, Propaganda Department
Wu Gaizhi, director, Counterespionage Department
Wang Xuewen (1940), director, Enemy Army Work Department

According to Hu Yaobang's own account, "Mao Zedong himself proposed that I become director of the Organization Department. I was then only twenty-three [thus, 1939]. The head of the Organization Department had to talk with high-level officers. At that time I went and talked with General Chen Geng, General Xiao Ke, General Xu Haidong, General Wang Shusheng, etc."[19]

Now at the center of the Chinese Communist army organization, representing Mao Zedong and the Military Commission of the Central Committee, Hu Yaobang would deliver orders of appointments and dismissals to generals and colonels. "When I sometimes criticized them somewhat severely, these high-level commanders would still listen."[20] During the five years that Hu held the post of Military Commission Organization Department director, he got to know well and understand the commanding officers in all areas of the Chinese Communist military, and he formed work and personal relationships with them. For Hu, this was another crucial step for his later task as secretary-general of the Central Committee of the CCP, the task of insuring that the military would follow the orders of the party.

At the same time, Hu also participated in the work of the Central Committee North and Central China Work Conference chaired by Wang Jiaxiang. The conference was set up as follows:

Wang Jiaxiang, chairman
Wang Ruofei, general secretary
Delegates:
Luo Ruiqing (Resistance University)
Xiao Jingguang (Garrison Command)
Hu Yaobang (Organization Department, General Political Bureau)
Xiao Xiangrong (Propaganda Department, General Political Bureau)

Yang Song (Central Propaganda Department)
He Qingshi (United Front Bureau)
Guo Huaruo (First District Military Commission)
Wang Heshou
Wang De, etc.[21]

From the structure of this list, one can see that the Central Committee North and Central China Work Conference, which had the duty of organizing the overall Chinese Communist leadership groups in North and South China for the day-to-day tasks in such areas as the party, military, united front, propaganda, and information work, was similar in form to the later regional secretariats after Liberation. Hu Yaobang's participation in the work conference again added to his experience and training in leadership work, and again broadened his range of connections.

It was during this period that Wang Jiaxiang first said that "Mao Zedong is China's strategic genius" and wrote a poem on "Mao Zedong Thought." Later, promoted by Liu Shaoqi and others at the Seventh Plenum, which helped systematize it, Mao Zedong Thought, with Mao himself at the center, became the central authoritative system of Chinese Communist ideology. Most certainly, Hu Yaobang, who had been supported and promoted more than once by Mao Zedong personally, at this time was a firm and loyal believer in Mao Zedong Thought and one of the central figures in Mao's system of authority.

For a young man of twenty-three to have already become director of the Central Committee Military Commission Political Bureau's Organization Department was indeed a very rapid rise in the world. But things were to become even better in Hu's early career. In 1942, he and Li Zhao, a graduate of the Chinese Women's University of Yan'an, declared their love for each other and were married.

In the late autumn of 1938, the seventeen-year-old Li Zhao had come to Yan'an from Anhui province to participate in the anti-Japanese movement. Having a clear record, she passed the political investigation and was admitted to the Chinese Women's University. Yan'an Chinese Women's University was founded July 20, 1939, with the eminent Wang Ming as its president. The great majority of Chinese Women's University students were young intellectuals about twenty years of age from the area around Yan'an or from parts of China that had fallen to the Japanese. A small number of the students were the daughters of workers or peasants, but there were also some daughters of the rich and famous families of China.

The guidelines under which Chinese Women's University was founded were: "To cultivate and train talented women cadres for the War of Resistance and the rebuilding of the nation," "to cultivate intellectual women cadres . . . who will have a revolutionary theoretical foundation and revolutionary work methods, who will be leaders of the women's movement and have good professional skills."[22] The school was divided into a general studies section, an advanced studies section, and a special section. The advanced studies section was to train cadres of a fairly high theoretical level. The special section was primarily for worker and peasant cadres with experience in the women's movement. The basic curriculum included the history of social development, political economics, Marxism-Leninism, and problems in the Chinese revolution. There were also electives such as the women's movement, military training, medicine and health, education, Russian language, English language, and Japanese language. The teaching methods included a combination of both class and individual studies. The students also participated in such manual labor activities as farming, road repair, and firewood gathering. Li Zhao was a graduate of the advanced studies section of Chinese Women's University.

Although by 1942 he was still only twenty-seven, Hu Yaobang had accumulated a great deal of experience about life and suffered many hardships. His marriage to this young woman was to bring him a great deal of comfort and happiness. They came together and fell in love in Yan'an's new atmosphere of mutual freedom and equality between the sexes. Li Zhao was also a good wife, bearing and raising their children, mediating and stilling the quarrels between the boys, cooking the Hunan dishes Hu loved so much, bringing him the true happiness of family life, leaving him free of worry, to devote his whole energies to his work.

Li Zhao worked in the textile industry for a long time, with women like Hao Jianxiu and Wu Wenying, who had risen from the textile industry and spoke the same language. Li understood the broader implications of things. When she reached sixty she retired from her position as party secretary of the Beijing Textile Bureau and was never the burden to Hu Yaobang that Jiang Qing was to Mao Zedong. She also went frequently to Japan and Hong Kong as an ordinary citizen, collecting informed impressions for Hu on both foreign affairs and domestic affairs.

The Yan'an period was the golden age of the rise of the Chinese Communist Party, and it was also a time of great satisfaction in young Hu Yaobang's career and personal life.

6
The War
of Liberation

In May 1945 the Allied Forces of Great Britain, the United States, and the Soviet Union entered and occupied Berlin, the capital of Nazi Germany. In June the American forces took the Japanese military base at Okinawa. Victory in the antifascist world war was on the horizon.

From April 23 to June 11, 1945, the Seventh Congress of the Chinese Communist Party was convened in Yan'an, nearly seventeen years after the Sixth Congress. Mao Zedong presented a political report to the congress, "On Coalition Government." This is the only article by Mao that contains outlines of a program for national reconstruction. In this report, Mao called on the entire Communist Party of "more than 1.2 million members; this time, no matter what happens, we cannot allow ourselves to be dispersed by the enemy. . . . By strengthening unity among all comrades within the party and by strengthening our unity with all the people outside the party, we can guarantee that not only will the enemy not be able to disperse us, on the contrary, we shall certainly resolutely and thoroughly destroy the Japanese aggressors and their faithful running dogs completely, and go on to rebuild a China of the New Democracy."[1]

The Seventh Congress affirmed Mao as the leader of the entire party. The International faction of Wang Ming, having been criticized in the Yan'an rectification movement, was already a thing of the past. Hu Yaobang was one of the 547 delegates who represented the entire party membership at the congress. Hu's first participation in a national party congress is a clear indication that he was one of the grass-roots cadre corps that was continuing to rise within the party under the leadership of Mao Zedong.

Meanwhile, in June Chiang Kai-shek convened the Sixth Congress of the Nationalist Party. He announced to the congress that he would end the martial law that had existed for seventeen years since the Northern Expedition, and that he had decided to convene a National Assembly on November 12 to return government to the people, following the principles of Sun Yat-sen, and move China into the era of constitutional government.

On August 10, 1945, the Japanese, after fifty years of aggression against China beginning with the Sino-Japanese War of 1895, formally announced their unconditional surrender. Pressed by the hopes of the nation and the urgings for reconciliation of the United States, Chiang Kai-shek and Mao Zedong met to shake hands in Chongqing on August 28. After more than forty days of talks, they signed the "October 10th Agreement" on a nationwide ceasefire. The historical record shows, however, that the Nationalists and Communists were both buying time to expand their forces as a prelude to another outbreak of civil war. The two protagonists knew each other very well from more than twenty years of bitter experience. Both had decided that China could be unified only by force.

Not long after the victory over Japan, Hu Yaobang was sent to the Shanxi-Chahar-Hobei [Jin Cha Ji base area] frontlines as head representative of the Political Bureau for the Shanxi-Jehol-Liaoning Military District. He was soon transferred to the position of political officer in the district. The commanding officer, Chen Zhenxiang, had been a tough general of the Fourth Front Army and had distinguished himself against the Japanese general Abe Narihide.

At that point the Communist strategy was to enter the Northeast with the Russian forces and to use the Anti-Japanese Democratic United Army of Lin Biao, Peng Zhen, and Gao Gang to take the Northeast and turn it into a relatively stable base area (*houfang*). When Hu Yaobang first took up his duties in the military district, he led troops in guerrilla attacks and mobile warfare, enlarging the liberated area, and actively trained and incorporated troops from the Japanese puppet army into the Communist forces. He was responsible for getting soldiers and matériel to support the army in its battle to move north of the Great Wall. Without doubt, seizing the Northeast was an important turning point in improving the Communists' strategic position.

Early Stages of the Civil War

In the summer of 1946, the civil war between the Nationalists and Communists exploded full-scale. At the time, Chiang Kai-shek's total troop strength numbered 4.3 million men, while that of the Chinese Communists was 1.2 million, a ratio of 3.5 to 1. In addition, Chiang controlled all the major cities of China and most of the railroad and transportation lines as well as most of the areas that were rich in resources, giving him overwhelming material superiority.

At the beginning of the hostilities, the Nationalist armies attacking the Shanxi-Chahar-Hebei Military District numbered about 162,000. The Beiping army of Fu Zuoyi, the Shanxi army of Yan Xishan, and the troops of Li Wen, Chiang Kai-shek's son by his first wife, aimed their vanguard toward Zhangjiakou [Kalgan], which was then held by the Communists. In the autumn of 1946, Hu Yaobang commanded troops that participated in the battle for the defense of Zhangjiakou. But under attack by the greatly superior Nationalist forces, they had no choice but to abandon the city and revert to guerrilla and mobile warfare tactics in eastern Hebei. The situation was truly precarious.

At this point, Mao Zedong drafted a telegram, "Surround the Cities and Attack Their Support," to be sent by the Central Committee Military Commission to the Shanxi-Jehol-Liaoning Military District, which read,

> Your battle guideline should emphasize destroying the enemy's life support system. Then, any place the enemy sets up base will revert to us naturally and easily. To implement this guideline, you should surround a city and attack its support lines. The object in surrounding a city is not to take it but to cut off its supplies. Concentrate seven to eight times the enemy's troop strength. For example, concentrate four or five regiments to attack a support force of one or two platoons. Be fully prepared before you strike. Don't strike on impulse. Make sure that when you strike you win. When attacking, encircle and outflank the enemy. Annihilate the enemy when the time is right. Cadres should be taught these points carefully and thoroughly.[2]

The Fourth Column of Hu Yaobang and Chen Zhengxiang turned the campaign to eastern and northern Hebei. They concentrated their forces, surrounding towns and cutting their supply lines. Especially in eastern Hebei they achieved a series of victories, regaining a number of places lost after the abandonment of Zhangjiakou and giving them the beginnings of a secure foothold.

At the same time as the CCP was implementing its strategic defense policy, on May 4, 1946, it announced the change in its policy of reductions in rents and interest rates to one of confiscating the lands of landlords and returning them to peasant ownership. Following this, on October 10, 1947, the party also announced its "Chinese Land Law Guidelines," which stipulated that the land and property of landlords and a portion of that of wealthy peasants was to be confiscated and distributed equally among the peasants. The ancient slogan of peasant rebellions, "land to the tillers" was now clearly inscribed on the red banner of the CCP. This measure helped to mobilize the peasants to join with the party in the revolution and fight successfully to win the right to land ownership. In July 1947, the Shanxi-Hebei-Shandong-Henan Liberation Army led by Liu Bocheng and Deng Xiaoping crossed the Yellow River and advanced to the Dabie Mountain area. This opened up a whole new world for the Communists who now began actively to engage the Nationalist troops in the final war for the central plains of China.

During its nine months in the Shanxi-Chahar-Hebei military district, from June 1946 to March 1947, the Chinese Communist Shanxi-Chahar-Hebei Army, using mobile warfare tactics, wiped out more than 80,000 Nationalist and local armed troops, bringing to a halt the Nationalist Army's offensive along the entire front and forcing it to retreat and defend the larger cities and transportation lines. During this period, after its enlarged Laiyuan Conference of October 1946, the Shanxi-Chahar-Hebei Central Department reorganized the leadership structure and increased the troop strength of the four columns belonging to the Shanxi-Chahar-Hebei Military District. The Fourth Column of the Shanxi-Jehol-Liaoning Military District became the Fourth Column of the Shanxi-Chahar-Hebei Field Army. Thanks to the land reforms, the column had added 10,000 new recruits and expanded from two to three brigades. Hu Yaobang was now political commissar of an army of 30,000 men.

Three Battles and Three Victories

From April to July 1947, the Shanxi-Chahar-Hebei Field Army fought in succession the campaigns for Zheng-Tai, Qing-Cang, and Bao-Bei. Hu Yaobang participated in directing these three campaigns, all of which were victorious.

In April, the army started the Zheng-Tai campaign, planning first to wipe out the Nationalist troops surrounding Shijiazhuang, including those stationed in Zhengding, Huolu, Yuanshi, Zanhuang, and Luancheng, thus isolating Shijiazhuang. At the same time, they began to wipe out the enemy's ability to increase its support services. To cut the enemy's supply lines, the main force turned west to strike the troops stationed along the Zhengding-Taiyuan railroad.

> On April 3 and 4, the troops split up to advance to the prearranged meeting place. The Second Column under Yang Dezhi and Li Zhimin and the Third Column under Yang Chengwu headed to the area north of Shijiazhuang. The Fourth Column under Chen Zhengxiang and Hu Yaobang headed into the area south of Shijiazhuang. On the 8th, the first stage of the campaign for the Shijiazhuang perimeter began. On April 10, the Fourth Column, coordinating with the Central Hebei Military District troops, attacked and took Luancheng. On April 12, the Second and Third columns joined to attack and take Zhengding. Thus a base of some ninety places in the neighborhood of the two counties was liberated. More than 15,000 enemy troops were eliminated.[3]

This done, totally ignoring the attack on the North Daqing River Liberated Area by the Nationalist 94th, 16th, and 53d armies and the 62d Division, which was calculated to draw the Communist forces back from Shijiazhuang, the main forces of the Second and Third columns secretly advanced along both banks of the Hutuo River, moving separately to Shouyang and Yangquan. At the same time, under Chen Zhengxiang and Hu Yaobang, the "Fourth Column advanced west from the Jingxing area and the three columns in close coordination with each other closed in, encircling the Shouyang vicinity west of Yangquan."[4] Between April 9 and May 10, the Communists had wiped out more than 35,000 Nationalist and local warlord forces and were in control of more than 120 miles of the Zhengding-Taiyuan Railroad and the territory paralleling it. This joined up the two large Shanxi-Chahar-Hebei and Shanxi-Shandong-Henan strategic areas and isolated Shijiazhuang.

Following the Zheng-Tai campaign, the Shanxi-Chahar-Hebei Field Army was reorganized, again giving it a new administration. Yang Dezhi was made commanding officer, with Luo Ruiqing and Yang Chengwu as first and second political commissars respectively. Geng Biao and Pan Zili were made chief of staff and head political commissar respectively, under which were three columns and a newly formed artillery brigade. Hu Yaobang was political commissar of the newly formed Third Column, whose commanding officer, Ying Rui, had been the leader of the famous "Night Tiger Brigade" and had risen to division-level political commissar before he was twenty. Assistant commander and chief of staff was Wen Niansheng. Chief of the political department was Lu Ping.

On June 12, 1947, in conjunction with the summer campaign of the Northeast Field Army, the Shanxi-Chahar-Hebei Field Army cut off the Nationalist supply lines from within the Great Wall and mounted the Qing-Cang campaign to destroy the Tianjin-Nanjing Railroad between Qing county and Cang county. Most of the Nationalist troops guarding this section of the railroad were demobilized soldiers from the puppet army of the Japanese, incorporated into the Nationalist Army. Their defensive and fighting abilities were not strong. The field army's Third Column under Hu Yaobang and Zheng Weishan and the Second and Fourth columns, "in coordination with local units from the Chahar, Central Hebei, and Bohai military districts, carried out the attack very smoothly, fulfilling their mission very nicely, liberating the three county seats of Qing, Cang, and Yongqing counties and destroying more than 13,000 enemy troops." The troops under Hu Yaobang's command were clearly well disciplined, ready to fight, and well led.

The Great Victory of Qingfengdian

After winning three victories in three battles, the Shanxi-Chahar-Hebei Field Army high command decided that the Third Column of Hu Yaobang and Zheng Weishan should attack the town of Laishui, and that the Second and Fourth columns should advance north of the Daqing River to surround and cut off the supply routes of the Nationalist 16th Army in the campaign known as the Daqing Hebei campaign.

However, although the Third Column was able to wipe out some of the local Nationalist militia in the vicinity of Laishui, it was not able to sustain the attack for long. The result was a stalemate of attrition. Thus the high field command in September ordered the abandonment of the campaign, and the Third Column was ordered to move back down into the river district of central Hebei.

Many years later General Zheng Weishan still remembered that, as they turned back, some soldiers said,

> "The others are all advancing but we are retreating." Some of the officers even said, "Got the front teeth knocked out before even getting a good bite of flesh." Political Commissar Hu Yaobang and I lay back in a big cart staring at all the stars in the sky and listening to the incessant cacophony of the night insects, feeling very depressed. This phrase, "Got the front teeth knocked out before even getting a good bite of flesh," kept

going round and round in my head. That really annoyed me. When you win, the troops immediately get cocky and high. But when one battle doesn't go well, everyone gets mad at each other. These two extremes in their feelings really weaken an army's fighting spirit. . . . I remember that I then turned to Hu Yaobang, who was likewise deep in thought, and said in a low voice, "How about calling a meeting?" He thought for a minute and then replied, "Headquarters may want to make a summary of this campaign. Let's get everybody's reactions and study it in a Party Committee meeting."[6]

That evening when they made camp they received a top-secret telegram from Mao Zedong in the name of the Military Commission of the Central Committee, which read, "Although the Daqing Hebei campaign did not succeed in annihilating the enemy, your fighting spirit was very good. Any victories, whether big or small, are good. It's not important that your casualties were rather high. . . . After a certain period of recuperation, there will be a new campaign based on the specific situation in the area. . . . Commander Nie Rongzhen has said in particular that having one's front tooth knocked out isn't important, it can be replaced with a gold one."[7]

Following this, the field command began the Baoding-Beiping [railway line] campaign in which eight brigades of the Second and Third columns mounted a fierce attack on Xushui while the rest of the troops struck at the enemy's supply lines. Sun Lianzhong, commander of the Baoding Nationalist Pacification Office, sent out reinforcements of five divisions and one armored regiment led by Li Wen, who was personally trusted by Hu Zongnan. This was called the Li Wen Corps. To avoid being split up and attacked piecemeal, this army used the tactic of staying together and moving back and forth in close formation. This made it impossible for the three columns of the Shanxi-Chahar-Hebei Field Army to surround and annihilate it. Thus it was a stand-off between the two armies in the little triangle of Xushui, Gucheng, and Rongcheng. Clearly this attempt to surround and cut off the town was not succeeding. The Fourth Column, which was striking at the town's peripheral supply lines, was the first to retreat. After several nights of all-out efforts with no results, realizing that there was no way to break the stalemate, Hu Yaobang and Zheng Weishan had no choice but to pull out. Their Third Column then joined forces with the Second Column of Chen Zhengxiang in mobile defensive actions against Sun Lianzhong's troops, trying to find some way to split up the enemy force. But Sun's forces continued to maintain their close formation, making it impossible to split off and destroy any piece of it. Should they once again leave the scene of battle and go looking for other opportunities, or should they continue to attack here, hoping to take advantage of any change in the situation?

As Zheng Weishan recalls,

> It was late at night. The sounds of rifle fire and cannon fire had already long fallen silent. Comrade Hu Yaobang, the political commissar, was pacing back and forth, talking to himself. "We can't retreat again. Another retreat would throw cold water on the troops' morale. The political work would be even harder!"
>
> I thought about it. The political commissar was right. We couldn't retreat. When we retreated just a few days ago, the soldiers' faces looked awful. So I said to Hu Yaobang, "Political commissar, what about waiting a few days to see if there are any changes in the situation?"
>
> "Great!", he replied. "We have a good battlefield position. If only the enemy would attack they would suffer heavy casualties! Although Sun Lianzhong won't let us take his five divisions one at a time, he also won't take lightly the loss of Xushui. If only he would stop being so stubborn. The enemy's bound to make a mistake. On this point, Mao Zedong saw through the mentality of these bastards long ago during the Red Army period."[8]

Finally their opportunity arrived. The commander of the Nationalist Third Army, Luo Lirong, who was stationed in Shijiazhuang with more than 13,000 troops under his command, left Shijiazhuang on October 16 headed for the battlefield north of Baoding, planning to join Sun Lianzhong's army in a pincer attack on the Second and Third columns, one from the south, one from the north, and wipe them out. Clearly this was a bold and audacious plan. Shijiazhuang was some 100 miles from the battlefield north of Baoding. On October 17, the Communist field command received the telegram: "Secret message received: the Third Army of Luo Lirong has left Shijiazhuang, has already crossed the Huduo River, advancing toward Xinle."[9]

In accordance with the orders of the field command, parts of the Third Column started out on the 18th and had to make a twenty-four-hour forced march of nearly seventy miles to reach Fangshun Bridge by the 19th. Otherwise, as soon as the army of Luo Lirong crossed the Fanshun Bridge it would be able to coordinate movements with the Baoding security forces and it would be impossible to surround and annihilate it.

On the 18th the Communist forces did engage Luo Lirong's army, but by the morning of the 19th, the battle at Fangshun Bridge was not going well. They were not able to split up Luo's troops. The field command sent an urgent telegram to the Third Column to send the Seventh Brigade as reinforcements immediately. The field command's intent was clear: When the Seventh Brigade reached the Fangshun Bridge battlefield, the twenty-four regiments of the Shanxi-Chahar-Hebei Field Army and the local troops were to surround and annihilate the army of Luo Lirong.

The Qingfengdian battle lasted from the 19th until 10 a.m. on the 22d. The victory of Qingfengdian extricated the Shanxi-Chahar-Hebei Field Army from its stalemate with the Nationalist troops, allowing it to regain the initiative in choosing its future battles. This is why this battle has been called the first North China strategic counteroffensive, and why it was cited for special recognition and praise by the CCP Central Committee. Looking at the whole of the campaign, although Hu Yaobang's argument that the Shanxi-Chahar-Hebei Field Army continue to maintain its difficult stalemate with the army of Sun Lianzhong was based on his concern for the political morale of the troops, he surely understood the principles of military leadership.

Shijiazhuang Is Taken

After the great victory of Qingfengdian, the city of Shijiazhuang was a stranded island surrounded by liberated areas, but at the same time it was also a nail wedged between them, piercing their very heart. Originally Shijiazhuang was an insignificant hamlet on the North China plain, but because of its location it had become the junction of three railroad lines, one leading west to Taiyuan, the other heading east into Shandong, and the third, the major trunk line connecting Beiping to Henan and Hubei in the south. Thus not only was it an important town for the province of Hebei, it was the most important hamlet in all of China.

Because of the importance of its location, in the war against Japan and when the civil war broke out again, its defenses had been continually strengthened. In the city, spread out like pieces on a chessboard, were more than six thousand watch towers forming a solid, three-tier defense system, an outer city barrier twenty miles in circumference, an inner city barrier more than ten miles in circumference, and a fortress in the center. After the army of Luo Lirong was annihilated, the Nationalist Army guarding Shijiazhuang consisted of 24,000 men under the command of the 32d Division commander, Liu Ying. The defense force of Shijiazhuang boasted that, "Given the city's fortifications, the Nationalist Army can hold Shijiazhuang for three years."

As soon as the Qingfengdian battle was won, the field command telegraphed the Military Commission of the Central Committee requesting permission to follow up the victory by taking Shijiazhuang. Mao Zedong, on behalf of the Military Commission, immediately telegraphed back, saying,

> Telegram of the 22d, 12 noon, acknowledged: great victory wiping out enemy at Qingfengdian enormously significant turning point in progress of struggle in your area. For present, if northern enemy comes south, annihilate part of them. If northern enemy stays put, then our army should now rest for 10 days or so, to reorganize and recuperate its strength. Study Shijiazhuang thoroughly, complete all preparations for attack on Shijiazhuang. After that, concentrate not only main force of several brigades, must also concentrate several local brigades. Attack Shijiazhuang giving appearance of striking supply troops, then attack the city.[10]

Zhu De, after a tiring trip, arrived at the front line on October 25 to hold a field command meeting of all officers of brigade rank and above. He stressed that "The attack on Shijiazhuang will require courage and also the techniques for assaulting heavily defended fortifications." At the meeting, Geng Biao laid out the battle tasks of all the brigades. "The Third Column from the southwest and the Fourth Column from the northeast will constitute the primary attack forces," said Geng. "They will be supported by the troops of the Central Hebei Military District in the southeast and the Hebei-Shanxi Military District in the northwest. The district artillery brigade will be divided into four groups to coordinate with the actions of each of the troop contingents."[11]

On November 6 at dawn the roar of cannons signaled the beginning of the attack on Shijiazhuang. The Third Column, advancing from the southwest, set its sights on the fortress at the center of the city where the enemy command was located. The attacking vanguard moved forward, quickly overcoming the first ring of fortifications outside the city and then the second ring inside the city, annihilating the southwest enemy defense corps. But as they approached the fortifications at the center of the city the fighting intensified into fierce hand-to-hand combat. Yang Dezhi of the field command has written, "The fighting for the central fortifications was very fierce, especially when the attackers reached the area of the train station where we came up against a counteroffensive from enemy tanks and armoured cars.''[12] After six days and nights of battle, the defending commander Liu Ying was forced to submit and order the few remaining defense posts to surrender. The battle for Shijiazhuang came to its victorious conclusion at noon on November 12.

Shijiazhuang was the first city attacked and taken by the Communists in the liberation war, the first assault on fortified defenses. This victory joined together in one solid piece the Shanxi-Hebei-Shandong-Henan and Shanxi-Chahar-Hebei liberated districts, and it gave the liberation war a rich supply base. It also cut off one of the flanks that the Nationalist defense forces of Beiping and Tianjin had relied on. This clearly had a profound influence on the development of the whole battle for northern China and was also highly significant in the development of Hu Yaobang's military experience.

Director of the Political Department

In 1948 a critical change took place in the civil war between the Nationalist and Communist forces. In the war areas north of the Yangzi River the Nationalist troops of Chiang Kai-shek lost battle after battle. Lacking the power to do what he had hoped to, he had no choice but to change his strategy from "defending local districts" to "defending important points."

On the North China battlefield, after the Shanxi-Chahar-Hebei Field Army took Shijiazhuang at the end of November 1947, Chiang dismissed Sun Lianzhong from his position as commander of the Baoding Pacification Commandery and appointed the Suiyuan warlord Fu Zuoyi, who had a good military reputation as commander of the five-province North China Bandit Suppression Headquarters. After Fu assumed this post, in an attempt to restore the deteriorating Nationalist position, he reorganized the local militia into a defense force and brought the main force of his own personal army in Suiyuan down to Beiping. He hoped to seek out the main forces of the Shanxi-Chahar-Hebei Field Army and destroy it in one decisive battle.

Nie Rongzhen, who was then on the general staff of the Shanxi-Chahar-Hebei Field Army, recalls, ''Less than two months after he [Fu Zuoyi] took the stage, in the middle of January 1948, the Third Column led by comrades Zheng Weishan and Hu Yaobang, in coordination with the First Column led by comrades Tang Yanjie, Li Baohua, and Wang Ping, gave his 'trump card,' the 35th Army, a serious jolt, wiping out his newly reorganized 32d Division and destroying the 101st Division, a total of more than 7,000 men. The commanding general, Lu Ying-qing, was forced to commit suicide, and . . . high officers . . . were hanged. For Fu Zuoyi, having just taken command, this was surely a severe blow.''[13]

Just after that, the Third Column joined forces with the Fourth Column and the Fourth Brigade to win a series of victories in attacks in eastern Hebei. They were successful in drawing Fu Zuoyi's main forces up into Northeast China beyond the Great Wall, making it easy for the Northeast Field Army to deal with the Nationalist armies within the Great Wall in preparation for the Liaoning-Mukden (Shenyang) campaign.

In early August 1948, Hu Yaobang was transferred and promoted to the position of chief of the political department of the North China Field Army's First Infantry Corps, a large army group consisting of the 8th Column, 13th Column, and 15th Column, a total of more than 100,000 troops. In charge of command headquarters were Xu Xiang-qian, commander and political commissar; Zhou Shidi, assistant com-mander and assistant political commissar; Chen Manyuan, chief of staff; and Hu Yaobang, political department director. Both Xu Xiang-qian and Yan Xishan, the warlord of Shanxi, came from Wutai Moun-tain. Both men, and also Assistant Commander Zhou Shidi, were graduates of Sun Yat-sen's Huangpu (Whampoa) Military Academy and former commanders of the Fourth Front Red Army.

Since coming to the Shanxi-Chahar-Hebei military district, Hu Yao-bang had served as political commissar with Chen Zhengxiang of the Fourth Column, as political commissar with Zheng Weishan of the Third Column, and now, as head of the political department with Xu Xiangqian of the First Infantry Corps. All three of these men had been hard fighting officers of the Fourth Front Red Army. Modeled after the political commissar system of the Soviet Union's Red Army, the politi-cal commissar and head of the political department in the organization-al structure of the Chinese Communist Army not only did ideological work with the officers of the field units and morale boosting with the troops, but also worked to guarantee that the party maintained complete authority and leadership over the army.

In late November 1948, Xu Xiangqian became seriously ill. A mem-ber of the secretariat of the Central Committee, representing Mao

Zedong, sent Xu a personal letter that read:

> Comrade Xiangqian,
> We have heard about your illness and are extremely concerned for you. We hope you will take good care and rest quietly. Do not worry about your work. Zhou, Hu, and Chen will take over for you. When your illness is a little better and you are able to move, you should come here and recuperate fully before returning to the front lines. In short, what is most important is that you get well and rest. When you are well everything will be fine.
> Mao, Liu, Zhu, Zhou, and Ren, November 29

From then until January 1949, when Xu Xiangqian was able to resume command, the Central Committee's Military Commission, of which Mao was head, would cable the battle decisions to Xu's subordinates.[15]

On March 1, 1949, all the Liberation armies of the country were brought under a unified structure. The name of First Infantry Corps of the North China Field Army was changed to the 18th Infantry Corps. The original Shanxi-Chahar-Hebei Military District Infantry Corps led by Yang, Luo, and Geng was renamed the 19th Infantry Corps, and that of Yang Chengwu and Li Jingquan was renamed the 20th Infantry Corps. On March 27, 1949, the three great North China infantry corps, a total force of more than 400,000 troops, descended on the city of Taiyuan, prepared to mount a general assault. Assistant Commander of the Liberation Army Peng Dehuai, representing the Military Commission, announced that a Party General Frontline Committee of the Taiyuan campaign would be formed by eight persons: from the 18th Infantry Corps, Commander and Political Commissar Xu Xiangqian, Assistant Commander and Assistant Political Commissar Zhou Shidi, Chief of Staff Chen Manyuan, and Political Department Chief Hu Yaobang; from the 19th Infantry Corps, Commander Yang Dezhi and Political Commissar Luo Ruiqing; and from the 20th Infantry Corps, Commander Yang Chengwu and Assistant Political Commissar and Chief of the Political Department Li Tianhuan. The command headquarters and political office of the 18th Infantry Corps would be the Taiyuan frontline command headquarters and political department of all three infantry corps. Thus, of all the high officers of the three infantry corps, Hu Yaobang was the only one to be selected to be a member of the Party General Frontline Committee who was only chief of a political department.

The Campaign for the Taiyuan Periphery

Hu Yaobang had been appointed chief of the political department of the First Infantry Corps to assist Commander Xu Xiangqian with training and ideological work and to carry out propaganda work and contact with the enemy that would ensure a smooth takeover of the city of Taiyuan. Taiyuan had been the seat of the Shanxi "kingdom" of the resilient warlord Yan Xishan for some thirty-eight years. The topography of Shanxi is very rugged and mountainous. The city of Taiyuan is located in a high mountain pass from which it "looks down on and dominates the world." Yan Xishan's guidelines for managing the defenses of the city had been "to strengthen its fortifications every day." After being defeated in central Shanxi, Yan had the four strategic strongholds east of the city—Niutuozhai, Xiaokutou, Naoma, and Shantou—repaired and strengthened so that Taiyuan city itself was a formidable fortress within a fortress.

On October 4, 1948, at Xiangli village in Yuzi county, Xu Xiangqian called an enlarged meeting of officers from the regiment level and up, at which he proposed the slogan of "attacking Taiyuan, capturing Yan Xishan alive, and liberating the whole of Shanxi." He also laid out the organizational and training work to be done in preparation for the assault on Taiyuan. Hu Yaobang chaired the meeting in his capacity as chief of the political department of the infantry corps, and after the meeting he immediately jumped into his leadership tasks of preparing the troops.

One note entitled "Hu Yaobang visits the 13th Column" records that on August 17, Hu

> came to the 13th Column and participated in the victory celebration meeting and congratulated the more than 1,100 model heroes who had shown their bravery in the Linfen and central Shanxi campaigns, and talked personally with unit representatives and column officers, asking in detail about the units' conditions. He also talked with the leaders and solicited their views on such important issues as how to strengthen the party's leadership and prepare ideologically and politically for the assault on Taiyuan.
>
> On August 18, Comrade Hu Yaobang exchanged views with the officers of the column and analyzed the Party Committee work, pointing out that among the important problems in party work were that the Party Committee lacked good organization and a regular schedule, that its work lacked concreteness, and its duties were not clearly spelled out. He asked

the committees at the regiment level and above to bring into their activities some of the major responsible party members from the lower ranks, and to strengthen further their organization.

In accordance with the spirit of Comrade Hu Yaobang's suggestions, on August 28 and on September 18 the column's Political Committee held enlarged Party Committee meetings to examine and improve the work of the committees. Between these two meetings, Comrade Hu Yaobang telegraphed political officer Xu Zirong daily to find out about the progress of the meetings and provide leadership based on a true study of the objective facts. On October 3, he again came in person to the 13th Column to see if those officers of regiment level and above, especially the top leaders of brigade level and above, had overcome the tendencies to be disorganized and anarchic. . . . Through training studies and investigations the Party Committee officers at all levels committed themselves to strengthening the committees' collective leadership and reporting system to overcome gradually the bad guerrilla warfare habits.

[At the same time,] because of the inexperience of newly recruited soldiers and newly promoted officers, Hu Yaobang proposed political work among the troops to struggle to do three things well, to fight well, to maintain discipline over policies well, and for the troops to work together well.[16]

In something over two months of organization and training, during which Hu spent a great deal of time working with the officers of the three columns at all levels and with the squads at the grass-roots level, the officers had mastered the system of collective leadership and of requesting orders and reporting, and the troops had come to understand the relationship between the party and the masses and the political outlook of good soldiers. This helped greatly to eliminate such problems as the tendency toward anarchy and the guerrilla mentality of the officers of new units made up of ''liberated soldiers'' who had come over from the Nationalist armies and of peasants who had become ''turned-over soldiers'' (fanshen zhanshi) recruited after local land reforms. It also helped improve the problems of desertion, lack of discipline, and tension between officers and men. The results of the ideological work showed up in the positive and enthusiastic attitudes of the troops. The two months or so of organization and training that Hu Yaobang had provided guaranteed effective leadership of the party over the troops, inspiring the phrases ''ideologically'' and ''in political work'' of Xu Xiangqian's call: ''Complete full preparations ideologically, in fighting skills, and in political work for the assault on Taiyuan.''

October in the central plains of Shanxi is high autumn, a time of clear, brisk weather, the ripening of rice and sorghum, the harvest season. But this year the quiet countryside was suddenly filled with the sound and scent of war and death. Xu Xiangqian had originally fixed the date for the beginning of the assault on Taiyuan as October 18. But when Yan Xishan heard the news that Jinan in Shandong had fallen to the Liberation Army, he put together an army of seven divisions which on October 2 attempted a surprise attack that would overrun the armies surrounding the city and retake the airport in the suburbs. Xu Xiangqian responded to this new opportunity and pressed the Taiyuan campaign right away, even though it was ahead of schedule.[17] At the same time, Hu Yaobang rushed to the columns of the infantry corps to determine the prebattle morale of the officers, telling them that the infantry command headquarters had decided to put the plan for the Taiyuan campaign into effect ahead of schedule. On the night of October 4, the three columns of the First Infantry Corps of the Chinese Field Army, together with the 7th Column detached from the Shanxi-Suiyuan Field Army (Peng Zhaohui, commander; Sun Zhiyuan, political commissar; and Yu Qiuli, assistant political commissar), attacked the forces of Yan Xishan as they were moving south. After twenty-four hours of fierce fighting, more than 10,000 of Yan Xishan's men were wiped out, totally eliminating the small base they had established outside Taiyuan. Next, Xu Xiangqian ordered the 7th, 8th, 15th, and 13th columns to attack the major strategic points of eastern Shanxi.

This was a terrible battle. Yan Xishan used East Mountain, rising more than 300 meters just outside the city wall, as his rear shield. He personally directed his troops to repel the attackers from behind the heavy fortifications, with deadly 105 mm howitzers spaced at intervals as his main organizational structure. He then directed his airplanes to strafe and bomb the attackers from the air. He used this massive firepower to pin down the advance of each one of the attacking columns. When any of the fortifications was overrun he would immediately detach one of his specially organized "elite corps" to mount an overwhelming counterattack so that a single fortification might change hands a dozen times in successive attacks and counterattacks.

In accordance with the new tactic of "individual soldiers bursting out and small detachments advancing suddenly under cover of fire," which Xu Xiangqian had developed in the assault on Linfen, Xu's soldiers sacrificed themselves willingly and kept rushing forward. The Liberation Army had few cannons, and cannon shells were even more scarce. Every shot was precious and had to be carefully planned and accurately aimed. Hand grenades and hand bombs made no dent in the heavy walls of Yan Xishan's carefully constructed fortifications. Some could even withstand anything up to a 750-pound bomb. The fighting was intense. Some platoons of the Liberation Army by the end had only a handful of men left. The well-known chronicler of the Chinese Communist Army, Ren Baige, in his *Under the Command of General Xu*, has written with a bit of dramatic flair:

> Commander Xu was on the battlefield in person, assessing the situation, refining tactics, directing the troops . . . and he also personally did propaganda work encouraging the troops, ''Advance and advance again before the enemy has a chance to rest.'' ''Hold on for the last five minutes and the victory is ours.'' The director of the political department of the infantry, Hu Yaobang, risked the dense fire of the enemy to come to the front line personally to distribute to the troops copies of the army paper *Sons of the People*. He shouted, ''Political work goes to the rank and file, to the front line.'' Our propaganda officers, and even the reporters and writers who experienced life with the troops, all went out to the front line. The actions of the infantry corps high command and of other high officers inspired the officers in the field boldly, courageously to kill the enemy, becoming stronger and stronger, refusing to admit that they had been hit, refusing to leave the firing line even when seriously wounded. Finally the attackers took East Mountain and all the strategic points south of the city, killing more than 50,000 of the enemy (the actual statistics are over 20,000).[18]

After nineteen days and nights of fierce attacks and counterattacks, Taiyuan was completely and tightly surrounded.

Mopping Up Taiyuan

The united front was one of the three major means used by the Chinese Communists to overcome the enemy and attain victory. During the assault on Taiyuan, Hu Yaobang, chief of the political department of the First Infantry Corps, was also responsible for united front work.

In November 1948, Hu had made plans with Huang Qiaosong, commander of the 30th Army, which was defending Taiyuan, for a secret revolt to hand over the city without bloodshed. But as the saying goes, "Armies have no permanent victory, water has no permanent shape." On the eve of the revolt, Huang Qiaosong's trusted officer Dai Bingnan told the secret to Yan Xishan, who immediately arrested Huang and his contact Jin Fu, who was representing Hu Yaobang. Yan Xishan thought that Jin Fu was Hu Yaobang and had him sent off to Nanjing under guard, where Chiang Kai-shek presided in person as his judge. Still thinking that this was Hu Yaobang, and the highest ranking Communist leader caught by the Nationalists during the civil war, Chiang passed sentence himself and had Jin Fu shot by a firing squad.

The true story of this historical riddle of the true and false Hu Yaobang is related by Hu himself as follows: After Huang Qiaosong had decided to revolt, he entrusted a letter to Wang Zhenyu,

> who frequently accompanied Wang Yujia in liaison missions to our army. They arrived at one of the frontline encampments of the 60th Army, I don't remember the name of the place. At the time, the commanding officer of the 60th Army and its political commissar was Wang Xinting. The assistant commanding officer was Zhang Zuqiong, and the director of the political department was Gui Shaobin. The commanding officers of the infantry corps were Xu Xiangqian, commander and political commissar; Chen Manyuan, chief of staff; and myself, head of the political department. When we were apprised of this situation, we discussed it together, and it was I who then went to this frontline encampment to talk with them directly and work it out. Xu Xiangqian did not meet with them. After talking it over with Wang Zhenyu, I originally was going to go myself into Taiyuan city to meet with Huang Qiaosong. I discussed it by phone with Xu Xiangqian, who thought that it was not necessary for me to go myself, so we sent instead Chief of Staff of the 60th Army Jin Fu, who, using the title of head of the propaganda office of the political department, then went into the city, taking staff aide Zhai Xuyou with him.[19]

After the revolt of Huang Qiaosong was aborted, Taiyuan remained surrounded and isolated by the 18th Infantry Corps for six months. In the spring of 1949, Beiping and Tianjin were liberated in succession. Then the Military Commission of the Central Committee decided to mount a powerful assault on Taiyuan. On March 27, 1949, under orders from the Military Commission, Peng Dehuai, vice-commander of the Liberation armies and adviser for the Taiyuan campaign, arrived at the command headquarters in Dagukou village, East Mountain, on the Taiyuan front line. At the opening of the military conference for the Taiyuan assault, attended by army officers and heads of artillery divisions, Peng announced that the Taiyuan Party General Frontline Committee would be composed of Xu Xiangqian, Zhou Shidi, Yang Dezhi, Luo Ruiqing, Yang Chengwu, Li Tianhuan, Chen Manyuan, and Hu Yaobang.

On April 21, 1949, Mao Zedong and Zhu De issued the "Order for Armies of the Whole Nation to Advance." On that day, the 100,000 troops of the Second Field Army under Liu Bocheng and Deng Xiaoping and the Third Field Army under Chen Yi and Su Yuhui crossed the Yangzi River and seized Nanjing. One day earlier, at dawn on April 20, the assault on Taiyuan began. After four days of attacks by their overwhelmingly superior forces, all the strategic points surrounding the city in all directions had been taken by the Chinese Communists.

The Taiyuan frontline command headquarters then mounted the general assault on the city before dawn on April 24. "On that day of the general assault, Peng Dehuai, who still had not left the Taiyuan front line, was worried and called Hu Yaobang, head of the Taiyuan frontline political department, at two o'clock in the morning to go with him to a forward position to observe the battle."[20] After a predawn assault by 400,000 People's Liberation Army soldiers, Taiyuan was taken that day. Xu Xiangqian was made chairman of the Taiyuan Military Administrative Committee, with Hu Yaobang as vice-chairman, responsible for restoring law and order in Taiyuan and getting industrial production and business started again.

Advancing into the Northwest and Southwest

Not long after the conclusion of the Taiyuan campaign, Peng Dehuai decided to send the 18th and 19th Infantry corps to the Southwest to join in the campaign there. At that time there were three armies under the 18th Infantry Corps. Following the assault on Taiyuan, it was again enlarged by absorbing a large group of "turned-over soldiers" and "liberated soldiers," giving it a total of more than 100,000 troops. For various reasons, including the fact that Xu Xiangqian was once again ill, the command structure of the 18th Infantry Corps was reorganized. Zhou Shidi was made commanding officer, with Li Jingquan as political commissar, Hu Yaobang as head of the political department, Chen Manyuan as chief of staff, and Wang Xinting as vice-commander. Li Jingquan was from Huichang in Jiangxi province, an intellectual from a landlord family. After joining the revolution at an early age, in 1929 at Jinggang Mountain, he had become secretary to Mao Zedong and was highly trusted by Mao. But because Li was at the same time assistant political commissar of the Northwest Field Army, the political and ideological work of the 18th Infantry Corps fell mainly to Hu Yaobang.

In May 1949, Hu proposed that the 18th Infantry Corps "quickly complete its postcampaign work and be ready to accept the glorious new responsibilities facing it in the future. . . . It must definitely be made a mobile and effective force."[21] At the same time, Hu took up the ideological and mobilization tasks for "the liberation of Xi'an, the liberation of the Northwest, and the liberation of all of China." According to the recollections of the current editor of the 18th Infantry Corps' *Sons of the People*, "Hu Yaobang organized and sent out the members of the political department to work with the troops, to understand their conditions and help out. Day and night he was either going out to work with comrades in making investigations, working with guiding the troops, holding meetings on deployment, or writing propaganda articles. In the two weeks of May 2 to 16, 1949, the *Sons of the People* put out twelve issues with eight articles written or edited by Hu Yaobang in the name of the political department of the infantry corps, laying out the conditions and preparations necessary for the army's advance into the Northwest."[22]

A common problem among the troops engaged in expeditions to distant parts of the country was that many of the soldiers had been recruited from among the local peasants and from local armies and did not want to leave their home areas or were unwilling to make a permanent commitment to soldiering. They wanted to return to their homes and their new fields acquired in the land reform. There was also the added problem that some of the lower-ranking officers, having tasted victory, had become very cocky and arrogant. Thus desertions among the soldiers had become a serious problem that was badly weakening the fighting ability of the army.

To deal with these problems, Hu Yaobang now abandoned the disciplinary methods of investigations, punishments, and forced confessions, replacing them with stressing that the lower officers must show real concern and love for their men as the main way to stabilize the attitude of the troops. Hu thought that, "In consolidating the troops, aside from strengthening ideological education, the basic item is that the cadres love the soldiers. . . . The responsible cadres must be able to attract the men to them like a magnet . . . so that every soldier sincerely and willingly wants to share the hardships of life with you."[23]

While Hu was engaged in these tasks of political and ideological work among the troops, the First and Second Infantry corps, led by

Peng Dehuai, attacked and took Xi'an and Xianyang but were stopped in the Baoji area by a joint pincer attack by the forces of Hu Zongnan and Ma Jiyuan. Hu Zongnan had joined with the two Mas from Qinghai and Ningxia (Ma Bufang and Ma Honglu) in proposing to "return to Xianyang and occupy Xi'an." The military situation was urgent. In early and mid-June, the 181st Division and the 61st Army of the 18th Infantry Corps reinforced the troops at Xianyang. As soon as the battle to defend Xianyang began, Hu Yaobang rushed to the front lines to rouse the troops. The Xianyang defense force successfully broke up the attack by Ma Jiyuan's forces.

After repelling the attack on Xianyang, Peng Dehuai immediately mobilized the four great infantry corps, the First, Second, 18th, and 19th, in a Fufeng-Meixian campaign that wiped out four armies under Hu Zongnan and swept west some 300 miles to Qinchuan in Gansu, winning a great victory. This was followed shortly by the taking of the strategic northwestern city of Baoji on the part of the 18th Infantry Corps under He Long, putting direct pressure on Hu Zongnan's Qinling defense line. By the end of September, the Northwest campaign of the 18th Infantry Corps was successfully completed. Under the leadership of Hu Yaobang, the corps had done an outstanding job fulfilling its mission in the Northwest.[24]

In the middle of September, Hu, as one of ten representatives of the Chinese New Democratic Youth League, left the northwestern front for Beijing to participate in the first session of the Chinese People's Political Consultative Conference. On September 25, in the Qinzheng Hall in Zhongnanhai, he was in charge of reporting procedures. On September 21, not yet thirty-four years old but already a participant in the revolution for twenty years, Hu took his place with the many different delegates representing political authority from throughout China and participated in the discussions of national affairs.

The nine other representatives of the Chinese New Democratic Youth League attending the conference were Feng Wenbin, Jiang Nanxiang, Song Yiping, Lu Ping, Wang Zhizhou, Zhang Ben (female), Yang Shu, Gao Jingzhi (female), and Wang Mingyuan. Hu was listed number three, and he attended the conference in the capacity of the New Democratic Youth League representative from the armed forces. On October 1, he also attended the first National Day ceremonies for the founding of the People's Republic of China. Hu says he was so excited that those several days the only thing he did was shake hands and clap.

On November 16, after returning from Beijing to the infantry head-quarters at Qinling, Hu called a meeting of all officers of regiment level and above at which he conveyed to them the spirit of the National People's Political Consultative Conference and reported on the army's acceptance of the mission to enter Sichuan province. He said, "We must explain to the troops clearly and thoroughly a few problems. First, it will be an honor to enter Sichuan. Second, it will not be difficult to complete this glorious mission. Third, Sichuan is a fine place. Fourth, we need to explain our army's responsibilities. Fifth, there will still be some difficulties." He also said, "This will be our last big battle. This is an unusual opportunity, and every comrade should take advantage of it to demonstrate his abilities and help us take this glorious mission into Sichuan."[25]

At that time, the 18th Infantry Corps and the 7th Army of the First Field Army, already under the command of He Long, were engaged in a defensive stalemate with the armies of Hu Zongnan on the Qinling-Dabashan line. The two sides had met in six engagements in which both sides made temporary gains, but the encounters had ended in a stale-mate.

Chiang Kai-shek and Hu Zongnan judged that it was most likely that the liberation armies would attack Sichuan mainly from the north. Thus Hu Zongnan had concentrated his main forces to meet an attack from this direction. However, while the 18th Infantry Corps and the 7th Army divided into three routes and moved slowly south through Shaanxi to attack and hold down the main concentration of Hu Zong-nan's armies in the northern foothills of the Qinling [mountains], the Fourth Field Army, which was poised to move south and take Guang-dong and Guangxi, and the main forces of the Second Field Army of Liu Bocheng and Deng Xiaoping, which were then resting in western Hubei, had already completed a wide detour, circling back so that they were now in position surrounding Guizhou and Sichuan.

In the middle of November, the opening shots of the Sichuan-Gui-zhou campaign shook the entire southwest of China, raising the curtain on this final great battle of the civil war. By the end of the month, the Second Field Army and part of the Fourth Field Army had taken Guiyang and Yibin, crossed the Wu River, and defeated the armies of Song Xilian and Luo Guangwen, more than 30,000 men strong, in the mountains of southern Sichuan. They then continued to attack and take Chongqing and began to close up all the escape routes of western Sichuan, to surround the Chengdu basin from the east, west, and south.

By this time Hu Zongnan, who was known as a very good strategist, realized that the Communist plan was to make a lot of noise in the north while striking from the east, so he immediately withdrew his main force from the Qinling-Dabashan defense line and moved it to Chengdu.

The 18th Infantry Corps and the vanguard of the First Field Army, under the separate commands of He Long, Zhou Shidi, Li Jingquan, Hu Yaobang, and Chen Manyuan, now moved down the mountains, chasing and attacking the retreating troops of Hu Zongnan all the way to Mianyang, liberating northwestern Sichuan and destroying 80,000 of Hu Zongnan's troops, right up to the outskirts of Chengdu.

By late December, the Second Field Army's Fifth Infantry Corps led by Yang Yong, the Third Infantry Corps of Du Yide, and the Fourth Field Army's 50th Army, joined by the 18th Infantry Corps, together began the campaign for Chengdu. By then, Chiang Kai-shek and Hu Zongnan had already left the city, and many of the Nationalist troops had lost their main officers and had little will left to fight. One after the other, the Nationalist army units gave up and came over to the Communists. Only Hu Zongnan's trusted commander, Li Wen, defending the northern battleline and facing the troops of Hu Yaobang, led seven armies in a surprise attack on the 24th. But the tide had already turned and the attack was futile. On the 26th, after two days of heavy fighting, the 30,000 men under Li Wen were either dead or taken prisoner. This crushing defeat affected the remaining Nationalist units, who came over to the Communists one after the other, finally liberating the entire Chengdu area and concluding the campaign.

On December 30, 1949, in accordance with telegraphed orders from Mao Zedong and the Military Commission of the Central Committee, the 18th Infantry Corps, as victors in the battle for Chengdu, led a victory parade into the city. After more than four years of the turbulent War of Liberation, crossing the mountain passes, rivers, and plains of China's ancient heartland and having risked his life in a hundred battles, Hu Yaobang finally put on the uniform of one of the commanding officers of this great army of more than 100,000 men and rode victoriously into the southwestern capital of Chengdu. With the birth of the People's Republic of China, the life and career of Hu Yaobang had turned a new page.

7
Liberation:
The Early Years

Mao Zedong now turned from the task of reunifying China to reach out with a hand very conscious of tradition to carefully weave anew the fabric of power and authority throughout the 3,700,000 square miles of this ancient land. Liu Bocheng, who commanded his troops like a rather aloof and haughty god, made decisions on his own, sometimes independent of the commands of his superiors. Mao appointed the more relaxed, urbane, and diplomatic Deng Xiaoping as his military political commissar to complement Liu's strengths and weaknesses, and act as a check on his power. The reputation of the great army under Liu and Deng is known throughout China. Both men were from Sichuan so, as in the case of Xu Xiangqian who commanded the attack on Taiyuan, when the troops under Liu and Deng entered Yunnan, Guizhou, and Sichuan they had the advantage of being on their home turf. This use of local leaders to fight in their own provinces was an ingenious way of dealing with the deeply ingrained Chinese psychological barriers of localism.

The Sichuanese are a very proud people and the province is well endowed and prosperous, justly famed nationwide for its natural beauty. But historically, it has also been the site of a number of independent feudal kingdoms or military states and peasant uprisings that have periodically challenged the central government. To make sure that the province would not once again provide the basis for an independent kingdom beyond the reach of the central government, it was of course essential that the army of Liu and Deng not be allowed to put down roots. It was partly for this reason that the 18th Army Corps was ordered to enter Sichuan. This was also the reason behind the telegram that Mao Zedong sent specifically ordering the 18th Army Corps to act as the victors in the battle for Chengdu and to hold a victory parade in the city.

In February 1950, the 18th Army Corps was assigned to the Southwest Military District. Deng Xiaoping was appointed political commissar of the district, first secretary of the Southwest Bureau, and chairman of its Economics and Finance Commission. Liu Bocheng was made chairman of the Southwest Military and Administrative Council and second secretary of the Southwest Bureau. He Long was made commander-in-chief of the district and third secretary of the bureau. This was a clever move that both acknowledged Deng's position and maintained a balance in the area. At the same time, the 18th Army Corps was split into three groups, with Hu Yaobang in command of the 61st Army to establish order in northern Sichuan, Li Jingquan remaining in Chengdu as head of the east Sichuan defense district, and Zhou Shidi's troops moving into western Sichuan. Under the Southwest Bureau there were seven provincial administrative districts, for Yunnan, Guizhou, Sikang, northern Sichuan, eastern Sichuan, western Sichuan, and southern Sichuan. In splitting up the original 18th Army Corps to occupy northern, eastern, and western Sichuan, Mao was using his familiar method of maintaining control over smaller, divided units.

Hu Yaobang, now thirty-five years of age, was made head of the Chinese Communist North Sichuan Administrative Bureau and chairman of its Economic and Finance Commission. At the same time he was also secretary of the North Sichuan District Chinese Communist Party and political commissar of the North Sichuan Military District as well as member of the Southwest Military and Political Council. Thus he represented the combined authority for northern Sichuan of the party, government, army, and economic administration. The headquarters for the North Sichuan Administrative Bureau was located in Nanchong, from which it administered four special districts, a total of thirty-five counties.

In March 1950, under the sponsorship of Deng Xiaoping, the Southwest Military and Political Council convened a conference on land reform in the Southwest. Based on the fact that the region had just been liberated and there were still some 270,000 local armed bandits at large in the area, plus more than 900,000 former Nationalist troops waiting to be reassigned, the situation was quite unstable. Thus Deng Xiaoping proposed a flexible policy, not carrying out land reform for the moment but first carrying out rent reductions. Hu Yaobang participated in the conference and also helped draft the "Articles on Rent

Reduction in the Southwest District.''

The general principles of these articles stated:

> Land reform is an essential condition for raising the productivity and for the industrialization of the nation. But our southwestern region has only recently been liberated and social order still needs to be more fully reestablished. Preparations for land reform work are as yet not completed. Therefore, during the next two years of 1950 up until the autumn of 1951, land reform will not be implemented in the Southwest District. During this period, to lighten the feudal exploitation, to begin the process of improving the life of the peasants, to restore and improve agricultural production, and to unite the people at all levels in support of united front reconstruction in the Southwest, we must carry out a program of rent reductions.[1]

Even so, there were some particularly stubborn local power groups, landlords, bandit leaders, and heads of cliques or factions that resisted this program, saying, ''As long as the Communists don't ask for rent reductions or security money returns in the Southwest, we'll let you in. If, however, you break the rice bowl, you won't be able to fix it without us.''[2]

The 61st Army mounted a bandit suppression campaign against local bandit groups. But during the spring campaign, because they ''were anxious to achieve quick success,'' they did not explain their policies and generally overlooked mass mobilization and the political fragmentation. Thus, although in the first four months the enemy forces they attacked turned and fled, few of them were eliminated. The campaign was not very effective. Some of the undercover Nationalist agents became very bold, even to the point that some of the troops were attacked by large guerrilla forces under Nationalist agents.

On May 16, at a meeting for officers of regiment level and above to summarize their experiences in the bandit suppression campaign, Hu Yaobang addressed the outstanding problems. He said,

> To prepare to deal with all the many schemes and devices of the Nationalist agents, with the rumors and acts of violence that they have already perpetrated, with the fact that they scatter and take cover . . . infiltrate our organizations, instigate divisions and schisms, and try to use women to entrap our people . . . it is necessary to combine courageous and firm struggle with skillful and flexible tactics. The party, government, army, and masses must unite. The higher levels of all organizations must unite with village and hamlet leaders. Military attacks have to be coordinated

with fragmenting the enemy politically. Fighting units have to coordinate with work teams. Mobilization of the masses must be combined with dividing the landlords from the self-defense brigades that control the villages. To eliminate the Nationalist agents requires digging up the bandits at their roots. Otherwise, they will continue to return, running away when we approach but returning as soon as we leave any particular area. To root the bandits out fully, it is necessary to catch those who are directing them from behind the scenes, the real leaders of the bandit groups and their accomplices, those who are giving them orders and money . . . it is even more essential to rely on mass mobilization, on organizing peasant associations, on implementing and enforcing rent and tax reductions, and on carrying out land reform. If the masses can be mobilized and brought over to us, the bandit units can be eliminated quickly, and the goal of totally eliminating the Nationalist agents from northern Sichuan by September is attainable.[3]

After Hu's talk,

each [antibandit] unit of over a hundred men set up a mass work brigade, and it was common for each platoon to have a mass work team which, in coordination with the military actions against the bandits, held meetings of local representatives from all classes of society and large mass meetings. They told the people about the plans and policies of the party and people's government and organized peasant associations and self-defense brigades. . . . The masses took the lead in reporting information about the enemy, in setting up interrogation and investigation groups. In Suining County Military District alone there were over 1,100 such groups, forming a broad network throughout the countryside. . . . [At the same time,] the bandit suppression forces held discussion meetings with the relatives of the bandits, using the bandits' relatives to urge them to surrender, to spread announcements and distribute leaflets, in a broadly expanding political offensive so that the bandit organizations were rapidly weakened and divided and came over one after the other. The commander of the ''Anti-Communist Save the Nation Army,'' Wang Yimin, and the head of his 7th Division, Xian Zhengxiang, under our strong offensive, realized they had reached a dead-end and voluntarily gave themselves up. By the end of August, bandit units of some 73,000 men had been eliminated, including more than 24,000 who gave up thanks to the political fragmentation campaign . . . and the gangs of bandits were eliminated one month ahead of the original plan. . . . Based on the mobilization of the masses, rent reductions, deposit returns, and land reform [also] proceeded smoothly.[4]

In one year, Hu's northern Sichuan district had very quickly accomplished the two important tasks of reducing rents and eliminating the bandits. In this district these tasks were carried out relatively peacefully and smoothly, without the large-scale disruptions and excessive number of arrests and bloodshed that occurred, for example, in the eastern Sichuan district administered by Li Jingquan.

After rent reduction and bandit suppression were accomplished, social order was stabilized in northern Sichuan, and beginning in 1951 Hu gradually shifted the focus of his work to improving production in the district's towns and villages. Having no background in economic reconstruction, he studied and learned even as he was directing this work. After investigation and research, Hu set out the following guidelines for restoring and developing production.

1. With the focus on reviving the original silk and cotton textile industries of the Nanchong area, other industries and the planting of mulberry and cotton in the countryside were to be promoted.

2. Under the guideline of attacking illegal speculation and hoarding and establishing state commerce and balanced trade, the normal economic activities of individual businesses were to be encouraged, and trade between northern Sichuan and other areas of China was to be organized, so that the supply of commodities would be stabilized and trade flourish.

During the two years and eight months that Hu Yaobang was the top administrator of northern Sichuan, agricultural production in his district doubled, while the attack on speculation and hoarding and the elimination or arrest of Nationalist agents made it possible for industry and commerce in the towns and cities to begin to recover and develop. Consequently, social order was stabilized and productivity increased.

It was during this time that Hu for the first time worked directly under the leadership of Deng Xiaoping. Deng appreciated Hu's ability to lead and plan realistically, and Hu in turn was greatly impressed with Deng's style of leadership, his sense of responsibility, and his decision making. It was Mao Zedong's careful selection of personnel that made this historical union of Deng Xiaoping and Hu Yaobang possible, a union that would eventually lead to their work together in the later reform movement.

The Little Guy Mounts the Stage

In August 1952, the situation in the greater southwestern area having already been stabilized, Mao decided to transfer Deng and Hu to the capital. Although Deng still maintained his position of responsibility for the Southwest District, Mao had already decided to give the major responsibility for the district to Li Jingquan, who had accompanied Mao ever since the Jinggang Mountain period and whom he personally trusted. By bringing Deng and Hu, both of whom had loyally followed the Mao Zedong line, to the capital and putting them in charge of the Communist Party and Youth League respectively, Mao further consolidated his authority and control at both the central and regional levels.

In September, thirty-seven-year-old Hu Yaobang became first secretary of the Central Committee of the New Democratic Youth League, replacing Feng Wenbin who had been demoted to local committee work in Tianjin. For the next fourteen years Hu would be solely responsible for the leadership of Communist youth.

Feng Wenbin had been a leader of youth work with a long background in the Communist Youth League and in the CCP. He had been Hu Yaobang's superior in the Jiangxi Soviet period when Hu first became involved in youth leadership work. When the New Democratic Youth League held its first National Conference from April 11 to 18, 1949, Ren Bishi had been elected honorary league chairman. Later, the first plenum of the Youth League Central Committee had elected Feng as secretary and appointed Liao Chengzhi and Jiang Nanxiang as assistant secretaries.

The reason for Feng Wenbin's expulsion from this position in 1952 has not been made public even today, but secondary sources offer some information. Two months after its founding, *China Youth News*, the official organ of the Youth League Central Committee, in a "July 1, 1951, report made an error. The page four pictorial was on the large meeting called by the party's Central Committee to commemorate the thirtieth anniversary of the founding of the CCP and included pieces commemorating the birth of the party written by Chinese youth. There were some inaccuracies in these reports and essays." This prompted Feng Wenbin to call together those responsible for the paper. Feng criticized them severely: "If you don't do it properly you might commit an error of vanguardism."[5]

Nearly ten months after Hu Yaobang was made first secretary of the Youth League, meeting with the executive delegation of the Second National Conference of the New Democratic Youth League, Mao Zedong noted, "The days of the Youth League arguing for independence from the party are long past. The problem now is a lack of independent work by the league, not one of arguing for independence. . . . In 1952 I spoke with the comrades of the Central Committee of the league and raised two topics that I wanted them to study. One concerned how the party leads the league, and the other concerned how the league does its work.''[6]

At the First Conference on Youth League Organizational Work, held after Hu Yaobang had already become first secretary of the league's Central Committee, Li Chang, secretary of the Secretariat of the league's Central Committee, said, ''From June through September 1952, the league has already gained 1,780,000 new members nationwide. One of the fairly common problems facing our membership expansion work at present is a lack of concrete understanding and guidance, insufficient guarantees that the league's quality remains high. In some regions we have already discovered large increases in the numbers. . . . In a few places we have discovered that 70 percent of the new members are not qualified.''

In the history of the CCP, the Communist Youth League has had tendencies toward vanguardism and of acting like a separate party. This is the reason that on November 1, 1935, the party's Central Committee announced the dissolution of the national organization of the Communist Youth League (except in the liberated areas). In April 1949, when reinstituting the national Youth League organization, to prevent the reoccurrence of this tendency, Ren Bishi, a member of the Politburo, was made honorary chairman of the Youth League, to guide the work of the Youth League. On June 27, 1950, after Ren died of a brain hemorrhage, Mao Zedong was worried about Feng, who wanted to rapidly expand the Youth League into a huge organization and create his own little leadership group. At the same time, Mao felt even more strongly that he needed someone who was capable, experienced, and trustworthy to bring the Youth League back and guarantee the party's leadership of it. Thus Feng Wenbin was dismissed on charges of making trouble in his attempt to make the Youth League independent of the party, and Hu Yaobang was appointed because Mao thought that he could be entrusted to guarantee the party's leadership over the league.

When Hu first took charge of the Central Committee of the two-million-member Communist Youth League, his task was not easy, particularly in the new circumstances following Liberation. And there were officers of the league at all levels who, having a fairly high educational level and good qualifications, were not very happy about having this young man from the military move in as their leader. As Hu recalls,

In 1952, I was transferred to Beijing to become first secretary of the Central Committee of the Youth League. Six months later, I attended a meeting called by Chairman Mao. Probably there were some who had said something about me, and Chairman Mao had investigated something of the situation before the meeting. As soon as the meeting came to order Chairman Mao asked, "Hu Yaobang, how long have you been here?" I replied, "Half a year." Chairman Mao then said, "When a little guy mounts the stage he doesn't inspire a lot of confidence does he!" He also said, "Half a year's no good. It'll take two years to solve the problem. Don't worry about it. Just do what you have to do!"[7]

A little later, at another forum, Mao also said,

Confidence is built slowly. . . . True respect of the masses for their leaders depends on the understanding that comes through revolutionary practice. They must truly understand before they will trust you. Confidence in the Central Committee of the Youth League is now already quite high. There are some who still don't respect it. They'll slowly learn to respect it. The little guy has just mounted the stage and confidence in him isn't very high yet. Don't worry. A bit of criticism and some grumbling are inevitable. There are "little speeches" because "big speeches" have not developed. If we are fully democratic and expose our wounds face to face and let people say their "little speeches," they may well say they don't have the time, they just want to rest.[8]

The appointment of Hu Yaobang as first secretary of the Central Committee of the Youth League was obviously the result of a lot of urging and support from Mao Zedong.

Taking Over Youth League Publications

Upon taking up his new position, Hu first put his energies into seeing to it that the publications of the league's Central Committee were well managed. These included *China Youth News*, *China Youth*, and *Youth League Work* (*Tuan de gongzuo*). Addressed to young people and to Youth League cadres, these periodicals quickly brought the policy guidelines and ideas of the Chinese Communists to officers of league organizations at all levels and to young people in general. By educating youths and explaining government policies, these publications attempted to bring the political ideology and activities of young people in line with the political guidelines of the CCP.

When Hu Yaobang went to Beijing to take up his new position he lived in the compound at Number 3 Zhengyi Road (originally Yuheqiao Road). According to the recollections of Xing Fangqun, former editor-in-chief of *China Youth*,

> Comrade Hu Yaobang came in 1952 to be first secretary of the Youth League. The moment he arrived he placed a great deal of emphasis on the work of the youth publications. As chair of the meetings of the Secretariat of the Central Committee of the league, he frequently discussed the ideological work of the league and the propaganda tasks of its publications. Beginning in the autumn of 1953, he held a meeting at his home every Sunday evening of those responsible for *China Youth News*, *China Youth*, the China Youth Press, and the propaganda office of the league's Central Committee. During the meetings he would always report on some of the important ideas and talks of leaders of the party's Central Committee, and then he would tie them in with the work of the Youth League and the writing of editorials, and he would examine the ways by which the Youth League should carry out propaganda and educational work in accordance with the spirit of the Central Committee policies. While he was talking he would suggest topics and tell the youth publications to write articles and organize reports.[9]

To keep the youth publications on a high plane yet communicate with and be attractive to young people in general, Hu thought that they should get two categories of leaders to write articles for them. One was influential old revolutionaries, well-known scholars, and specialists; the other was young communications personnel and selected outstanding and capable young people. During Hu's time as director of the Youth League, and influenced by his insistence on the importance of these guidelines, the editorial staffs of the youth publications actively took the initiative to solicit manuscripts. It was for this reason that many of the older revolutionaries, including Mao Zedong and Liu Shaoqi, and a number of writers, scholars, and specialists like Guo Moruo and Qian Weichang contributed poems and comments on manuscripts and documents and even wrote articles themselves for *China Youth News* and *China Youth*. Some of those that had a far-reaching influence on youth in the 1950s and '60s were Tao Zhu's ''A Life of Ideals, Feelings, and Spirit,'' Chen Yi's ''To the Graduating Class of the Capital High School'' on the question of being red and expert, Guo Moruo's ''Genius and Hard Work,'' Qian Weichang's ''Scientific Inventions in Ancient China,'' and Li Rui's ''The Early Revolutionary

Activities of Comrade Mao Zedong.'' Among those students and other young people whose manuscripts were printed in *China Youth News* and *China Youth* and who then went on to become special reporters and professional writers were the ''rightist'' student Lin Xiling and the ''rightist'' writer Liu Shaotang.

Thanks to Hu Yaobang's supervision of Youth League publications, their lively and interesting articles made them popular and respected among young people and other readers. When Hu started working with these publications, the circulation of *China Youth* was less than 200,000, but by the mid–1950s it had rapidly increased to more than a million, and by the early 1960s it broke the 2 million mark. Before the Cultural Revolution it had already reached 2.6 million. Likewise the circulation of *China Youth News* increased very rapidly, topping 1 million well before the outbreak of the Cultural Revolution.

Ideals and New Recruits

Being only thirty-seven years of age when he took over the position of first secretary of the Central Committee of the Youth League, Hu Yaobang of course aroused the skepticism of some old hands. In carrying out his leadership responsibilities, he had to explore new paths.

Hu's main philosophy guiding his leadership of the youth work was to emphasize teaching young people the real practical uses of Communist thought, to promote an atmosphere of growth and vitality and of the search for truth that would help develop a rich diversity of activities for young people. To attain this objective and implement fully his goals for youth leadership work, in addition to supervising the youth publications, Hu took over the supervision of the propaganda and educational work among young people. At the same time he also moved to set up a coherent organizational system that could reach out in all directions and provide responsive communication at all levels.

In June 1953, at the Second National Conference of the Chinese New Democratic Youth League, Hu obtained the approval of the Central Committee of the Communist Party headed by Mao Zedong to recruit some 25 percent of those representing the various larger schools and institutes, local areas, and the armed forces who were no more than thirty years of age and had demonstrated outstanding abilities in real work, to be selected as Youth League Central Committee members and alternates, and to reorganize the older ''veterans'' of the Standing Committee and Secretariat and establish a new, younger Secretariat headed by Hu himself. In 1954, Hu also chose Hu Qili to fill the position of secretary of the Youth League Committee of Beijing University. With these reforms, Hu Yaobang had already begun to set up the core leadership of the Youth League that in the 1950s and '60s was known among Youth League members and young people in general as the "three Hu's and one Wang" (Hu Yaobang, Hu Keshi, Hu Qili, and Wang Zhaohua). Most of the important members of the Youth League faction who are the mainstream of Chinese reformers today and now occupy key posts at all levels of the party's Central Committee were at that time already working under Hu Yaobang [see appendix]. The "little guy" had already set his feet firmly upon the stage and gained widespread confidence and respect.

8
Rightist Tendencies and the Antirightist Campaign

In the early 1950s a split appeared in the Chinese Communist Party over the policy of agricultural collectivization. By the mid-'50s the debate within the inner circles of the Communist Party over which road the Chinese peasants should take, over where Chinese agricultural policy had come from and where it was going, reached a crossroads.

The moderates, led by Liu Shaoqi, Bo Yibo, and Deng Zihui, advocated that the direction of Chinese agricultural development should be first the mechanization of agriculture and then collectivization, and that this process should span three five-year plans (i.e., fifteen years, or eighteen years counting from the date of Liberation). They argued that to lead agriculture toward collectivization in China, the revolution in production should be the impetus. In the spring of 1955, because of the implementation of the state monopoly on grain and foodstuff purchases and requisitions, and because local cadres in some areas forced the peasants into collectives, the "productivity explosion" (*shengchanli baodong*) occurred in which it became common in the countryside for peasants to slaughter livestock, cut trees, and sell all their extra grain, thus destroying future production. For this reason, Deng Zihui, who was in charge of agriculture, with the support of Liu Shaoqi released the "Announcement Concerning the Reorganization and Consolidation of Agricultural Cooperatives" on January 10, 1955, in the name of the Central Committee. The document stated that one of the following three measures should be adopted, depending on the individual conditions in different places: (1) In areas that had already fulfilled the plan, halt further expansion and put all energies into consolidation; (2) in areas that had already exceeded the plan, implement appropriate reductions or retrenchments; (3) in areas in which preparations were inadequate and had been hastily pushed forward, reorganize. Deng also stressed that even within the collective agricultural economics of cooperatives, the main system of production responsibility should be a "labor and production contract system." Liu Shaoqi, Bo Yibo, and Deng Zihui adamantly opposed the policy of rapidly pushing agricultural collectivization, so as to avoid taking the disastrous road of Stalinist agricultural collectivization. The result of the reorganization was the elimination of 200,000 cooperatives that did not meet the necessary conditions.

The radicals, including Mao Zedong and Chen Boda, thought that the position of Liu Shaoqi, Bo Yibo, and Deng Zihui was one of "having one foot planted in a socialist industry and the other foot planted in a small-scale peasant economy."[1] In China "cooperatives must come first, and only then can we use large machines." The mechanization of agriculture "will not be possible, or become possible on a large scale, until agriculture has achieved a foundation of cooperativization on a large scale." Furthermore, "The accumulation of the large amounts of capital that will be required for fulfilling the industrialization of the nation and the reform of agricultural technology must in large part come from agriculture."[2] Thus on October 11, 1955, Mao Zedong convened the Sixth Session of the Seventh Congress of the Chinese Communist Party at which he criticized Deng Zihui for the error of "rightist tendencies" and proposed the rapid completion of agricultural cooperativization in less than three years' time. Mao agreed that the social revolution should be used to spur on the revolution in production. The congress approved Mao's point of view in its "Decision Concerning the Question of Agricultural Cooperativization."

Having come from a peasant family with a small amount of land, and with experience in carrying out land reform in northern Sichuan, Hu Yaobang had a good understanding of the peasant's desire to have his own land, and of the real conditions in the villages. It was for this reason that under Hu the Youth League organizations in the countryside had upheld the policy of Liu Shaoqi, Bo Yibo, and Deng Zihui and opposed moving too rapidly.

Nonetheless, not long after the congress, in an article entitled "Actively Organize the Young People to Participate in the Agricultural Cooperatives Movement," Hu wrote:

> In regard to the agricultural cooperativization movement, leading organs of the Youth League at all levels still maintain varying degrees of a rightist

viewpoint. This is true not only of the Central Committee of the Youth League, but also of local league committees at all levels. The most prominent example took place recently during the unhealthy fad of "oppose adventurism" [*fandui maojin*] and "firmly retrench" when some league committee members widely denounced the enthusiasm of young people who set up cooperatives as "hasty adventurism" and "impure motives." They forced those who had joined a cooperative into leaving, and they even used such strange tactics to make the masses quit the cooperatives as setting up banners for those who left, calling them "model league members."[3]

On the question of the usefulness of agricultural mechanization, Hu clearly tended to agree with the view of the Liu Shaoqi group. In 1960, after the failure of the Great Leap Forward and the people's commune movement, in an article entitled "A Generation of New People Formed in the Great Struggle on the Agricultural Battleline," Hu said, "From our valuable experience in the Great Leap Forward, and with the realization of mechanization, we shall be able to raise greatly the productivity of agricultural labor, and we shall be able to change totally the present backward situation of '500 million people growing food to eat.'" He also argued that, "Beginning with last year, in ten years, over the whole land machinery will be used wherever the use of machinery is possible."[4] In other words, Hu Yaobang too thought that it would take fifteen years (from 1955) for agriculture to become basically mechanized, and that only after mechanization was achieved would China be able to solve its backwardness of 500 million people working in the fields in order to have enough to eat. This clearly was close to the view of the Liu Shaoqi faction.

In the mid–1950s another important point that Hu Yaobang suggested relating to the question of the development of agricultural production was his call to young people to continue and to develop upon the Yan'an spirit of "taking the offensive against adversity," to bring agricultural production to China's wastelands. Thus the January 16, 1955, issue of *China Youth* carried an editorial, "Comrade Khrushchev's Address to the Moscow Conference of Young Volunteers for Cultivating the Wilderness." At Hu's suggestion, the editorial office added the line, "Comrade Khrushchev's address has deep educational significance for our Chinese young people as well."

In June 1955, at a meeting to send off the "Beijing Young Volunteers to Cultivate the Wilderness Brigade," Hu Yaobang said, "In the last several thousand years, our ancestors have turned 160,000 mu of wasteland into arable fields, leaving 150,000 mu out there deep in sleep. . . . We young Chinese certainly cannot let those wastelands sleep for long. . . . We shall certainly with planning call on them to grow grain, and bring them into the socialist service of our nation."[5] After this, the Central Committee of the Youth League sent out a group of cadres to mobilize a large number of young people who had left school and were out of work into a brigade to participate in farming in China's border regions and wastelands.

In the Youth League publications of the mid–1950s, Hu Yaobang tended to lean toward the "rightist" position of first carrying out the mechanization of agriculture and opposing pushing quickly for collectivization, and also of supporting the struggle against adversity by going out to cultivate the wilderness.

Becoming a Member of the Party Central Committee

From September 15 to 27, 1956, the Eighth Congress of the Chinese Communist Party was held in Beijing to consider the revision of the party constitution and discuss proposals for the second five-year plan. The presentations to the congress included Liu Shaoqi's "Political Report of the Central Committee of the CCP," Deng Xiaoping's "Report on Revising the Party Constitution," Zhou Enlai's "Report on the Draft of the Second Five-Year Plan Concerning the National Economy," and "The Role of Education in the Youth Movement" by Hu Yaobang, representing the Central Committee of the Youth League.

Hu proudly proclaimed that "As of the end of June this year, the membership of the Youth League had already reached 20 million men and women, about 17 percent of the total young people in the entire country, and there are 700,000 grass-roots league organizations located in peasant villages, factories, schools, state organs, and the armed forces spread throughout the entire nation. In the last eight years, 2,150,000 Youth League members have joined the Chinese Communist Party. We can say without any exaggeration that the Youth League has already become a reliable reserve army for the party. It effectively guides the minds of the young people of the entire country ever higher."[6]

It was at this congress that Hu Yaobang was elected to the Central Committee of the CCP, becoming one of the ninety-seven members who formed the core of the leadership of the party. Clearly, Mao Zedong and also Deng Xiaoping, who had been instrumental in eliminating the "Gao Gang and Rao Shushi Antiparty Bloc" and had just been promoted to the position of secretary-general of the Central Committee, awarded this important promotion to Hu for his outstanding leadership of the Youth League.

Two months before the convening of the Eighth Congress, Deng Xiaoping had returned from Russia, carrying with him Khrushchev's address to the Twentieth Congress of the Communist Party of the Soviet Union opposing the cult of the individual. The secret report denouncing Stalin aroused an intense reaction. With the support of Liu Shaoqi and Peng Dehuai, Deng Xiaoping presented to the Eighth Congress his "Report on Revising the Constitution," which struck out the passages on "taking Mao Zedong's thought as the highest guiding principles of the entire party," which had been added to the constitution by Liu Shaoqi at the Seventh Congress in 1945. Deng further emphasized that "The major significance of upholding collective leadership and opposing the cult of the individual has been forcefully explained by the Twentieth Congress of the Communist Party of the Soviet Union. This explanation has had an enormous influence not only on the Communist Party of the Soviet Union but also on Communist parties throughout the entire world.''[7] The Eighth Party Congress was to have an enormous influence on the personal career and intellectual development of Hu Yaobang, on the development of the Chinese Communist Party, and on the Chinese political situation.

The Hundred Flowers Period

Following Khrushchev's secret speech criticizing Stalin, violence broke out in Poland and Hungary. This worried Mao Zedong. Mao supported Zhou Enlai's proposal that the party should relax its relationship with the intellectuals. Mao further proposed the policy of "Let a hundred flowers bloom, let a hundred schools contend." He thought that the authority of the Communist Party was secure enough that this movement for greater freedom of expression would simply make the party more enlightened and stabilize its rule.

Mao's proposal for the Hundred Flowers movement did not receive a positive response from leading members of the Central Committee such as Liu Shaoqi, Deng Xiaoping, and Peng Zhen. They believed that such a movement would create all kinds of problems, and that greater democratic freedoms would make life difficult for party cadres and adversely affect the rule of the Communist Party. Thus, the Politburo did not pass Mao's proposal. The famous nuclear physicist Qian Wei-chang, who had studied in the United States, has said that "This faction of Liu Shaoqi and Peng Zhen did not support the hundred flowers idea." Nonetheless, in May 1956 and again in February 1957, Mao instructed Zhou Enlai to convene two Supreme State Conferences, which announced to the whole nation the Hundred Flowers policy, inviting all democratic parties and people at all levels in the society to speak out.

Hu Yaobang, too, was greatly influenced by Khrushchev's secret speech and by Deng Xiaoping's report to the Eighth Congress. Furthermore, because of his experience in admitting large numbers of intellectuals into the party as administrator of Resistance University in the years 1937–38, Hu reacted positively to Mao's Hundred Flowers policy. In 1956 he gave a talk to the editorial staff of *China Youth News* in which, according to the recollections of Chen Mo (then assistant editor in chief), he said, "A newspaper must exhibit a spirit of struggle, must open up and be critical, must be prepared to go to court. You mustn't be afraid. I see that you are somewhat afraid right now." Chen noted that Hu then "quoted at length from Gorky's high school condemnation of the times, and also from Comrade Deng Xiaoping's talk, encouraging us with 'A newspaper must be a trumpet, a voice that is prepared to go into battle. . . . The struggle between the old and the new, between progress and stagnation, retreat, this is a great ideological struggle. If we are to win the struggle we must must be strong, we must be prepared to lose our black velvet caps, to lose our jobs.'"[8]

Hu Yaobang's speech undoubtedly had an influence on the attitude of the editors and reporters. In the spring of 1956, *China Youth News* began putting out a "Hot Pepper" supplement (*fukan*), edited by Shu Xuesi, which, with a spirit of "making revolution in every issue," printed a number of sharp, biting articles attacking bureaucratism and exposing social evils. For example, Liu Binyan, the famous reporter for *China Youth News*, wrote three pieces courageously attacking bureaucratism and the harm it did. These were printed in *Renmin wenxue* (People's Literature): "Working on the Bridge" (April) and "The Inside News of the Newspaper" (in two parts, June and October). In April 1957, a leadership group of the CCP accompanied the former president of the Soviet Union, Voroshilov, on a tour of the Beijing Agricultural Exhibition Hall. The guide, Zuo Ye, an assistant to the minister of agriculture, got into a violent fight with a photographer who was trying to take pictures. Consequently, a reporter with the group wrote a news article entitled "Assistant to the Minister and the Photographer," which was printed in *China Youth News*, arousing a furor nationwide. These articles and the special "Hot Pepper" supplement of *China Youth News* brought an excited response from the public and were received very favorably by young people and other readers.

With Hu Yaobang's support, the Central Committee of the Youth League reported to schools and institutes and league members throughout the country the content of the Hundred Flowers policy and of Mao Zedong's February 1957 speech, "On the Correct Handling of Contradictions among the People." Hu personally gave reports to the Central Committee of the league and to various universities on mobilizing people for the Hundred Flowers movement. In the versions of Mao's speech first circulated, to allay the fears of the intellectuals, Mao guaranteed that "Those who have knowledge should speak out. If the words are not perfect, the speaker should not be blamed. The listener can judge, changing those ideas that are faulty and trying to carry out those that are right." He also clearly stated that "Democracy is both an end and a means," and there is no so-called absolute standard for separating the fragrant flowers from the poisonous weeds.

Lin Xiling got a copy of Khrushchev's secret speech from the office of Hu Yaobang's secretary, Cao Zhixiong, and used it in talks given at People's University and Beijing University, tying it in with strong criticism of the defects in the Chinese Communist system. In many schools throughout the nation, students even held demonstrations, boycotted classes, and voiced their grievances. In the spring of 1957, the voices of students and young people demanding democracy and freedom reverberated throughout all of China.

These far-flung waves all had a direct or indirect cumulative effect on the "position" and "attitude" of Hu Yaobang and the Central Committee of the Youth League, in their position of ultimate responsibility for league members and students. The situation was fluid.

Evolution of Hu Yaobang's Antirightist Views

Mao Zedong's essay of May 15, 1957, "Things Are Beginning to Change," was addressed to party cadres, telling them that he wanted to change the original focus of the Hundred Flowers movement and return to the old road of restraint and suppression, and declaring that he wanted to seize up to 15 percent of the rightists at large in society.

On the same day, the Chinese New Democratic Youth League

opened its Third National Conference. It was at this conference that the league's name was changed to the "Chinese Communist Youth League," reflecting the fact that socialist industry and commerce in the cities and the cooperative movement in the countryside had both been basically achieved. At this conference Hu Yaobang continued as first secretary and Hu Qili continued to be an alternate member of the league's Central Committee. On May 25, 1957, Mao Zedong addressed the conference, saying, "Any words or actions that depart from socialism are wrong."[9]

However, Hu Yaobang's report, "Unite with All the Young People of the Nation to Establish a Socialist New China," took a somewhat different tack. In part four of this report, Hu said,

> Getting all our young people rapidly to discard all unproletarian opinions, and getting them to accept the basic viewpoint of Marxism-Leninism, definitely cannot be accomplished in a short period of time. Any attempt to use simplistic, rigid, hasty, or crudely violent means to revolutionize the thought of young people would be futile. We must fully recognize the fact that this task will be a long and difficult one. Only then shall we be able seriously to study the correct way of implementing this task. In teaching Marxism and Leninism, in teaching Communism, we have to make them lively and tie them in closely with real life. And we have to let young people having all kinds of different opinions talk freely.[10]

Hu's actions and his words are enlightening. In a talk he gave on January 17, 1983, he stated that "In 1957, I had a talk with Lin Xiling for four hours. She wouldn't listen to me, but I never thought she should be arrested." On October 27, 1979, in another talk, Hu said, "At the time, I had a talk with Lin Xiling and pointed out to her that her thinking was so dominated by the ideology of individualism, and that there was no future in this kind of approach. At the time she still didn't believe me, so I just said to her, 'You don't believe it? We'll see what you think in twenty years.'"

On June 19, 1957, Mao Zedong brought out his revised version of "On the Correct Handling of Contradictions among the People." The line "Democracy is both an end and a means" was changed to "Democracy as such sometimes seems to be an end, but it is in fact only a means." At the same time, he also added to the text six criteria for judging errors, which took the place of legal criteria. Mao even tried to justify having gone back on his word by saying that this was being open and above-board. But under the slogan of "beating back the attack of the bourgeois rightists,'' Mao was clearly trying to protect his own position of power as well as all levels of the party bureaucracy.

Hu Yaobang was trapped in the middle of a storm from which it was difficult either to advance or to retreat. But Deng Xiaoping helped him out by sending him to Moscow on July 16, at the height of the Antirightist campaign, as the head of a delegation of Youth League students to participate in the Fourth World Youth and Student Peace and Friendship Festival. While he was out of the country, his own Chinese Communist Youth League seized a large number of rightists at all levels in the organization. It is possible that even more might have been seized. After the Antirightist campaign was over, Hu emphatically stated, ''In 1957 the problem with the *China Youth News* was really enormous, but the general secretariat managed to see to it that it squeaked by.''[11]

Looking back on the past, Hu has observed that ''Before the Great Cultural Revolution, I too was wrong about some young writers. Some of those comrades were also very talented, though their writings were not mature enough and they needed help. But our policy for dealing with them was wrong. Now they have returned, and have become excellent writers. If now, as middle-aged writers, they should say in their writings that some old guy had been wrong about them, I would agree, because that's a fact.''[12]

In early 1978, Hu gave a talk at the Central Party School in which he said, ''I now am really sorry that in the Antirightist campaign of 1957 I regarded a group of talented cadres who were on the Central Committee of the Youth League as rightists. I would like to offer them my genuine apologies.''[13]

It was with this in mind that twenty years later, as head of the Organization Department of the Central Committee of the Chinese Communist Party, Hu overturned the cases and cleared the names of 500,000 who had been accused of being rightists during the Mao Zedong era.

9
From the Mao Line
to the Liu-Deng Line

The period from the elimination of Wang Shiwei in the Yan'an rectification movement to the arrest of the rightists in 1957 was one of historically inevitable double punches that developed in proportion to the amount of power and degree of control wielded by Mao Zedong. The antiright hurricane toppled 500,000 bright intellects and stifled the free thought and creativity of 600 million people, covering China with a dark cloud. The nation was exhausted, morally bankrupt, and moaning in pain.

But Mao was intoxicated with the victory of his own turbulent storms. Always victorious, Mao thought that he was the great communist man, standing at the pinnacle of victory. In November 1957, vaunting the self-conceit of his ambition to wrest from Khrushchev the new leadership of the communist movement, Mao flew to Moscow to take part in the ceremonies celebrating the fortieth anniversary of the Russian Revolution. At the meeting of the Communist and Workers parties he announced his monumental thesis that "the east wind prevails over the west wind." But Khrushchev did not buy this line and sent him packing. Mao returned in a huff. He now became convinced that the reason he had not prevailed was that he did not have in his hands enough steel and grain.

Mao Zedong fantasized that "the liberated man, the Chinese people as masters of their own nation," "propelled by the great liberating force of Communist thought, contained an inexhaustible supply of energy" that "like 'atomic energy' would explode in a 'nuclear chain reaction.'" Thus he proposed that "in the struggle for production, all revolutionary and construction tasks must be realized through the mass movement."[1]

With this hypothesis as his foundation, beginning in January 1958 at the Nanning Conference, he roamed around, everywhere proclaiming the great idea of catching up with England, overtaking the United States, and surpassing the Soviet Union. At the first meeting in the afternoon of May 8, 1958, Mao said, "I think that in a dozen years or so our nation can become an industrialized nation. . . . It now looks like it will take only fifteen years to catch up with England, and even to catch up with the United States."

On the evening of May 18, he put it even more concretely. "Next year 10 million tons of steel, the year after, 17 million tons of steel. The world will be shaken. If in five years we can reach 40 million tons, we might even catch up with England in seven years, and in another eight years, with the United States."[2]

On November 21, at a meeting in Wuchang, Mao stated: "Khrushchev is very cautious. He already has 55 million tons of steel and more than 100 million tons of oil. He is so cautious he still needs twelve years to prepare for the transition. . . . They've already been at it for forty years, and in another twelve years they still won't have made the transition. They'll be behind us. They're already frantic now. They don't have any people's communes. He can't do it."[3]

It was during this time that the *People's Daily*, on October 13, reprinted Zhang Chunqiao's essay "Break the Legal Rights of the Bourgeoisie," which was the first call for discarding gradualism and patience and beginning the transition to the communist society. A crazy man and crazy followers together made up crazy words to go with Mao's crazy three-stage theory of catching up with England, overtaking the United States, and surpassing the Soviet Union, which, together with the Great Leap Forward and the people's communes, formed the Three Red Banners of the general line that led off into the sky.

In Wuhan, at the Sixth Plenum of the Eighth Central Committee of the CCP, which met from November 28 to December 10, 1958, Mao proposed after thirteen days of debate that he not be nominated as candidate for chairman of the People's Republic of China, thus compromising with and receiving the support of the pragmatic faction headed by Liu Shaoqi and Deng Xiaoping. The session passed the "Resolution on Some Problems Concerning the People's Communes," approving the great experiment in which China was to begin the early transition to a communist society under the leadership of Mao Zedong and the mass movement. Following the antirightist tragedy of 1957, the stage was now set for an even greater tragedy to be played out across the countryside of China.

The Central Committee of the Youth League
During the Great Leap Forward

Under the leadership of Hu Yaobang, the Communist Youth League and the student movement were caught up in the fanaticism of Mao Zedong's ultraleftism and followed more or less the opportunistic line of Mao Zedong. On June 28, 1958, the Third Plenum of the Third Central Committee of the Communist Youth League adopted a "Resolution on Organizing a Broad Youth Program to Study and Put into Practice Marxism and Leninism and the Works of Mao Zedong." This resolution stated:

> This is a great period of development by leaps and bounds in which "one day is equal to twenty years." Under the leadership of the Communist Party, our nation's people have raised the curtain on a new socialist high tide of rapid and economical construction. . . . The several decades of the history of the revolution prove that under the guidance of the thought of Mao Zedong the revolutionary struggle proceeds from one glorious victory to the next. Under the guidance of the thought of Mao Zedong, the socialist construction of the nation can proceed at a fast rate and change the backward face of China's several thousand years of poverty and ignorance. The works of Mao Zedong are the lamp that leads forward the victory of the Chinese people; they are the socialist, the communist compass of the Chinese people's national construction.[4]

Not long after this resolution was passed, cadres Xing Chongzhi and Sha Chenggui went to the poorest parts of China in Henan province to observe and learn from the earliest communes, which had been set up in April 1958 and enthusiastically flew the Three Red Banners of socialist construction. In their report on this visit Xing and Sha wrote,

> Our deepest impression and greatest lesson from this trip to Henan are that all the people are forging steel. At the office, our understanding of the masses making steel was simply that every county, every commune, and every work brigade was engaged in making steel. But when we went out to look for ourselves, we discovered that this was not the whole story. Not only is every county, every commune, and every brigade engaged in this task, every family and every person is doing it. Every older person up to sixty and seventy years of age, and every child of seven or eight is directly participating in the mass movement. At the sixth brigade of the Surpass England Commune in Shangcheng County we walked around the hillside terraces. There really were furnaces on the terraces and steel was

flowing everywhere. The furnaces were given all kinds of names, too many to count—Youth Leap Forward Furnace, Magnolia Furnace, Surpass England Furnace, Good Women Furnace, Overtake America Furnace. . . . Every one of the people struggling beside the furnaces was pleased and confident, working day and night with enthusiasm and satisfaction, bare footed and bare shouldered.[5]

In November of the same year, *China Youth News* and *China Youth* were already announcing active preparations for the transition to communism and discussing the distribution methods of the supply system.

During this period of fanaticism, *China Youth* published a series of reports on "Unimaginable Miracles, Selected Examples of Agricultural High Production Satellites." These reports were filled with truly amazing marvels. Here is one of the most exaggerated of these reports:

Jiang Shaofang, a young worker at the Yulin Botanical Normal School in Guangxi province, overcoming his inferiority complex, has already crossed Chinese sorghum with corn to produce a kind of plant that produces sorghum at the top and ears of corn in the middle. Also, the grains of sorghum are as big as those of corn, one full spike weighing one pound. And one stalk may have several ears of corn, giving a yield much greater than normal corn. . . . Jiang Shaofang now plans, by cross-breeding and grafting sorghum and corn and sugar cane, to produce a plant that will be all three, sorghum, corn, and sugar cane. He also is preparing next year to plant a high-yield field of wet rice that will produce 60 to 100 pounds of rice per mu [one-sixth acre]. The method he will use is primarily: (1) to breed a very high yield wet rice, and (2) to apply highly advanced agricultural techniques.[6]

"The bolder man gets, the more the land will produce." Each cadre exaggerated more than his neighbor. In the Great Leap Forward, Mao Zedong used his own imagination to direct the activities of the Chinese people, and the masses, pushed on by the movement, raised the figures at each level, developing their creative story-telling and literary abilities, and replied to the marvelous fantasies of Mao Zedong with these "miracles."

On November 25, 1958, at the Second National Conference of Socialist Youth Activists, Hu Yaobang delivered his report, "Develop the Communist Spirit, Work Hard to Establish Socialism." In this report, he described for the first time his views concerning the Three Red Banners movement and the current youth movement. He said,

Thanks to the high tide of the mass movement that has mobilized all the people to participate in industry, mainly in making steel, this year our national steel production by November 20 has already reached nearly 9 million tons, doubling steel production this year and guaranteeing that we will reach the goal of producing 17 million tons. The national output of coal exceeded that of England, putting us in third place in the world. In agriculture, the very impressive performance of the combined factors of high yield and large acreage production of "satellite fields" is estimated to give us this year a total output of grain and cotton double that of last year. Some people said that the twelve-year national agricultural development goal was unattainable, but we have today, within just three years, already basically reached it.[7]

Hu's assessment of the Three Red Banners and mass movements was basically positive, but he was also keenly aware of the spreading tendency toward exaggeration and phoney claims. It was for this reason that he repeatedly warned young people that "True thought and speech and work must be combined with a spirit of seeking the facts. The search for the facts must respect objective laws, so that thought is in accord with objective reality, giving you the ability to grasp objective truth. Breaking with superstition does not of course mean breaking with science. We must fully accept all scientific principles, because they can help us solve real problems, help us create new things based on the new realities. All one-sided, outdated, unrealistic views must be discarded, because they can only impede and hurt our thought and actions."[8]

Indeed, in May of that year, Chen Yun, in a letter to Mao Zedong on the question of steel production goals, had also said, "Virtually all the comrades attending the conference feel that setting the production figure for steel at 9 millions tons is too low [the figure had been set at 13 million tons], and can make people discouraged. . . . Setting the production figure somewhat lower will not necessarily discourage people. Just as Liu Shaoqi said to the Politburo, on the contrary, setting it too high can discourage and frustrate the people. Of the 9 million tons produced by the homemade forges . . . 4 or 5 million tons are substandard raw iron that is not suitable for casting, that cannot even be reprocessed into usable steel. This is a waste of the people's energies."[9]

From July 2 to August 18, 1959, the Central Committee of the CCP met first in an enlarged conference of the Politburo and then in the Eighth Plenum of the Eighth Central Committee at Lushan. At the beginning of the conference the atmosphere was quite relaxed, with meetings during the day and dance or theatrical performances at night. Under the clapping and applause of those sychophants who were stirring up Mao Zedong's psychology of euphoria, men like Ke Qingshi, Chen Boda, Lin Biao, Kang Sheng, and Zeng Xisheng, the conference, which was originally supposed to bring the excessively leftist tendencies under control, turned into a litany of praise and congratulations for their achievements. The Lushan conference was really a victory parade with no thought at all for the sufferings of the people.

It was Peng Dehuai who stood up and on July 14 wrote a letter expressing his opinions to Mao Zedong. In this letter Peng pointed out that the Great Leap Forward of 1958 and its continuation in 1959 had "given rise to some irregularities," that the business of having all the people forging steel "had some good points and bad points." His reasons were, "First, the atmosphere of overexaggeration has become widespread. . . . [It] has engulfed all parts of the country and all institutions. The appearance of unbelievable miracles published in the media really hurt the credibility of the party very badly. . . . Second, the petty bourgeois fanaticism makes it easy for us to make 'leftist' errors. . . . Some targets have been increasingly raised to the point that goals that can only be achieved in several years . . . have become targets to be achieved in one year or a few months. Consequently, they have become totally divorced from reality and cannot receive the support of the masses."[10] Zhang Wentian, Huang Kecheng, and Zhou Xiaozhou spoke out in support of Peng's position.

On July 23, August 2, and August 16, Mao came out with his treacherous lies, opposing the alleged rightist opportunism and attacking Peng Dehuai's and Zhang Wentian's criticism of the rash left opportunist line. Mao spuriously argued that "This struggle at Lushan is a class struggle, a continuation of the life and death struggle between the bourgeoisie and the proletariat, part of the process of the socialist revolution of the past ten years."[11] Mao even threatened those attending this enlarged conference of the Politburo by saying that he was prepared to return to the mountains and take up guerrilla warfare all over again over this issue. His threats had their intended effect.

Deng Xiaoping left this quarrelsome place on the excuse that his leg hurt. Zhou Enlai and Chen Yun were intimidated by Mao, who knew they "would stand firm at the conference." Liu Shaoqi, who only in April had become president of the nation, was not of course in a strong position. Only Zhu De maintained the attitude of a true soldier and stood up and spoke truthfully. All the rest were just followers and sychophants. The truth be damned! Let reality go to hell! This is how Peng Dehuai, who had stood up for the people, was struck down. The Eighth Plenum of the Eighth Central Committee issued a public announcement that, "At the present time, the main danger is that rightist opportunism is spreading among some cadres."

Hu Yaobang did not attend the meeting of the enlarged Politburo. From July 13 to 18, in his capacity as first secretary of the Central Committee of the Communist Youth League, he was at Qingdao chairing the Third Plenum of the Third Central Committee of the Youth League. In his work report as representative of the Standing Committee, he talked mainly about motivating youth throughout the country to become active and to participate in the movement to increase production and economize, about strengthening the grass-roots organizations of the Youth League and further improving the league's capacity to struggle.

On August 2, however, Hu arrived at the Eighth Plenum of the Eighth Central Committee of the Communist Party and cast his vote in agreement with Mao Zedong. Why did he do so? Hu thought:

> The general line is the product of our party and Chairman Mao and combines the universal truth of Marxism with the revolutionary realities of the Chinese people. It is the concise expression of the great determination and wisdom of our people who want to change the "poverty and ignorance" of our nation. This general line will further arouse the latent socialist activism of our young people.
>
> There are some who close their eyes to the spirited communist attitude of our young people and to the great achievements this has accomplished. They overemphasize particular shortcomings of young people that are the result of a lack of experience, and they throw cold water on the positive attitude of the masses. This is the intolerable attitude of bourgeois paternalism. In our view, first, under the correct leadership of the party, it is the achievements of young people that are most important, and their mistakes are only secondary. . . . We should look at the basic nature of something, . . . not just at its defects. We should not attack one small problem and ignore all the rest. Second, these mistakes occur in the process of great strides forward. The important thing is progress. With continued progress all mistakes can be easily overcome. This is why we should enthusiastically praise the communist spirit of our young people, why we should enthusiastically support their revolutionary activism.[12]

Not until later would the seriousness of the damage done by the

Great Leap Forward reveal the truth of Peng Dehuai's message, which was at the time smeared with mud. The lesson of reality would also change Hu Yaobang's view of the Lushan Conference.

In his first talk of 1985, Hu said, "The *People's Daily* printed an article on the 1959 Lushan Conference saying, 'At the time Comrade Liu Shaoqi said that the Central Committee should take 50 percent of the responsibility for the errors of the Great Leap Forward, and the *People's Daily* should take the other 50 percent. If the exaggerations of what was happening in the Great Leap Forward had not been so blindly encouraged by the *People's Daily*, the errors would not have become as great as they did.'"

Actually, the *People's Daily* should take some of the responsibility, but was it not the original editor-in-chief, Deng Tuo, who was hounded in 1958 by Mao for "pedantic, lifeless, rigid editing" and then kicked out and sent to the Three-Family Village?![13] In 1957 the *Wenhui bao* was made an example of a rightist paper; Deng Tuo was kicked out as an example. Everyone knew that he should report only good things to Mao, that Mao encouraged leftism and would not tolerate any "rightism."

Eighteen years after the Lushan storm, when Hu Yaobang became director of the Organization Department of the party's Central Committee in December 1977, he was responsible for the first case of redressing an unfair grievance within the party, the case of Peng Dehuai. The truth will out.

Emphasis on Agriculture in the Early 1960s

In 1960 the Communist Party called on the entire nation to "continue to leap forward." But the leaping horse already had no more grass to feed on and its rider, Mao Zedong, fell off and hit the ground. Mao's blind pushing of the Great Leap Forward had already led the Chinese people into disaster. In the latter half of 1960, China entered the period known as the three years of famine, during which at least ten million people starved to death. The tragedies recorded in the *Twenty-four Dynastic Histories* of "selling sons and killing daughters," of "leaving home and family," "dying from eating earth," and "man eating man" appeared again under the "glorious Three Red Banners."

In 1960, Hu Yaobang's attitude toward the Great Leap Forward took a great leap forward. According to one of the Red Guard papers of the Cultural Revolution period, Hu said then that "The Three Red Banners are no good."

In March 1961, the CCP Central Committee met in Guangzhou to analyze the serious situation prevailing throughout the country and to form a new policy. But because there was no consensus among those attending the conference, they were not able to formulate a new policy. Consequently, they announced that they would first study the problem before coming to a decision.

All the high-ranking officials of the party became involved in implementing a grass-roots investigation and study program. Through an investigation by Wang Dongxing of the soldiers of the Central Security Forces who came from the countryside, Mao was informed that "The ordinary people in the countryside are now not eating as well as dogs. In the past dogs were able to eat chaff and grain. The people are so starved they have no energy. Little children are so starved they cannot stand up. The reaction of commune members is: is Chairman Mao telling us to starve to death?"[14] Liu Shaoqi went to investigate the Tianhua brigade in Changsha county of Hunan, and to his hometown, Tanzichong, in Ningxiang county, Hunan, after which he admitted that "Life for our rural relatives is very difficult . . . and the root of the problem still lies with the Central Committee." Zhou Enlai, Zhu De, and the others also went down to the countryside to investigate. Even Peng Dehuai, who had been stripped of office, was allowed to go home to Wushi to study the situation.

In the latter half of 1961, Hu Yaobang went to Tang county in Hebei, which had once been the base of guerrilla operations under his leadership. The investigation he carried out there was not just a cursory survey. He really got down and examined the conditions closely.

Back in the days when Tang county was the location of the headquarters of the North China Field Army, the people of this base area, to win a few mu of land of their own, had risked their lives and invested their grain in the Communists' land revolution, using wheelbarrows to carry Mao Zedong victoriously into the Hall of Abundant Wealth in the Imperial Palace in Beijing.

In Tang county, now bleak, desolate, and broken, Hu Yaobang walked through the villages and mountain hamlets. He found cadres he had once known well, and country friends. He interviewed illiterate old peasants, women, and children. He saw the empty hands and broken rice bowls of the people and investigated the free markets. He realized that the blind leftist opportunist line of Mao Zedong had created this devastation among the people, that the "people's communes" had robbed the peasants of everything they had, destroying their hopes and dreams. This was undoubtedly a severe blow that led Hu to a profound reexamination of his ideas.

In accordance with the spirit of the "Twelve Emergency Directives for Work in the Peasant Villages," formulated by Liu Shaoqi and Deng Xiaoping in November 1960, Hu guided the cadres of Tang county in formulating a law of "Family Management of the Fields" which was quickly put into effect throughout the county. Hu told the cadres: agriculture has to turn back. We must seek truth from facts. Food supplies have to be liberated. The principle of to each according to his labor must be fully implemented. Free markets must be started. Ways must be found to solve the problems of managing the forests, of private plots, and of housing. At the same time he also encouraged the peasants to open up wasteland to cultivation, telling them that "a little freedom" would make things go better. Realistic policies such as these made it possible for the peasants of Tang county to turn around and start on the road back to recovery. They welcomed these ideas. Many years later, they still remembered the time Hu Yaobang came to Tang county.

On January 30, 1962, at the "Central Committee Enlarged Work Conference" chaired by Liu Shaoqi, in front of seven thousand Communist Party cadres, Mao Zedong was forced to give a disingenuous examination of himself in which he admitted, "In socialist construction we are still very ignorant. There are still a number of essential fields of socialist economics that we do not understand. Speaking for myself, there are a number of problems concerning economic construction work that I still do not understand." But in reality, there were many people, from the Central Committee down to the grass-roots organizations, who were still following the ultraleft line of Mao Zedong, and Mao himself still sided very much with their "sincerity." The Anhui incident was typical.

The secretary of the Anhui Provincial Committee, Zeng Xisheng, one of Mao's most reliable supporters, had ruled Anhui for thirteen years. During the fanaticism of the Great Leap Forward, the exaggerations had been most severe in Anhui and Henan (under Party Committee Secretary Wu Zhipu). In the countryside of Anhui north of the Huai River and in the mountains of northern Henan the death rate in villages and communes had reached more than 30 percent. According to Li Baohua's report to the Central Committee,

> The number of those who died abnormally [i.e., from starvation] reached two million. At the time, Liu Shaoqi and Deng Xiaoping were in charge of the everyday work of the Central Committee. When they received the report of the disastrous situation in Anhui, they twice sent high officials to investigate the disaster, but both times the investigating teams were

stopped and detained politely but forcefully in a hotel. They were not allowed to make contact with the people at the grass-roots level. When this was reported to Liu and Deng, they felt that without primary source information it would not be possible to deal with Zeng Xisheng, who was covering the situation up so firmly. Thus they decided to send Hu Yaobang to lead the third investigation team to Anhui to find out the facts of the disaster and the problems and bias in the work of the provincial committee.

When Hu Yaobang arrived in Anhui, Zeng again tried to use his tricks to deal with him. But Hu had a scheme of his own, to meet openly with Zeng and the provincial committee while covertly carrying out the real work. . . . Hu had already ordered his investigation team to split up and go to Anhui by different routes . . . and quietly to start a real investigation. When their reports came back and Hu had their materials in hand, he informed Zeng that he wanted to investigate three counties, Wuwei, Tianchang, and Quanjiao. Upon arriving in each of these counties, he called a meeting of the county committee members and immediately laid out his concrete evidence before them so that . . . they found themselves with no recourse but to admit the truth one by one.

His mission accomplished, Hu Yaobang returned to Beijing. When Liu Shaoqi and Deng Xiaoping received this solid evidence they proposed that Zeng be relieved of his position and that Li Baohua be sent as his replacement. Seeing that he could protect Zeng no longer, Mao Zedong had no choice but to agree. When the people of Anhui heard the good news that Zeng Xisheng was being stripped of his duties, they . . . praised Hu Yaobang's work style of seriously digging for the facts.[15]

This took place in the first half of 1962. Because the people of Anhui province remembered Hu's successful battle with Zeng and his policy of really looking out for them, in July 1979 they elected him as Anhui's representative to the Fifth National People's Congress.

In the latter half of 1962, Hu Yaobang participated in the work on the "Revised Draft of the Articles on the Peasant Communes" sponsored by Liu Shaoqi and Deng Xiaoping. This document moved the basic accounting unit from the commune down to the production brigade, and it also declared that the commune was not a system of public ownership. In actuality the people's communes had already reverted to the level of advanced agricultural production cooperatives.

From the lesson of Mao Zedong's failure, Hu strongly felt that to understand the socialist stage of agricultural work and comprehend fully the way in which economic construction must be carried out would require much energy. In the early 1960s he read many books on agriculture and became friends with a number of agricultural scientists. Not afraid to ask questions, he accumulated a good deal of knowledge about agricultural theory. Based on his belief in tying together theory and practice, Hu reported to the Secretariat of the party's Central Committee that he wanted to spend some time in a rural area to study a real agricultural situation. In early 1963 his proposal was approved, and Hu went to Hunan province as local committee secretary for southern Hunan.

Hunan is an area of many mountains, little water, and tiny fields. During his time in southern Hunan, based mainly on his observations of the real conditions in mountainous areas where there are few arable fields, Hu came to believe that a one-track policy concentrating on grain production was undesirable, but rather that it was necessary to promote general economic development and management. He felt it was essential to make use of the many different kinds of resources of the mountains, rivers, and fields, that those who could run sideline occupations should do so. He also raised the idea, "Who cares whether a cat is black or white as long as it catches mice." Hu proposed setting up large ranches on the grassy slopes of southern Hunan, and he even suggested obtaining a small number of dairy cattle from abroad to start a modern dairy industry.

In March 1965, Hu was made second secretary of the Northwest Bureau of the CCP and first secretary of the Shaanxi Provincial Committee. The Central Committee was intentionally increasing the area under Hu's administration and giving him more practical experience in real situations. This broadened the scope of his leadership and study to the provincial level and to that of the large Northwest region.

During this period Hu continued to learn more about the agricultural problems of Tang county and southern Hunan. Based on this extended contact with the realities of some of the more poverty-stricken and desolate parts of the country, he felt that it was essential to put a great deal of energy into planting grass and trees in the Northwest, to bring soil erosion under control and create a good ecological environment, and that at the same time it was essential to implement agricultural guidelines that would encourage different kinds of enterprises suited to the particular resources of different areas. Hu had already begun to form a concept for dealing with agricultural questions: to make impoverished rural villages wealthy, the main thing was to address specific problems head on and formulate realistic policies; you could not rely on administrative orders or on national plans or quotas, nor could you rely on national investment. It was necessary to mobilize the energies of all the villages and families and let the peasants themselves take over.

In the spring of 1966, Hu was transferred back to Beijing again to take over the work of the Communist Youth League.

The Movement to Learn from Lei Feng and
Study the Works of Mao Zedong

The three years of great famine were a time of crisis for the prestige of Mao Zedong and the CCP and for the impoverished, starving Chinese people. The economic crisis inevitably led to a crisis in confidence that threatened the stability of rule of the party. In the words of Peng Dehuai, "If it hadn't been for the goodness of the Chinese workers and peasants, another Hungarian incident would have broken out long ago."

It was the realistic policies of the Liu Shaoqi and Deng Xiaoping line that brought the economic crisis under control. The spring harvest of 1963 was the turning point in the recovery. And it was the movement to learn from Lei Feng and study the works of Mao Zedong that turned around the crisis of confidence that had been created by the repeated mistakes of the leadership.

Before the victory of the Chinese Communist revolution, Lei Feng was a poor orphan shepherd boy. In 1958 he became a worker in a factory, and in 1960 he joined the army. Lei Feng died suddenly in public service in 1962. His simple feelings of love and hate were directly tied to his experiences. Following the victory of the Chinese Communist revolution, the lives of many young people were much like that of Lei Feng.

At the beginning of 1963, some of the papers and magazines of Beijing and the Northeast ran stories introducing the life of Lei Feng, but these did not attract widespread attention. It was the Central Committee of the Youth League under the leadership of Hu Yaobang that grasped the "model" significance of Lei Feng's death and shaped it into what would become an inspiring and oft-used piece of propaganda. In a double issue of 1963, *China Youth* published all of the facts known about Lei Feng and articles praising his example as well as Mao Zedong's poem, "Learning from Comrade Lei Feng." Liu Shaoqi, Zhou Enlai, and Deng Xiaoping, among others, also wrote poems on this theme. Luo Ruiqing wrote a long essay on learning from Lei Feng. The Central Committee of the Youth League issued an "Announcement on the Educational Activities of Young People Throughout the Nation to Learn from Lei Feng." This was how the very influential and long-lasting movement to learn from Lei Feng began.

On May 1, 1963, Hu Yaobang published in *China Youth* an article on "Raising the Proletarian Consciousness of Young People to a New and Higher Level." In it Hu talked about the significance of learning from Lei Feng, saying:

> The discovery of the facts of Lei Feng's life and the fact that there are many young people growing up like Lei Feng are highly significant. This indicates that the young people of China are indeed moving forward toward the goal of becoming strong proletarian warriors. . . . Looking through Lei Feng's diary we can discover one point that is extremely enlightening, his spirit of self-examination, self-criticism, and self-motivation. Even while we are working to change the objective world, we must also exert ourselves to change our own subjective worlds. Lei Feng was precisely this kind of a person who grew up always changing himself. Young people from working families who study Lei Feng must also develop a self-conscious awareness of changing oneself. Those young people who do not come from manual labor backgrounds must all the more strengthen their self-conscious awareness of changing oneself. We are confident that all young people who come from the exploiting class need only to separate themselves thoroughly from the ideology of that class, genuinely learn from the working people, and truly take their stand with the proletariat, in order likewise to become that kind of good young person. . . . Raising the socialist consciousness of all the Chinese people . . . will inevitably give our national economic construction a new face. We predict that our task of socialist construction will surge forward to victory![16]

At the same time, the movement to study the works of Mao Zedong, which was to give direction to the actions of so many maturing young people, was also beginning to spread throughout China. These movements, from the point of view of the leadership skills and energy involved, were indeed very large and painstaking operations. Like an emergency blood transfusion, they seemed to restore the people's lost confidence in the leadership of the Communist Party. With the success of the line of economic realism pressed by Liu Shaoqi and Deng Xiaoping, they rescued the rule of the CCP from its severe material and morale crises.

But the politically and economically self-regulating social system that had been set up so carefully by Liu Shaoqi, Deng Xiaoping, and Hu Yaobang, and which was bringing stability again to the rule of the Communist Party, was to become an effective means for Mao Zedong to seize control of the power to issue directives, and to stir up an estimated 100 million small Lei Fengs to rise in "revolt" against Liu, Deng, and Hu. The Cultural Revolution would prove that the movements to learn from Lei Feng and study the works of Mao Zedong were a tragedy for the Chinese people that should be condemned.

Deng Xiaoping and Hu Yaobang: Thirty Years of Struggle

The beginning of the relationship between Deng Xiaoping and Hu Yaobang can be traced back to 1937 when Hu was first a student at Resistance University in Yan'an. At the time, Deng was also lecturing at the university, which is the reason it is said that there is a teacher-student relationship between Deng and Hu. At the beginning of 1938, when Hu became assistant director of the Political Office of the university, Zhuo Lin, Deng Xiaoping's wife, was one of the persons Hu was concentrating on as a prospective candidate for party membership. Zhuo naturally had a very good impression of Hu Yaobang. In early 1938, Deng became political commissar of the 129th Division of the Eighth Route Army, and shortly afterward Hu was also sent to do united front work in Suide, so the two were working in different parts of the country from this time. But both belonged to the central rising core of the Mao faction, and the common tie with Resistance University proved to be the beginning of what was to be a long relationship of common understanding.

In March 1949 Hu Yaobang was head of the political department of the 18th Infantry Corps. Before his troops entered Sichuan, Hu delegated someone to write an article for the corps' paper, *Sons of the People*, on a talk by Deng Xiaoping, who was then political commissar of the Central China Military District, on the question of discipline in the ranks. The article gave a serious summary of Deng's ideas.

At the end of 1949, soon after the 18th Infantry Corps entered Sichuan to do battle, it was formally incorporated into the organization structure of the Second Field Army under the leadership of Liu Bocheng and Deng Xiaoping. In early 1950, when Hu Yaobang led the army to restore law and order in northern Sichuan and was made head of the administration with full responsibility for northern Sichuan, he was a great deal of help to Deng Xiaoping, who was responsible for Southwest China. Deng's hometown of Guang'an and Zhu De's hometown of Yilong were both in northern Sichuan. Hu governed northern Sichuan very benevolently and achieved brilliant political results. He was decisive but not without consideration for the people's feelings. This was the beginning of Deng's direct strong appreciation of Hu Yaobang.

In the early 1950s, Deng and Hu were together transferred to Beijing where they became two bright stars in the national government. For his capable handling of the "Gao Gang and Rao Shushi Incident," Deng was promoted to secretary general of the party's Central Committee in 1956. Because of his experience and abilities working with young people, Hu replaced Feng Wenbin as first secretary of the Youth League. In their respective responsibilities for the work of the party and league, Deng represented the party supervision over the league in which Hu Yaobang acted as Deng's right-hand man. From this point on the two worked in close harmony with each other and weathered the storms together.

During the Cultural Revolution, the Qinghua University *Jinggang-shan* Red Guard paper and other Red Guard papers published some of the communications between Deng and Hu from as far back as the mid–1950s.[17] These reflect the relationship of close ties and support, of common views and attitudes between the two. For example, it was reported that in 1956, when Hu was organizing so-called youth production brigades in the countryside, this gave rise to contradictions between the young people and older people in some places. When this came to Mao Zedong's attention, he said, "You must not set up strictly young people's production brigades." But Deng Xiaoping then replied, "The youth production brigades in the countryside have a special and positive role to play in production. They are good." Right up until March 1959 Deng continued to support Hu's project.

Another report said that in the spring of 1957, when *China Youth News* started the special "Hot Pepper" editions, Deng supported this, saying, "The *China Youth News* now has more criticism of faults than it used to have. This is good. . . . If you dare not to criticize, dare not to speak just because the criticism contains some defects, then you'll return to the lifeless silence of the past. That kind of silent frustration is not good."

In July 1958, speaking to Hu Yaobang and the officers of the Central Committee of the Youth League, Deng reportedly declared that "The key issue is that there is only one party. If you hold firm on this item, then though you make ten thousand mistakes, you are basically correct. This principle will always be true, right down to the time of the withering away of the party and the league. The league has not gotten off track. Its mistakes are the party's mistakes."

In October 1961, Deng gave a report to a meeting of provincial and city Youth League committee secretaries in which he totally rejected the 1958 campaign to eliminate bourgeois ideas and thinking. He emphasized strongly "a change in work style" and pointed out that their work method must be to "examine thoroughly," to "make fine, careful adjustments," to "seek truth from facts," to "bit by bit, drop by drop" make "gradual small changes." Fully appreciating this, Hu Yaobang stated, "Ever since the secretary general first made contact with us, he has always brought up this problem." Deng Xiaoping's view of their work methods had a very great impression on Hu's leadership work.

In the same year, with the support of Deng Xiaoping, Hu approved the "Thirty-eight Articles" of guidelines for Youth League work, which were criticized during the Cultural Revolution as opposing class indoctrination among young people.

In 1962, at the first meeting of the Youth League Central Committee, talking about restoring individual farming in the countryside, Deng uttered his famous line, "Who cares whether a cat is white or black, as long as it catches mice." Reflecting back on that time, Hu has said that beginning in 1956, Deng told the Youth League Central Committee that "You have worked hard and have achieved results. Your mistakes haven't been as bad as those of the party. Even when you have made mistakes you have still worked hard." Consequently, Hu has said, "The secretary general has never said one word of criticism about us."

During the Cultural Revolution, Mao Zedong's Red Guards accused Deng and Hu of going to play bridge at the officers' club on Yangfengjia Road in order to organize a "Beethoven Club." They said that the relationship of Hu Yaobang with Yu Qiuli and Liu Lanbo[18] was that of a fanatical "reactionary gang."

From the middle of the 1950s to the outbreak of the Cultural Revolution in the mid-1960s, through the concrete study of society, Hu Yaobang gained an increasingly better understanding of the damaging nature of Mao Zedong's left opportunist line of rash, sudden change. In gradual stages, he separated himself from Mao's erroneous line and self-consciously supported the realistic line of Liu Shaoqi and Deng Xiaoping.

But because of his historical background and work relations with colleagues above and below him, and because of a similarity in personalities, rather than saying that Hu was a member of the Liu-Deng faction, it would be more accurate to say that he was one of the close friends of Deng Xiaoping's "Beethoven Club." Yet Hu never completely separated himself from the enormous attraction of Mao Zedong. Hu's revised attitude toward and relationship with Mao was not one of total rejection. It was the exploding sounds of the Cultural Revolution set off by Mao that prompted the change in Hu Yaobang's thought and understanding.

10
In the Wild Storms
of the Cultural Revolution

As both a great military strategist and a politician, Mao Zedong was used to mounting surprise attacks, but he never had a head for constructive planning. After Liberation, every one of his political movements and surprise political attacks hurt China badly, spreading chain reactions of disaster throughout the impoverished and naïve countryside, like falling dominoes.

The tragic failure of the Three Red Banners movement [of the Great Leap Forward] forced Mao, who could not admit failure, to call out his first line of command power against the realist faction of Liu Shaoqi and Deng Xiaoping. The Liu-Deng realists then attempted to enshrine Mao, to "honor and keep him at a distance," in order to put a stop to his blind idealist rule. To Mao, who had sat upon the high throne of imperial power, who had been master over all, who had "wanted to be higher than natural law," this was like a fish bone caught in the throat that had to be spit out. Day and night he plotted his counterattack.

When Mao unfurled the banner of the Cultural Revolution, the cannons of his surprise attack aimed at the command headquarters of the Liu-Deng line; his immediate goal was to recover his lost power, and his secondary goal was to use the hundreds of millions of Chinese people in a monumental experiment to create in China the ideal kingdom that would last for a thousand years.

On November 10, 1965, in accordance with Mao's guidelines, Yao Wenyuan published in the Shanghai *Wenhui bao* his "Critique of the New Historical Drama *Hai Rui Dismissed from Office*." As this black cloud settled heavily over the city, the Central Committee of the Communist Youth League also sensed nervously that they were about to be inundated by a fierce storm. In February and March 1966, faced with the rapidly increasing pressure of the reverence for Mao Zedong that was being whipped up in the schools and in society at large, the Secretariat of the Youth League Central Committee twice asked Deng Xiaoping to issue a general edition of the *Quotations from Chairman Mao Zedong* [the "little red book"] for young people. Deng resisted, giving the excuse that he was "waiting until after volume five of the *Selected Works of Mao Zedong* comes out before editing a new work."

In March 1966, to deal with the increasingly precarious situation, the Secretariat of the Central Committee of the CCP under Deng Xiaoping urgently ordered Hu Yaobang, who had the ability to take charge, to return to Beijing and personally assume command of the Youth League Central Committee. In Beijing, Hu convened on April 10 the Ninth Plenum of the Second Central Committee of the Communist Youth League at which the work of the Central Committee and the direction it was to move in were adjusted. According to one resolution, "the first secretary of the Youth League Central Committee, Hu Yaobang, gave a talk at the conclusion of the meeting. The meeting passed unanimously the 'Resolution to Further Promote among the Youth of the Entire Nation the Movement to Study the Works of Chairman Mao.' . . . All the work of the Communist Youth League will concentrate on one point, to teach and organize young people to read the works of Chairman Mao, to listen to the words of Chairman Mao, and follow the Chinese Communist Party."[1] After the meeting, the league also began publishing numerous propaganda reports on youth who were enthusiastically studying and putting into practice the works of Chairman Mao.

But the flames of the Cultural Revolution, spreading like a prairie fire, became more and more intense. On June 1, 1966, after the successive attacks on "Hai Rui Dismissed from Office" and "Sanjiacun" (Three-Family Village), Mao also announced his approval of the big-character poster "What are Song Shi, Lu Ping, and Peng Fengyun Really Doing in the Cultural Revolution?" written by Nie Yuanzi and six others from Beijing University. Mao called this "The first Marxist-Leninist big-character poster in China."

In mid-May 1966, under the repeated vicious attacks of Mao Zedong, Liu Shaoqi and Deng Xiaoping hastened to appoint Li Xuefeng as the new first secretary of the city of Beijing, replacing Peng Zhen. At the same time they reorganized the Beijing City Council. On June 15 a meeting of the Secretariat of the Youth League Central Committee chaired by Hu Yaobang also decided to reorganize the Beijing Committee of the Youth League. Several new appointments were made: Li

Ligong, originally secretary of the Shanxi Communist Youth League Committee, was appointed first secretary of the Beijing Committee, replacing Wang Zhaohua (of the "three Hus and one Wang"). Wang Qinghan, formerly secretary of the Jiangsu Provincial Committee, was made second secretary; and Yu Chonghao, previously secretary of the Ji'nan City Committee, became secretary. Wang Jialiu was relieved of her duties as assistant secretary.[2] This reorganization shows that the Central Committee of the Youth League had already suffered its first attack in the storm of the Cultural Revolution. But an even greater battle was about to take place.

The Youth League Central Committee Is Overthrown

On June 3, 1966, Liu Shaoqi and Deng Xiaoping jointly decided to use the traditional method of the Chinese Communists and send a large number of work teams to the universities and middle schools to replace the Party Committee leaders in order to get control of the developing Cultural Revolution. The Youth League Central Committee also sent a proposal to the CCP Central Committee on sending out work teams. After June 3, the Youth League Central Committee assumed responsibility for taking over the Cultural Revolution movement among middle school students throughout the nation, and important members of the Youth League Central Committee acted as leaders of work teams that entered many of the key middle schools to take control of the movement. Hu Yaobang's effective assistant, Hu Qili, took over the leadership responsibilities for the movement in Beijing middle schools.

In mid-June Mao Zedong traveled around the South igniting fires. In response to Mao's exhortations to do battle, Liu Shaoqi and Deng Xiaoping felt that they had to use quick and decisive measures to quell the spreading chaos. It was for this purpose that they ordered the work teams to "oppose disruptions" and seize "false leftists." The Central Committee of the Communist Youth League set about carrying out this order.

In early July, however, the situation suddenly changed. The army troops of Mao Zedong's comrade in arms, Lin Biao, were at that time in control of Beijing. On July 7 Mao himself returned to Beijing, and in the latter part of July he ordered the dissolution of the work teams. From August 1 to 12, supported by military force, Mao convened the Eleventh Plenum of the Eighth Central Committee at which he released his big-character poster, "Bombard the Headquarters." Dubbed as representing the capitalist roaders within the party, Liu Shaoqi and Deng Xiaoping were attacked, and the formation of work teams was rejected as an action of the bourgeois counterrevolutionary line. On August 18, Mao for the first time publicly reviewed the Red Guards at Tiananmen Square, where he called on them to "Fight! Rebel!"

At the same time that this was happening, on August 15, 1966, at a "Full Central Committee Working Members Meeting" of the Youth League, Li Fuchun, a member of the Politburo's Standing Committee, addressed the meeting and criticized the responsible persons of the Youth League Central Committee (headed, of course, by Hu Yaobang) for having made the following serious mistakes:

1. Failure to lift high the banner of Mao Zedong thought, and having turned their backs on Mao's directives.

2. Failure to take a firm proletarian stand, and even still maintaining a bourgeois stand.

3. Giving lip service to the mass line while in reality making sporadic attacks on it.

4. Having been responsible for all the middle school work teams, most of which incited the students to make trouble; having pressured and coerced the students.

At this meeting, Li Fuchun argued that Hu Yaobang, Hu Keshi, Wang Wei, Hu Qili, and others had stopped examining their own actions, and that dismissals could only be decided by the entire Central Committee of the Youth League. At the same time, in accordance with the suggestion of the party's Central Committee, a "temporary secretariat" would be set up composed of the former secretary Lu Jindong (of poor peasant background) and Wang Daoyi (of worker background) to be temporarily responsible for the everyday work.

But the framework of the Central Committee of the Youth League continued to exist, and Hu Yaobang continued to be influential as its leader. The "Youth League Central Committee Revolutionary Rebel Brigade" was not able to control the committee entirely. Guan Feng and others of the Central Committee Cultural Revolution Team incited the Beijing Red Guards to attack the Youth League Central Committee, but they were not able to destroy it.

In December the former alternate secretary of the Youth League Central Committee Secretariat, Li Shuzheng, led a work team into the Number 12 Middle School and got into a fight with the Red Guards in which one of the teachers, Zheng Taonan, was killed. In response,

Guan Feng and Wu De of the Central Committee Cultural Revolution Team held a meeting of over 100,000 Red Guards in one of the gymnasiums in Beijing. Billed as a memorial for Zheng Taonan, "the hero who had sacrificed his life defending the revolutionary line of Chairman Mao," the meeting was the beginning of the punitive expedition against the Central Committee of the Youth League.

After the meeting, some 100,000 Red Guards, under a number of "separate individual" leaders, excitedly pushed right into the meeting of the Youth League Central Committee. Rushing in the front gate, they surrounded all the rooms and warned Hu Yaobang and the others that they had better start listening to "the criticism, struggle, and wisdom of the revolutionary masses." Thus was Hu Yaobang's fourteen-year leadership of the Youth League overturned.

Days of Criticism, Manual Labor, and Forced Retirement

The red wave overwhelmed the Youth League Central Committee. Under enormous pressure, the officers were turned around until even Hu Yaobang's personal secretary changed sides and criticized Hu.

Beginning in January 1967, the rebel faction of the committee "locked Hu Yaobang up in a cowshed for two and a half years." He was dragged out to be paraded on the streets and insulted. At the same time, his wife, Li Zhao, was criticized and indicted by the rebel faction in the Beijing textile offices. His children were all branded as the children of "reactionary elements." Some were locked up and interrogated, some were sent down to the countryside to be reformed through "reeducation among the poor peasants." The family was broken up and separated, a sad and tragic humiliation for all of them.

According to Li Zhao's recollections,

> Overnight I was transformed from a revolutionary cadre into a "counterrevolutionary." Yaobang was separated out for "investigation" and "public exposure." Our eldest son was seized and confined to a "counterrevolutionary compound" where they attempted to force him to confess to anything that would implicate his father. Even my little twelve-year-old daughter was not spared. She was singled out and attacked at school. During those dark and painful days . . . I said over and over to the children, "Your father and mother are innocent. We have done nothing to be ashamed of, either toward the party or toward the people, or toward you. No matter what happens you must not do anything toward the party

or toward our family that you would be ashamed of. Remember that your father and mother care for you.'' . . . Our little daughter had to bear the humiliation every day of bringing food and medicine to her father who was locked up as a "counterrevolutionary." Later, she would ride her bicycle over to the "counterrevolutionary compound" to send clothes to her older brother, inside of which would be a note from their mother telling them that they must always "seek truth from facts."[3]

Regarding the Red Guards and the rebel faction, Hu Yaobang has commented, "I still don't say that locking up people like us for more than ten years during the Cultural Revolution was 100 percent wrong. Maybe it was 98 percent wrong and 2 percent right. That's still pretty wrong!"

By September 1968 the Cultural Revolution was already a fanatical religion. The revolutionary team of the Central Committee was so red it was blazing hot. Mao Zedong had been transformed into a god. There was a revolutionary committee in every province and city of the entire nation.

On October 30 and 31, 1968, taking advantage of the fact that all of China had been dyed red, Mao convened the Twelfth Plenum of the Eighth Central Committee. To legitimize its resolutions, in accordance with the Eighth Congress regulations, more than half of the members of the Central Committee were required to be present. Hu Yaobang, as a member of the Central Committee elected by the Eighth Congress, was of necessity temporarily released from the "cowshed" to participate in this plenum.

In accordance with the wishes of Mao Zedong, the session passed the "Report on the Investigation of the Crimes of the Renegade, Enemy Agent, and Scab, Liu Shaoqi" and resolved that "Liu Shaoqi is to be dismissed from the party for life and stripped of all positions both in and outside the party." When it came time to vote on this, only one female Communist Party member, Chen Shaomin, showed that she "would not bend to force" and refused to go along with the crowd. After the meeting, Kang Sheng asked her why she had not raised her hand, to which she replied, "This is my right!" Seeing the historical meaning of this, Hu Yaobang was greatly moved and said, "This was an extraordinarily great act!"[4]

Following the plenum Mao Zedong issued another directive. "Participation in manual labor is a great reeducation opportunity for all cadres. Except for those who are old or incapacitated or ill, everyone should do this. Even those cadres who are on active duty should in groups go down and join in manual labor.'' In accordance with this directive, the heads of the rebel faction of the Youth League Central Committee sent Hu Yaobang to a "May 7th" cadre school to do manual labor and be reeducated. Angrily, Hu told Zhu Zhongli, the wife of Wang Jiaxiang, "When the heads of the 'rebel faction' of the Youth League Central Committee send you to do manual labor in the countryside, they always make you carry things weighing more than a hundred pounds, which is quite beyond your physical ability. . . . That's really hard! All right, I'll use this as an opportunity to get in shape.''⁵

During his two years of manual labor, Hu would go walking in the villages near the "May 7th" cadre school and was able to see the real conditions under which those at the grass-roots level in the countryside lived. He also became friends with some of the peasants and with young intellectuals who had also been sent down to do manual labor. Under their influence Hu's thoughts and feelings underwent a great change.

In the early spring of 1971, still at the cadre school, Hu fell ill. His request to return to Beijing for treatment was granted. There he remained at home, unemployed for a long time. During this period of "convalescent" forced retirement, he did a great deal of serious thinking and reflecting, and he threw himself into reading. Zhu Zongli has said that "Hu Yaobang's study had several large bookcases filled with all kinds of books, ancient and modern. The books lying on his desk were all marked and underlined in red ink showing that he had read them carefully. One time I saw quite a few ancient works and asked [him], 'You also read the ancient texts?' to which he enthusiastically replied, 'Now that I am standing to the side and without a job, this is a rare opportunity for me to read the old works and learn a little.' ''⁶

On September 13, 1971, the "Lin Biao incident," which shook both China and the rest of the world, took place. The myth of Mao Zedong's greatness now instantly burst, pricked publicly for all the people to see by the hand of Mao's own close comrade in arms, Lin Biao. The Cultural Revolution was headed for a dead-end; the people, the army, and the party were greatly shaken. In late November Mao fell ill. Although he had escaped the crisis, the scars were deep and his health and spirit badly damaged.

On January 10, 1972, Mao attended a memorial service for Chen Yi. He clearly hoped to change his political image, to calm the hearts of the people, the army, and the party. Mao told Chen Yi's children that Deng Xiaoping was a good comrade and a talented person. This was the prelude to his decision to use Deng, and it was also a way to block the power of Zhou Enlai, whose position had risen rapidly following the Lin Biao incident.

Hu Yaobang, too, heard about the changes taking place and made his move. He wrote to Mao and the Central Committee on his position, declaring that he wanted to "continue the revolution"; he also urged Wang Jiaxiang "to write a long position letter . . . to Chairman Mao and Premier Zhou."

On March 2, 1973, Mao personally had Deng Xiaoping recalled to Beijing from his house arrest in Jiangxi. In the same month, in the capacity of a member of the Standing Committee of the Third National People's Congress, Hu Yaobang attended a memorial service for Zeng Zesheng. Mao also organized a "veteran cadres study class." Deng Xiaoping, Wang Jiaxiang, Zhu De, Chen Yun, Li Fuchun, Tan Zhenlin, Nie Rongzhen, Xu Xiangqian, and others were called to participate in this study class because of "the 'Lin Biao incident' and to redress the vacuum and imbalance that had appeared in the organs of government.

On April 23 Deng Xiaoping, escorted by Mao Zedong's niece, Wang Hairong, dramatically appeared with the title of vice-premier at a welcome banquet held for Prince Sihanouk of Cambodia. On May 1, the name of Wang Jiaxiang appeared in the *People's Daily* on a list of leaders of various organs of the Central Committee. Whether or not Hu Yaobang had previously been a renegade, he became extremely active in the "soft struggle" that was now being led once again by Deng Xiaoping and Wang Jiaxiang in Beijing.

The Warrior Returns: Hu and the CAS

In June 1973, not long after Deng Xiaoping was rehabilitated, he replaced Zhou Enlai, who was ill from cancer, in supervising the everyday work of the Central Committee.

In January 1975, after the conclusion of the Fourth National People's Congress, Deng Xiaoping held three concurrent Central Committee posts: vice-chairman, first vice-premier, and commander in chief of the armed forces. In replacing Zhou Enlai in overseeing the real work of the party, Deng had become a new power.

Deng brought the two Hus up with him. In July 1975, Hu Yaobang and Hu Qiaomu became Deng's trusted aides. Hu Yaobang was assigned responsibility for the party organization at the Chinese Academy of Science (CAS), and he was also made vice-president of the academy (the president, Guo Moruo, was resting from an illness). His first task was to restore order and get the academy back on its feet. At the time there were ninety-three departments and organs under the CAS with more than 36,000 researchers and staff. As one of the "nine bastions of conservatism" it was a Cultural Revolution disaster zone.

Hu Yaobang, who had been grinding his sword for ten years in forced retirement, immediately took up his task. He threw himself head first into the job of reorganizing the academy. Upon first taking up his new position, he told people that, being already sixty years old [by Chinese reckoning], he did not have very many years left. In the limited number of days of work still left to him, he would do just as much as he could for the party, for the nation, and for the people. He would "die only when he dropped from exhaustion."

Hu Yaobang's actions were consistent with his words. He worked thirteen or fourteen hours every day. He held a nonstop series of interviews and discussions. Based on his feeling that the single-minded ultraleft line of the Cultural Revolution period had pushed Chinese science and technology to the brink of disaster, he made a number of impassioned statements that were perhaps somewhat excessively sharp and overshot the mark. Among them:

"Red is red, and expert is expert. Why make so much fuss about it!"

"The dictatorship of the proletariat does not apply to science and technology. If you apply the dictatorship of the proletariat to science and technology, then you'll find yourself opposing the intellectuals."

"If the Party Committee secretary doesn't understand some project then he should say, 'Comrade Department Chairman, I don't understand. You come take charge. I'll listen to you.'"

"Too much contact with reality suppresses theory."

"To emphasize close relations with industry and agriculture will stop people from doing theoretical work."

"We shouldn't make generalizations about open-door schooling. A little less of that kind of creativity would be fine."

"If open-door schools mean opening all the doors wide so that anyone can walk in, then the schools would just become tea houses."

Deng Xiaoping's trust in Hu Yaobang was not misplaced, however. In September he took charge of drafting a "Summary Report on the Work of the Chinese Academy of Science." From the style and content of this report it is clear that Hu's mastery of the art of political struggle had already matured. He flexibly used quotations from Mao Zedong and "praised" the Cultural Revolution. But in reality this report overthrew the three aspects of the "dictatorship of the proletariat" that weighed most heavily on the intellectuals: forcing people to study the works of Mao Zedong, the empty discussion of politics, and the black and white class struggle. It further explained the necessity and importance to the modernization of China of training talented scientific specialists and of greatly developing science and technology. On September 26, while listening to Hu talk about this report, Deng Xiaoping praised his effort and insight. At a time when leftism dominated the country and stifled the truth, the "strange words and perverse theories" of Deng Xiaoping and Hu Yaobang played a very influential role in restoring the confidence and courage of intellectuals and of the people in general.

At the same time, Hu raised a number of specialists to positions of leadership in the various departments and organs of the academy. He set up Chen Jingrun, a brilliant mathematician, as the model of a good specialist. This made it possible for the research work and programs of the CAS to get back on the right track.

Hu also involved himself in a good deal of support work. He wrote to Wu De, head of the Greater Beijing municipal government, requesting a solution to the problem of bottled gas tanks for researchers at the CAS. He called for a raise in the salaries of scientific research personnel and set up two nurseries for the children of families in which both parents worked. In the five months that Hu Yaobang was responsible for the administration of the CAS he gained a wide reputation for being an honest administrator who encouraged bright young people in the sciences.

Prelude to Spring

Deng Xiaoping and Hu Yaobang wanted to put a halt to the ultraleft line of the Cultural Revolution. Mao Zedong wanted to maintain the Cultural Revolution line and continue to make revolution. It was only a question of time until the inevitable conflict between the two opposing camps broke out.

In September 1975, when the "Summary Report on the Work of the Chinese Academy of Science" was being put together, the spies of Chi Qun at the CAS (Chi Qun was originally assistant head of the propaganda office of the Zhongnanhai Security Police and one of those trusted and relied upon by Mao Zedong during the Cultural Revolution) secretly sent a copy of meeting records to Chi Qun. Chi Qun then sent these materials to Shanghai for Jiang Qing and Zhang Chunqiao; they were then turned into a white paper (minus any indication of their origin) and disseminated to cadres and to the masses in an attack that accused Deng and Hu of rehabilitating the rightists and bringing them back into power. The March 9, 1977, issue of the *People's Daily* later noted that "Not since Liberation had a local party organization attacked the leading comrades of the Central Committee in this way."

On January 8, 1976, the death of Zhou Enlai set off the conflict between the two sides. Zhou's corpse was hardly cold before a wave of big-character posters appeared at Beijing University and Qinghua University striking back at the movement to rehabilitate the rightists and criticizing Deng Xiaoping.

The February 1976 issue of *Red Flag* also directed its fire against Hu Yaobang. An essay entitled "Strike Back against the Movement in the Science and Technology World to Rehabilitate the Rightists," written by a large organized group at Beijing and Qinghua universities, claimed that "Recently, the strange words and perverse theories in the science and technology world and the strange words and perverse theories of the education world have reinforced each other and they have gotten together to create a movement to rehabilitate and bring the rightists back into power."[8] Such words dripped with hostility toward Hu Yaobang.

Hu's report on the CAS and Deng Xiaoping's "General Outline of the Work Projects of the Whole Party and Nation" and "Some Problems Concerning Speeding Up Industrial Development" were dubbed by the Central Committee revolutionary committee as three antiparty, antisocialist poison arrows aimed at the proletarian headquarters of Mao Zedong. In the movement started by Mao to strike back against the rehabilitation of rightists, Hu Yaobang, Deng Xiaoping, and others were once again struck down as "capitalist roaders who refuse to change their ways."

But the criticism of Deng and Hu now had the effect of, in the words of Hu Yaobang, "reverse propaganda." The more Hu and Deng were attacked the better they looked in the eyes of the people. At the beginning of the Cultural Revolution, among all those who were struck down from the Central Committee, Hu Yaobang had been one of the least noticed of the "big reactionary gang." The criticism of him was limited to youth and those who worked with youth. But in this movement to strike back against the rehabilitation of rightists, the "strange words and perverse theories" made a strong impression on the people, and the name of Hu Yaobang became known throughout the nation.

11
Bombarding
the "Whatever" Clique

On January 21 and 28, 1976, Mao Zedong twice sternly ordered the Politburo of the CCP Central Committee to pass his "not stupid" proposal that Hua Guofeng be appointed premier of the State Council. On February 3, the Central Committee released its (1976) Document Number 1 announcing this "not stupid" decision to the nation.

Making Hua Guofeng premier was indeed not stupid. On February 25, at a conference of top leaders of all the provinces, municipalities, autonomous regions, and large military districts convened by the Central Committee, Hua proclaimed that at present they should criticize Deng Xiaoping. "We can talk about the problems of comrade Deng Xiaoping and criticize him by name." Then, following closely the orders of Mao Zedong, he used bloody measures to suppress the one million people who gathered in a mass demonstration in Tiananmen Square [on April 5] ostensibly to commemorate the death of Zhou Enlai but really to oppose the reactionary rule of Mao Zedong and his "gang of four."

The people, however, made the angry accusations that "China is no longer the China of the past. The people are not incurably stupid. The feudal society of the First Emperor is gone for good." On September 9, 1976, cursed and damned by the people, Mao Zedong went off to join the other emperors of China's hoary past. The poem of Yu Youren, one of the founders of the Nationalist Party [Kuomintang], reads, "From the rivers and mountains successive generations of talented men appear, each in turn bringing misery to the people for a few years." On October 16, barely one month after Mao's death, the "gang of four," whose power had depended on the fearsome banner of Mao Zedong, were toppled by the autumn wind of the Beijing coup and thrown into prison.

But their followers were still at large. In a charade supported by the remnant forces of the Cultural Revolution, Hua Guofeng continued to dance to the old tune of "We must uphold every policy of Chairman Mao, and carry out every directive of Chairman Mao."[1] This "whatever" policy, which was simply a reprint of Lin Biao's fallacy that "every word is the truth," continued to keep China bound up inside the shroud of Mao Zedong. Headed by Hua Guofeng, the "whatever" clique (*fanshi pai*) tried hard to keep Deng Xiaoping from coming back again, but they were destined to fail. In May 1977, in what seemed like a miracle, Deng Xiaoping came back for the third time. And Hu Yaobang too came back to life again.

In August, at the Eleventh Congress of the CCP, Hu was elected a member of the Central Committee. At the beginning of October, he was appointed vice-president of the Central Committee's Higher Party School. Hua Guofeng, who was then chairman of the Central Committee, was also president of this school, and Wang Dongxing, vice-chairman of the Central Committee, was first vice-president. Hu Yaobang was responsible for the day-to-day work of the school. It was from this position that he started arduously to work his way back up to the top once again.

Operating on the Henchman, Kang Sheng

Kang Sheng was vicious and totally amoral. In his whole life he had had two moments of glory: one was the brutal role he played in Mao Zedong's Yan'an rectification campaign, about which Hu Yaobang has angrily commented, "For the past twelve years Kang Sheng has been one of the divisive factors in the party organization. Politically he was not revolutionary. He had no philosophical commitment, and he was totally depraved in both his work and his studies. He undermined the organizational integrity of the party and was one of those criminals most responsible for setting the Chinese revolution back fifteen years. Furthermore, in a real way, the role he played was worse than that of any of the 'gang of four.'"[2]

After Mao Zedong's death, control over the armed forces had already passed to the old veterans like Deng Xiaoping, but others of the pillars of Mao's power, such as the security police forces and the propaganda organizations, remained in the hands of the "whatever" clique. The first, second, and third departments of the Central Special Security Forces, which had formerly been under the control of Kang

Sheng, were now headed by Wang Dongxing and Li Xin (Kang Sheng's secretary). The Central Committee Propaganda Department was in the hands of Zhang Pinghua (a close friend of Hua Guofeng) and Li Xin. The head of the Organization Department of the Central Committee was Guo Yufeng, a confidante of Kang Sheng. After the death of Xie Fuzhi, Hua Guofeng became head of the Department of Public Security. The 6341st Corps (the Zhongnanhai Military Police force) was commanded by Wang Dongxing. Wu De (a follower of Kang Sheng in the Yan'an period and the person then responsible for the rectification campaign in the north Shaanxi school) was the key person in the Beijing City Committee. This shows that Kang Sheng and the "whatever clique" had a firm grasp on the means of power. Hu Yaobang put it very clearly when he said that Hua Guofeng, "for a long time, held control of propaganda and personnel matters, primarily through Wang Dongxing, Wu De, Su Zhenhua, Li Xin, and Guo Yufeng."[3]

After Hu Yaobang took up his position at the Central Party School, he immediately clashed with Hua Guofeng and Wang Dongxing by encouraging the students to criticize the "Tang Xiaowen" (a pun on "Party School writings" [*dang xiao wen*]) writing group, which had been organized by Kang Sheng's follower, Li Guangwen. He pointed out the relationship between Kang Sheng and the "whatever clique," revealing the framework of their control and ambitions.

Next, Hu Yaobang supported the article "Has the Cadre Line that Overturned the 'Gang of Four' Been Corrected?" which was written by Yang Fengchun and others. The first purpose of this article, which was published in the *People's Daily*, was to call for the liberation of all those cadres who had been persecuted by Mao Zedong, Kang Sheng, and others. It also attacked the "whatever" faction's control over the media and the organizational structure of China. After operating on Kang Sheng, Hu pushed forward in an unrelenting attack on the "whatever" kingdom.

Debate over the Standards of Truth

The overthrow of the "whatever" clique was essential to discarding the Mao Zedong style of socialism and reforming China. Otherwise, Hua Guofeng's pet idea of "with you in charge, I can relax" would continue to impose the Mao style of dictatorship upon the people, and the infinite number of sacred directives from Mao that Wang Dongxing had in his hip pocket would continue to hang over the heads of the people like the sword of Damocles.

Deng Xiaoping was the first to point out this serious problem. After the *People's Daily* on February 7, 1977, came out with the duet of Hua Guofeng and Wang Dongxiang on the theory of the "two whatevers," Deng opened fire on them. On May 24, 1977, speaking to Hu Yaobang and others, he said, "These 'two whatevers' are no good. [They] can't explain away the question of my rehabilitation, nor can they explain away the question of the 'sympathy' demonstration of the masses at Tiananmen Square in 1976. You just can't take what Mao Zedong said about one problem and apply it to some other problem, or take what he said at one place and apply it to some other place, or take what he said at one time and apply it to some other time! . . . There's no such thing as one man being absolutely right."[4] If Deng was the great commander who designed the strategy for overthrowing the political line of the "whatever" clique, then it was Hu Yaobang who led the troops into the front lines of the battle.

In February 1978, the *People's Daily* published the article "There Is Only One Standard of Truth." Obviously, this was only a preliminary shot, a first step in formulating the thesis that truth must pass the test of practice. Hu Yaobang then organized the writers on theoretical research at the Party School to revise an essay written by Hu Fuming, a lecturer in the philosophy department of Nanjing University, entitled "Practice Is the Criterion of Truth." When approving the final draft of this essay, it was Hu Yaobang who changed the title to "Practice Is the *Only* Criterion of Truth."

However, the troops of the "whatever" clique still crouched low behind the fortress of their theory. On May 4, 1978, Hua Guofeng rushed off on a visit to North Korea, and just as Hua was being submerged by the welcoming chants of the North Korean people, "Long live Hua Guofeng," Hu Yaobang unsheathed his broadsword. On May 9, 1978, the essay "Practice Is the Only Criterion of Truth" appeared in *Lilun dongtai* (Trends in Theory), a classified (*neibu*) publication of the Central Party School. Two days later, on May 11, 1978, the day that Hua Guofeng returned to Beijing from North Korea, Hu had this essay printed in the *Guangming Daily* under the name of "special editor of the *Guangming Daily*." The next day it was reprinted in the *People's Daily*. Like a tidal wave, this essay generated a great debate throughout all of China on the criterion of truth.

The essay stressed that "Whether or not a theory accurately reflects objective reality, whether or not it is true, can only be determined by the test of social practice." Regarding the limits, the "restricted zone," set up by the "gang of four," it declared that "we must dare to reach out, dare to clarify the difference between true and false. Science knows no boundaries, no restricted zone."

Wang Dongxing saw this essay as

> startling and disturbing. In talking with a few comrades of the Politburo [Hua Guofeng, Ji Dengkui, Wu De, etc.], it was our view that the danger of this essay was that it inferred that the thought of Mao Zedong was "a set of shackles," a "forbidden zone" that was theoretically false, ideologically reactionary, and politically opportunistic. I directed the comrades responsible for managing propaganda, Zhang Pinghua, Li Xin, and others, to suppress such articles in the *People's Daily*, *Guangming Daily*, and *Liberation Army News*. And I organized several people to write opposing essays to be published in inner party publications that would forcefully denounce this essay, saying, "If you say that practice is the only criterion for testing the truth, then is the party's present eleven-item policy true or not? Do we have to wait until after the four modernizations are implemented before we can really prove that these policies are true?[5]

Hua Guofeng also directed *Red Flag* not to take a position on this question, nor to criticize the stand of others.

The realists, led by Deng Xiaoping and Hu Yaobang, and the "whatever" faction, led by Hua Guofeng and Wang Dongxing, all understood that this was not a purely theoretical debate, but rather a contest to see which of the two sides would win out politically. Thus both sides threw all their energies into this decisive battle.

On June 2, at an Armed Forces Political Work Conference, referring pointedly to the attempt of the "whatever" faction to regain the initiative, Deng Xiaoping said, "There are also some of our comrades who talk about Mao Zedong's thought every day, but who always forget, throw out, and even go so far as to oppose Mao Zedong's fundamental viewpoint, his basic method of searching for the real facts, and recognizing that everything starts in practice, that theory must be united with practice. Some of them even believe that those who do search for the facts, who do start with practice, and unite theory with practice, are terrible criminals."[6] On June 24, the *Liberation Army News*, under the name of special editor to the *Liberation Army News*, printed an essay, written by Wu Jiang and revised personally by Luo Ruiqing (who was very powerful in military circles), entitled "A Fundamental Principle of Marxism." This article came down on the side of "practice is the only criterion for testing the truth.'' In July, at a meeting of the State Council to discuss basic guidelines, Li Xiannian stated that this proposition was indeed correct. After this, the main responsible persons of every province, city, autonomous region, and military district throughout China began contributing a succession of articles or speeches supporting the proposition.

Seeing that this position was snowballing and that it was a serious threat to the "whatever" clique, in early September Wang Dongxing created an incident by suppressing the circulation of a supplementary issue of *China Youth*, hoping that he could prevent the situation from developing further. Wang Dongxing "telephoned the Central Committee of the Youth League proscribing the circulation of this issue of the magazine, and giving four reasons: (1) It did not include Chairman Mao's poems. (2) It did not include Chairman Hua's dedicatory poem. (3) It contained poems on the Tiananmen incident. (4) It included an article by Han Zhixiong. *China Youth* rejected every one of these items. Wang then roundly cursed them, saying, '*China Youth* wants to challenge the Central Committee.'"[7]

When Hu Yaobang had returned to power after the Cultural Revolution, all those like Hu Qili who had worked under him during his long period of managing the Chinese Communist Youth League had been restored to their original positions in the league's Central Committee and its organs, including *China Youth*. Clearly, Wang Dongxing's attack on *China Youth* was an attempt to reduce Hu Yaobang's power. But Wang, who did not understand what was going on in the country, had bitten into a piece of hard bone. The veterans then under Hu Yaobang's command stood up and refused to budge. First, they firmly rejected on principle Wang Dongxing's reasons for wanting to suppress the magazine issue. Second, they called on the people to support them. The entire editorial staff of *China Youth* put up in public a big-character poster explaining the background and reasons for the suppression of the magazine, showing that they would refuse to give in even if it meant they would be fired.

News of the *China Youth* incident immediately rocked Beijing and, spreading throughout the entire nation, evoked the widespread support of the people. Hu Yaobang was able to force Hua Guofeng to rescind Wang Dongxiang's order to suppress circulation of *China Youth*, defeating once again the attempt of the "whatever" clique to regain lost territory. The circulation of that issue of *China Youth* exceeded 2.7 million copies.

After the *China Youth* incident, the defeat of the "whatever" clique was certain. By the end of November 1978, the heads of all the provinces, cities, autonomous regions, and military districts of the entire country had expressed their unanimous support for "practice is the only criterion of the test of truth." Hua Guofeng was forced to make a self-criticism and agree to stop saying that "the two whatevers are good."

From December 18 to 22, 1978, the Third Plenum of the Eleventh Central Committee of the CCP was held in Beijing. The public report of the session read, "The conference gave high marks to the discussion concerning practice as the only criterion to test the truth and recognized that this has far-reaching historical significance for liberating the thought and correcting the ideological line for all party comrades and for all the people of the entire nation."[8]

At the Third Plenum Hu Yaobang stood out in the debate as a superior political strategist with the ability and courage to defend the truth, for which he won the widespread praise of those assembled. At this historic conference, which has been called "the second Zunyi Conference" of the Central Committee, Hu was promoted to the Politburo and was elected third secretary of the Central Committee Discipline Inspection Committee. Later he was elected secretary general of the Central Committee and director of the Central Committee Propaganda Department.

Restoring Order and Vindicating the Unjustly Accused

After writing his "Vindicating Those Cadres Who Were Overthrown by the 'Gang of Four'" in support of Yang Fengchun and others of the Central Party School, Hu Yaobang was immediately attacked by the "whatever" clique. According to a report published in the Hong Kong journal *Zhengming*,

> Comrade Guo Yufeng, who was at the time director of the Organization Department of the Central Committee, said, "This article is a really big poisonous weed." He also said, "This is the opinion of a leading comrade of the Central Committee." Of course, comrade Guo Yufeng didn't have that much guts. This then stirred up the other comrades of the Central Committee Organization Department who pasted up a lot of big-character posters which Guo Yufeng then suppressed. Then several of the veterans got hold of the original drafts of these posters and sent them to the

People's Daily, where we put the situation together and sent over our report to the Standing Committee of the Central Committee. It was published on October 7, and Guo Yufeng was dismissed on December 10. This had been a big obstacle. Once the big obstacle at the Organization Department was removed, it became relatively easy to deal with the cases of unfair, false, and wrong treatment. When comrade Hu Yaobang became director of the Organization Department, a whole new atmosphere emerged.[9]

Making Hu Yaobang director of the Organization Department was an important step in the attack on the "whatever" kingdom, and he was the right choice for rectifying the many serious cases of unjust grievances that had accumulated since Liberation. Hu's record of vindicating those who had been unjustly accused goes back to the early 1960s. When he went to Anhui in the name of the Central Committee to investigate the evidence against the "black tyrant" Zeng Xisheng, he "also investigated two cases in which justice had been miscarried," those of Zhang Kaifan and of Li Shinong and Yang Xiaochun, and proposed that the Central Committee should clear them. Zhang, Li, and Yang were all high officials in Anhui province who were upstanding and honest and consequently ruthlessly purged by Zeng Xisheng. Overturning the cases against them had a great deal of influence in the exoneration of unjustly accused persons throughout the country, and it helped promote the work of strongly opposing the "five winds" in the countryside throughout China.[10]

As soon as Hu took office he immediately went into action. Taking up the debate over "practice is the only criterion for testing truth," he also took hold of the task of rectifying the mountain of cases of injustice that had accumulated. The part Hu played in exonerating those who had been unjustly accused will go down in history. His attitude was that "No matter what the circumstances, no matter what organization or what person made the accusations, if it was wrong then it must be corrected."[11] Himself having been hurt by the Cultural Revolution, having been repeatedly accused, Hu Yaobang, in carrying out his duties as director of the Organization Department, had a sense of historical responsibility, of sympathizing with the anxieties and viewpoints of others, of extending justice to the people. Under his leadership and supervision, the personnel of the Central Committee Organization Department ignored the pressure and interference of Hua Guofeng and Li Xin and went out to examine the complaints and find the documents that overturned a large number unjust cases, even though they were in turn accused by the "whatever clique" of creating an atmosphere of "the miscarriage of justice."

On November 9, 1978, talking to the trainees on the question of Kang Sheng, Hu Yaobang said,

> In the last year we have reexamined a number of accumulated cases and cleared up a number of phoney problems. We have set free a large number of comrades and exonerated and restored the good names of cadres and and people both within and outside the party who had been wrongly accused. Although we cannot bring comrades who have died back to life, we should clear their names, give them proper funerals, hold memorial services for them, and deal with the effects of their cases, so that that they may lie in peace, as the Chinese proverb says, "shining like the white snow." . . . Some of those with high positions in the party and government have been dealt with quickly, but there are also more than ten million cadres and ordinary people who need to be vindicated and rehabilitated. The corpses of some have long since turned to dust, but they have not yet been cleared of their alleged crimes as spies or special agents. Their families still bear this burden. Even if the Central Committee Organization Department was much larger, it still would not be able to clear each of these cases one by one. It is for this reason that I hope that all units and organizations from the province down to the grass roots will actively take up this task of reexamining such cases so that the problems of these people may be more quickly cleared up. Those who can be released should be freed right away so that they aren't kept hanging in limbo."[12]

There were, however, some special cases in the first, second, and third offices that were under the control of Wang Dongxing and Li Xin and were beyond the power of the Organization Department to do anything about. This continued to be true right down to the convening of the Third Plenum of the Eleventh Central Committee. It was not until Hu Yaobang became secretary-general of the Central Committee that the work could be extended to all branches of the government, including the first, second, and third offices of the Central Committee.

Around the time of the Third Plenum, the Tiananmen incident finally became publicly recognized as a revolutionary action. The cases against Peng Dehuai, Tao Zhu, Bo Yibo, and Yang Shangkun were overturned, and those who were already dead were publicly exonerated and the reputations of those who were still alive were cleared. On December 15, the *People's Daily* printed an article signed by the editor entitled "Search for the Facts, Wrongs Must Be Righted," which elaborated on Hu Yaobang's thesis that "If it is wrong it must be corrected.'' On January 2, 1979, the *People's Daily* article entitled ''The Requisite Qualities and Character of a Chinese Communist'' said that the rightists should be rehabilitated so that the spring winds could bring an end to the ice age that had existed since 1957.

The ''class struggle'' of the dictatorship of the ultraleft that Mao Zedong had pushed for so long had left many deep scars. After the Third Plenum, the task of rehabilitating those who had been wronged was pursued throughout the nation. Petitions, big-character posters, grievances, demonstrations, sit-ins, and cries for democracy created a mounting tidal wave. In the ensuing tumult, from the central government down to the local levels, some of the ''orthodox factions,'' ''whatever cliques,'' and ''local emperors'' thought this was pure anarchy. Consequently, each group devised its own schemes to resist the work of exonerating the wrongly accused within their own spheres of influence. The combination of this overwhelming social movement and the trouble stirred up by ''local emperors'' attempting to resist it, combined with the complex problems of making economic readjustments, began to create doubts even in the mind of the reformer Deng Xiaoping. Deng became ambivalent about continuing the work of rehabilitating those who had been wronged and was worried about pressing forward so rapidly.

To clear away such obstacles, Hu Yaobang appointed more than a thousand cadres from the various departments of the Central Committee, the Central Committee Military Affairs Commission, the State Council, the Standing Committee of the National People's Congress, and the Central Committee of the Communist Youth League to spread out across the nation to handle the cases of unjust accusations. On September 6, 1979, accompanied by Hu Yaobang, Deng Xiaoping addressed more than a thousand cadres, saying,

> Comrade Hu Yaobang has scolded me, saying that ''writing a bad check is worse than not repaying a loan.'' I accept this. Since coming back from Japan, I have visited several universities and seen the big-character posters, and said a few words. The result is that everybody is putting up big-character posters. Everyone with a grievance of any kind is expressing it, making accusations. This has happened very suddenly. A number of them have not thought things out fully and are confused. Some are holding demonstrations. Others are making trouble, saying that this is an omen that the world is becoming even more chaotic. Such claims are premature, aren't they? . . . Generally speaking, the situation is already very different today than it was two years ago. For me, and for you too, we must go out confidently to complete this task.[13]

In the process of righting the world's most grievous wrongs, Hu Yaobang began getting rid of the extremists, diehards and opportunists, and camp followers of the "gang of four" who were taking advantage of the unrest. As soon as he took office, Hu immediately dismissed the first secretary of the Heilongjiang Provincial Committee, Liu Guang-tao, who was a diehard follower of Mao Yuanxin (nephew of Mao Zedong). Then he dismissed a number of the followers of the "gang of four" in the Northeast, Tianjin, Shanghai, and Beijing. Hu's move-ment to clean house was carried out in a rational and restrained way. It was for this that he was called the rationally controlled nuclear-powered bulldozer clearing out all the "trash" of the previous dynasty, and opening up the road for the new era ahead.[14]

However, as the situation developed, it was inevitable that these tasks would run into the bureaucratic machinations of the "whatever" clique and the "local emperors" and their multitude of interwoven relationships with the "gang of four." Just as in the case of Mao Zedong and the "gang of four," the image that the people had of the political role played by the "whatever clique" was exactly the opposite of the real situation. Thus in the early stage of this decisive battle to clean house and start anew, it was inevitable that Hu would run up against the hostility and attacks from these corrupt and degenerate forces.

After the Third Plenum, on

March 29, 1979, a printed leaflet appeared in Beijing that was pasted up at Shatan and at the Democracy Wall and signed, "The Society for the Study of Marxism, Leninism, and Mao Zedong Thought." This leaflet read, "It is essential that the revisionism of Hu Yaobang and Hu Qiaomu be criti-cized. It is because of the revisionist philosophy of Hu Qiaomu and Hu Yaobang that the Great Cultural Revolution has been criticized. They have now risen to high positions and are deeply engaged in revisionism, opposing Chairman Mao, opposing the line of the Eleventh Party Con-gress, opposing the party regulations, opposing the constitution. . . . There is even one province that in March suddenly convened a 'Party training session' chaired by the director of the Propaganda Department, at which it was asked, 'Where is China going? Where does Deng Xiaoping want to take China? What is Hu Yaobang up to? Their policy is the opposite of that of Chairman Mao. Hu Yaobang is a revisionist of the old school.'" One secretary of the Youth League says that "Everything's in chaos now. Let's go liberate thought! With Deng Xiaoping's support, Hu Yaobang has opposed Chairman Mao and he can't deny it." . . . In the early morning of May 1, at an important city in one province (a city under provincial control), 1,400 reactionary big-character posters suddenly appeared in twenty-three places reading, ''Down with Deng Xiaoping. Give us back our Mao Zedong,'' and ''Down with Deng Xiaoping and Hu Yaobang. Give us back Mao Zedong Thought.''[15]

From the central government to the countryside, the forces of the ''whatever clique'' did indeed look upon Deng Xiaoping and Hu Yaobang as their greatest enemies.

''A thousand sails pass by the sinking ship, the sick tree has ten thousand springs ahead.'' These declarations were the swan songs, the elegies to a past dynasty. The people called Hu Yaobang the hero who destroyed the modern superstition.

> *Liberated with the people,*
> *Sharing the nation's suffering,*
> *Restoring order to the world,*
> *Knowing the people's hearts,*
> *Court of justice,*
> *Righting the wrong.*

> *To be forever known in the history of youth,*
> *From "Organization" to "Propaganda,"*
> *To "Publishing," to "Examiner," surrounded by spring.*
> *Only wish you had made the decision earlier.*[16]

Hu Yaobang did not turn his back on the hopes of the people. When the Fifth Plenum of the Eleventh Central Committee struck down the ''gang of four,'' Wang Dongxing, Ji Dengkui, Wu De, and Chen Xilian also fell from power.

In July 1980, Mao Zedong's portrait was removed from the Great Hall of the People. On July 12, at the memorial service for An Ziwen, Hu Yaobang said for the first time publicly that ''Lin Biao, Jiang Qing, and Kang Sheng'' were wild animals, thus stripping off Kang Sheng's mask and revealing him as the vicious gangster he really was.

In September, at the third session of the Standing Committee of the Fifth National People's Congress, the policies of Hua Guofeng were criticized, and the successful economic reformer, Zhao Ziyang, was made premier. Hua Guofeng was isolated.

On December 12, the trial of ''Lin Biao and the Gang of Four'' began. At the same time, at a meeting of the Central Committee Politburo, Hu Yaobang read a long criticism of the political errors Hua Guofeng had committed over the years. He also said, ''Many comrades within the party do not agree that Hua Guofeng should continue to hold the positions of chairman of the party and head of the Central Committee Military Affairs Commission. Thus, Hua Guofeng has asked to resign from these two positions."[17]

On December 14, Hu announced the thorough denunciation of the Cultural Revolution. At this point, the final demise of the "whatever clique" was simply a matter of time.

From June 27 to 29, 1981, the Sixth Plenum of the Eleventh Central Committee met in Beijing. Speaking to the second meeting of the session, Li Xiannian announced the following proposals:

1. To accept the resignation of Hua Guofeng from the positions of chairman of the Central Committee and head of the Military Affairs Commission.

2. To elect Hu Yaobang chairman of the Central Committee.

3. To elect Deng Xiaoping director of the Military Affairs Commission.

4. To elect Zhao Ziyang vice-chairman of the Central Committee.

5. To confirm Hu Yaobang, Ye Jianying, Deng Xiaoping, Zhao Ziyang, Li Xiannian, Chen Yun, and Hua Guofeng as chairman and vice-chairmen of the Standing Committee of the Politburo of the Central Committee.[18]

In the afternoon of June 29, Hu Yaobang delivered his acceptance speech to the entire conference. His speech centered on three main points, the outlines of which were:

> The first point is the question of who has made the greater contributions in the past few years.
>
> After the "gang of four" was shattered, each of the members of the Politburo and Standing Committee made their own individual contributions, but the older veterans of the revolution made somewhat more and greater contributions.
>
> The second point is that two things have not changed.
>
> I have been raised to this high position in the party under very special historical conditions. Originally, in accordance with the wishes of the majority of the party as a whole, it was Comrade Deng Xiaoping who should take this title. . . .
>
> That it has now been decided to do it this way does of course constitute a big change. However, I feel that it is my duty to explain to the entire conference that two things have not changed: first, the role of the older revolutionaries has not changed; second, my level of ability has not changed.
>
> The third point is where should we focus our energies.

In the past several years, we have spent a great deal of energy clearing up the mountain of problems that have accumulated over the years. We have also spent a lot of energy putting together the historical resolutions passed by this conference. . . .

Clearing up the accumulated problems, from the point of view of leadership, is now completed. I would ask the comrades to note specially this statement in our "Public Announcement": "This conference has completed the historical task of correcting the confusion and corruption in the party's ideological leadership." . . . In what direction, then, should we now turn our leadership energies? Our energies should focus mainly on examining the problems of improving the national economy. At the same time we should think about how effectively to create a socialist spiritual civilization.

I have taken a total of eighteen minutes sketching the outlines of these three positions. I'm finished. (enthusiastic applause)

Finally, in his concluding speech to the conference, Deng Xiaoping pointed out, "This brief talk that Hu Yaobang just presented proves, I believe, that our choice of Hu Yaobang for chairman of the party is indeed the right choice (enthusiastic applause)."[19]

12
Historic Steps
in the New Long March

The Fifth Plenum of the Eleventh Central Committee in February 1980 decided to reestablish the Secretariat of the Central Committee. In addition to his position on the Standing Committee of the Politburo, Hu Yaobang became secretary-general of the Central Committee.

When he first took over the management of the Secretariat, Hu, with the realists of the reform group, Zhao Ziyang and Wan Li, set off three successive bombs. The first bomb removed from the Beijing city construction plan the Eastern Chemical Engineering Project of Lin Hujia, then first secretary of the Beijing City Commission, and Hu Jiaman. The second bomb set out a plan for the development of education. The third bomb eliminated the Mao Zedong era ultraleft rule of Tibet. Of these three, it was the Central Committee Tibet Investigation Team that proved to be the most significant.

On May 23, 1951, representatives of the Central Committee and of the local Tibet government had signed a "Seventeen Article Agreement" on the peaceful liberation of Tibet. On October 26 of the same year, Mao Zedong had sent the People's Liberation Army into Lhasa. On December 20, Tibet had been declared peacefully liberated.

Although Mao had not set foot in Tibet since passing through its borders in the Long March, under the rule of his "Great Leap Forward" policy the feudal serfdom of the roof of the world was instantly transformed into socialism. Mao's policy shattered Stalin's theory of the stages of social development, and Tibet was described as a paradise in which a million serfs sang and danced with joy. The facts, however, were quite different. In March 1959, a tight-knit organization led by the Dalai Lhama, the religious leader of Tibet, started an armed uprising. During the Cultural Revolution period, Ren Rong, first secretary of the Tibet Autonomous Region Committee, pushed the ultraleft "twin policies" of class struggle and emphasis on grain production to the point that the people of Tibet were left without *zanba* [barley flour blended with tea and butter], butter, beef, or mutton, their staple foods.

On April 7, 1980, the "Tibet Work Seminar Summary," drafted by the Central Committee Secretariat under Hu Yaobang's direction, was approved by the Central Committee. On May 22, the Central Committee Investigation Team led by Hu and Wan Li boarded a plane for Lhasa.

> In spite of severe altitude sickness, Hu Yaobang and Wan Li together analyzed what they were learning. By the fifth day, his reaction to the high altitude lessened somewhat and he read documents, examined the map, and listened to reports. Later he went to the local Party Committee conference hall, where he addressed several hundred cadres for 170 minutes, proposing six ways to improve the economy of Tibet. On May 30, the day before leaving Lhasa, he paid a visit to the Naji hydroelectric station some five miles outside Lhasa. There he said to the cadres and workers that every party member and every official must constantly think about how to do good things for the people.[1]

From his trip to Lhasa, Hu realized that the greatest problem was poverty, and that the standard of living was much lower in Tibet than in any other part of China, worse than any other of the autonomous regions. At the same time, he had "seen very clearly that the scars that a long history of feudal serfdom had left on society were very deep and could not be erased overnight. Many things that are the products of history will take time. One cannot hope to change them in just a day or two."[2]

Thus the Tibet Investigation Team on the one hand admitted to the Tibetan people that "the ultraleft party line has severely damaged the party's policy toward the Chinese minorities, its economic policy, its policies toward religion, toward the united front, and toward cadres. The Tibetan people have suffered as have all the other peoples of China."[3] At the same time, two measures were adopted to cure the situation and expand Tibetan autonomy. One was to replace Ren Rong with Yin Fatang, a realist who understood both the Tibetan language and its customs, and to attempt to bring more Tibetans into the government positions. The second measure was to improve the economy by fully encouraging self-government in the minority regions, by encouraging them to recuperate and build up their strength, to formulate economic policies based on regional differences, and to develop educational policies that would strengthen Tibetan culture and education. In addition, it was announced that the State Council would exempt Tibet from taxes on agriculture and livestock for two years, raise the quota for state purchases of Tibetan barley, eliminate all forms of apportionment plans, and cancel commercial taxes on collective enterprises and various other businesses. The implementation of these measures achieved big results the very next year when, "on the Tibetan new year, the streets of Lhasa were filled with people of all nationalities, dancing and singing, a moving sight that had not been seen for twenty years. They said, this year there is lots of beef and lamb, lots of butter, lots to eat. The Central Committee has given Tibet new hope, a new spring."[4]

When Hu Yaobang met with the Dalai Lama's older brother, Jiale Dunzhu, in 1981, he suggested the five articles for reconciliation and a forward-looking plan welcoming the Dalai Lama to return and offering him a position corresponding to assistant deputy chairman of the National People's Congress, to work at tasks useful to the unification of the country.

All this was welcome news to the Dalai Lama, who was still drifting around abroad. Consequently, in September 1982, upon Hu Yaobang's reelection as secretary-general of the Central Committee, he sent a telegram of congratulations, saying, "When Hu Yaobang in 1980 visited Lhasa, I trusted him fully, because he had the courage to admit that the Lhasa problem had been managed badly. This is a commendable attitude." He also said, "I still believe in Hu Yaobang, and hope one day to be able to meet him."[5]

The reform policy proposed for Tibet was a model for reconciliation, friendship, and cooperation between the CCP and the minority nationalities throughout the nation and the beginning of a dialogue with China's minority peoples.

Models of Agricultural Reform

The resolution of the Third Plenum of the Eleventh Central Committee to implement agricultural reforms on a nationwide basis called on peasants to divide the land and institute the contract responsibility system at the individual family level (*baochan daohu*). The red flag of the people's communes faded.

In September 1980, the Central Committee Secretariat convened a national agricultural work conference to formulate and pass Central Committee 1980 Document No. 75 on further strengthening and improving the agricultural responsibility system. On September 27, Document No. 75 was distributed throughout the nation, bringing a sense of stability to Chinese peasants. But there were some places that resisted this policy, especially in Hebei. There, ever since 1958, Liu Zihou had continued to carry out an ultraleftist line. Under his autocratic rule, Hebei was well-known as a political and economic disaster area. The Taihang Mountain area of the province was a base of the old revolutionaries, and beginning with the establishment of the people's communes its peasants had had a consistently hard life of "half a year of chaff and half a year of grain."

It was for this reason that

> It was very difficult to implement fully some of the important policy guidelines, and with the gradual development of the first series of problems with the realistic policy of restoring order and correcting past mistakes, there were more people coming from Hebei to the capital to ask for help than from anywhere else in the country. After several unsuccessful attempts to straighten things out, the Central Committee finally sent a couple of loyal comrades (i.e., Jin Ming and Jiang Yizhen) who had long experience and no connections with the two Hebei factions to assume the main party and government positions of leadership. Unfortunately, these old comrades soon became overwhelmed and immobilized by the complex situation in Hebei.[6]

In the eyes of the capital, realizing the agricultural responsibility system at the family level seemed unattainable.

Meanwhile, in Hebei there was an outcry by those who still held onto the "whatever" theory against the dismissal of Hua Guofeng, and a movement to attack the reform faction of Hu Yaobang. Addressing this problem, in December 1980, at an enlarged meeting of the Politburo, Hu presented a tightly reasoned, factual report criticizing Hua Guofeng. This report was distributed in the form of a Central Committee document to county organizations throughout the country to counter the influence of this movement.

At the same time, meetings of the Central Committee Secretariat specifically discussed the problem of Hebei and decided in June 1982 to send to the province a nine-man work team headed by the strong Communist Party reformer Gao Yang, to turn the situation around. Between Gao and Hu Yaobang there was a strong bond of mutual understanding. As early as 1979, when Hu had become director of the Organization Department of the Central Committee, he had sent Gao "to Jilin province as secretary of the provincial committee, even though he still had not been cleared of the label of being a 'three-anti element.' Hu Yaobang said, 'Who cares! We'll worry about that later!' "[7]

After Gao Yang took up his position in Hebei, because Hebei was so severely factionalized and the leftist atmosphere was so vicious, he adopted measures to diagnose, isolate, and cure the disease. With the approval of the Central Committee Secretariat, Gao's prescription was to put into effect the actions specified by Document No. 75, and then later to decide what or who was right or wrong. This "directive to test their honesty by their actions" effectively turned the situation completely around. Hebei was immediately engulfed in an enthusiastic movement to divide the fields among individual peasant families, contracting for production at the family level and dividing all assets among individual families. Public property was also divided wherever possible, and where not possible the people bid on contracts. The peasants called this the "second land reform."

After six months, Gao Yang and his nine-man work team had diagnosed the disease of the cadre brigades and proposed to the Central Committee Secretariat a large, corrective "surgical operation."

"On the afternoon of March 18, 1983, the Secretariat of the Central Committee smoothly approved in just five minutes the decision on dealing with the leadership of the Hebei Provincial Committee. Secretary-general Hu Yaobang quietly described this event in four words, '*feng ping lang jing*' [the winds are calmed, the waves stilled]."[8] The new Secretariat of the Hebei Provincial Committee was composed of Gao Yang as first secretary and Zhang Shuguang, Xing Chongzhi, Gao Zhanxiang, and Xie Feng as secretaries. Except for Gao Yang, all had belonged to the Communist Youth League organization back when Hu Yaobang was first secretary of the Youth League Central Committee.

Gao Yang and the new provincial committee leadership group, in addition to retiring or dismissing the worst and most obvious of those cadres who had been Liu Zihou's main supporters at the provincial, county, and local levels and those who had profited by stirring up factionalism in the name of the "Cultural Revolution," also took on cases that were not so clear and had them sent to other provinces, thus rooting out thoroughly Liu Zihou's power base and divisive factionalism. The Central Committee Secretariat then filled the many positions thus left vacant with young and middle-aged trained cadres brought in from other provinces and with cadres from all levels in Hebei who had demonstrated ability by being active in the reforms. To implement a policy that is truly in tune with the feelings of the people it is essential to have a good system of feedback. The establishment of a new leadership system in Hebei made it possible for the agricultural reforms to take off.

In the spring of 1983, addressing the fact that the peasants were afraid that future changes might threaten their present land use rights and therefore would not think in terms of improving the soil or setting up long-term businesses, Daming county in Hebei began issuing "contract land use certificates," contracting the land to peasants for periods of up to twenty years. This policy was then implemented in the whole province, with unused mountain lands being contracted to the peasants for even longer periods of time. Based on the experience in Hebei, the Central Committee Secretariat then extended this policy to the whole nation through 1984 Document No. 1.

In the Baoding area, which had been hit hard by the Cultural Revolution, the changes were even greater. In 1984, the average per capita income in the countryside of the twenty-two counties in the Baoding area rose by more than 100 yuan. On January 4 and 5, 1985, the Secretariat held a special conference in the Zhongnanhai Conference Hall [in Beijing] which included the local Baoding committee and responsible persons from the twenty-two county committees. At the meeting Hu Yaobang enthusiastically said,

> The fact that the average income of the peasants in the Baoding area increased by 100 yuan is highly significant. Our domestic market is mainly in the countryside. If all 800 million peasants raise their income 100 yuan per year, that makes a total of 80 billion yuan, which is equal to one-fourth the value of China's total agricultural output. Even half that would be 40 billion yuan. This would be an enormous market! It would provide a powerful force for our four modernizations. It is precisely for this reason that we continue to watch closely the question of doubling agricultural production. The basic confidence in doubling China's output lies in the countryside. . . . [I] approve of the report in the papers by the counties of Baoding district pointing out their plans to get a firm grip on the development of local county and township enterprises and to continue to readjust the structure of agriculture and develop different kinds of business.[9]

After the meeting, local industry in the Baoding area took even greater strides forward. By the end of 1984, the total number of family-run factories in the area had reached more than 100,000, and nearly forty interprovincial specialized markets had been formed. In June of the same year, in the great Hebei tide of agricultural reform, the rapidly emerging 10,000-yuan peasant households [i.e., with 10,000 yuan or more yearly income] sent sixty-five persons (mostly specialized households) to Japan at their own expense. For a Chinese peasant to pay his own way for a trip abroad was previously unheard of in Chinese history. This indicates that the Chinese peasantry has already taken a great stride forward, leaping from antiquity into the modern world.

In 1980 Hu Yaobang had said, "Beijing is within the borders of Hebei. Hebei, under the eyes of the Central Committee, should become a model area." When the Twelfth Congress of the CCP met in September 1985, Gao Yang gave up his position to Xing Chongzhi. In February 1986, Zhang Shuguang was appointed secretary of the Party Committee for the Autonomous Region of Inner Mongolia, and Gao Zhanxiang was appointed assistant director of the Ministry of Culture. Jie Feng was promoted to governor of Hebei province. In just these few short years the agricultural reforms in Hebei had successfully fulfilled Hu Yaobang's plan to make this a model province.

In Hu's philosophy of agricultural reform there is one point of difference with the philosophy of large-scale mechanized agriculture stressed by Marx, Engels, Lenin, and Stalin, which is that Hu Yaobang stresses the role of agriculture in protecting the environment. As early as the mid–1950s, he had already begun stressing this point very strongly and had mobilized young people and Youth League members throughout the nation to plant trees and create forests. After becoming secretary-general of the Central Committee, every time he went out on an inspection tour, wherever he saw barren hills, bald ridges, and soil erosion, he would always repeat his "grass and trees story," telling people to contract the hills to families, use different forms of the responsibility system, and use every effort to plant grass and trees. Hu also considered environmental protection in the Taihang Mountain district of Hebei to be very important. He had climbed Taihang Mountain three times, and he told the Hebei cadres, "In the past in the mountain areas we only paid attention to investment in engineering or construction projects. We paid no attention to biological investment, with the result that the biological environment was destroyed. . . . We must as soon as possible turn Taihang Mountain, this 'yellow dragon,' into a 'green dragon.'"[10]

The creative spirit that Hu Yaobang demonstrated in his leadership of agricultural reforms in Hebei is a typical reflection of his philosophy of agricultural reform.

Putting a Halt to the "Spiritual Pollution" Campaign

In October 1983, yet another Cultural Revolution-style storm swept China, the campaign to eliminate "spiritual pollution." The vanguard of this "decontamination" movement was made up of Deng Liqun, Hu Qiaomu, Wang Zhen, Bo Yibo, and others, under the command of Deng Xiaoping.

As early as June 4, 1983, Deng Liqun, who was then director of the Central Committee's Propaganda Department, in a lecture at the Central Party School said, "On the ideological front and on the artistic front . . . there are still many problems, some of which are still quite serious. There is a small minority of people, including a few individual party members, who, under the flag of 'the complete liberation of thought,' have written erroneous essays and put out incorrect propaganda on the topics of 'Marxist humanism' and 'socialist alienation,' which have already had a very bad influence. They have had a very great negative influence on some young students in particular. All of us involved in propaganda work have the responsibility to adopt a Marxist-Leninist attitude, analyze seriously all kinds of intellectual movements, and work hard to eliminate *spiritual pollution*."[11] Deng Liqun and others proclaimed that, "Except for the five-starred red flag, nothing in Shenzhen is socialist. It's practically like Hong Kong." The ghost of Mao Zedong still had a hold on some of the cadres of the Communist Party.

On October 12, 1983, at the Second Plenum of the Twelfth Central Committee, Deng Xiaoping gave his speech calling for the elimination of "spiritual pollution." In this speech, Deng elaborated on the ideas of Deng Liqun, emphasizing, "Don't think that a little spiritual pollution doesn't mean anything, isn't worth getting alarmed and worried about. For some things, you can't see right away how terribly harmful they are, but if we don't take notice of them right away and adopt stern measures to control them . . . they can influence even more people to take the wrong road with results that may be extremely serious. Taking a long-term view, this problem is related to the question of what kind of people take over our tasks in the years ahead, and to the fate and future of the party and the nation."[12] At this conference, Chen Yun also gave a speech in the same vein and sponsored a resolution on party rectification and eliminating spiritual pollution that was passed by the whole conference.

On October 24, the Central Committee formally sent to all county Youth League and party organizations its Document No. 36 on eliminating spiritual pollution. This document said that they must "seriously investigate the actual situation concerning problems in ideology and spiritual pollution in all organizations and units. . . . All kinds of pornographic video recordings, pornographic books, pamphlets, pictures, pieces of folk art, and hand copied manuscripts . . . must be decisively, quickly, and thoroughly cleaned up." In the process of eliminating pornography, "important violators can be dealt with by the courts in accordance with articles 160 and 170 of the legal code, and if they are guilty of other crimes their punishments can be increased."[13]

Pushed forward by the accomplices of the ghost of Mao Zedong, the spiritual pollution campaign caused a second "Cultural Revolution" to appear, which in many places led to the forced cutting of long hair, banning of skirts, confiscation of tape recordings and books, and excessive criticism struggles and incidents of violence. But the Chinese people, intellectuals, and resolute party reformers were no longer as naïve as they had been during the early days of the Cultural Revolution. Throughout the country there was resistance and opposition to the spiritual pollution campaign. In this movement to eliminate "spiritual pollution," Hu Yaobang stood among the leaders who mounted the counterattack.

On October 25, in a discussion meeting on the spiritual pollution problem with people from outside the party, Hu Yaobang quietly "listened to their views and proposals." The next day, in his talk concluding this meeting, he obliquely questioned the theory of "pollution" held by those like Deng Liqun, saying, "The fact that in general in the past seven years we have done things fairly smoothly and properly is the main reason this has been one of the best periods since Liberation. . . . With a correct line and direction and policy, a correct method and procedure and order, our work has great promise."[14]

On November 17, after the Secretariat had received information from all over China on incidents of red terror, like those of the campaign against the four old things, and reports of the interruption of foreign trade, investment, and joint venture negotiations because of foreigners' worries about political instability in China, Hu Yaobang lost no time selecting a strategic opening for a counterattack opposing the spread of the "spiritual pollution" campaign. Breaking through the obstacles set up by Deng Liqun's control over propaganda, Hu published an article in *China Youth News* by a well-known editorialist entitled, "Pollution Must Be Eliminated, Life Must Be Beautified." This article criticized the mistaken notion that the beautification and fulfillment of life (including hair styling, colorful clothes, make-up, and healthy dancing) were to be identified with spiritual pollution. The article was in turn reprinted in the *Workers' Daily* and other papers, letting the country know Hu's political stand. This greatly strengthened the courage of those who opposed the spiritual pollution campaign. At the same time, Deng Liqun, who thought he wielded an invincible sword, was surrounded in a meeting of the Central Committee Secretariat.

On November 23, during a trip to Japan, in answering the questions of Chinese students studying abroad and of the Japanese, Hu Yaobang again unequivocally opposed any expansion of the spiritual pollution campaign, and through the international news media he broadcast this message loud and clear to the whole world. Upon returning to China, he joined Zhao Ziyang and Wan Li to report to Deng Xiaoping that the spread of the campaign to eliminate cultural pollution had already created a serious crisis that threatened the reforms, was affecting the confidence of the people and of the party, and was severely undermining China's international reputation. Faced with this unanticipated serious error in political judgment, Deng was forced to order a suspension of the campaign for more than a month. Later this was explained as a farce resulting from having listened to "false information."

The reform faction took advantage of this victory to push ahead. On January 1, 1984, Central Committee 1984 Document No. 1 approved extending the time limit for peasant land contracts and further relaxed controls on the circulation of rural commercial products. On April 30, a conference of the Politburo chaired by Hu Yaobang and Zhao Ziyang approved the summary of a forum of selected coastal cities that had been held under the auspices of Hu and Zhao and announced the further opening of fourteen coastal cities, including Dalian, Shanghai, and Guangzhou, and of Hainan Island, and the implementation of certain policies making them special economic zones. On January 1, 1985, the Secretariat approved Central Committee 1985 Document No. 1, which announced ten policy decisions granting more freedom to peasants in crop selection, commerce, transportation, mining, and industry. In his strong opposition to the spiritual pollution campaign and in pushing the reforms steadily forward, Hu Yaobang demonstrated his ability to stem an adverse tide.

Operating on the Cancer in the CCP Succession System

Looking back over the history of the Chinese Communist Party, although the Communists entered the imperial palace with "modern" strides, the question of the succession of power has remained a cancer in the one-party autocratic system. Not one of the old party leaders would voluntarily step down from the stage of history, and not one new leader mounted the stage except by a "coup d'etat." It was very much the problem of succession that had caused China to be soaked by the bloody storms of the Cultural Revolution for ten years.

Hu Yaobang, however, courageously wielded the scalpel and operated on the "cancer," the succession system of the Communist Party. After the Cultural Revolution, the first to raise the question of solving the succession problem was Chen Yun. On July 2, 1981, at a national conference of secretaries of the party committees, he said, "Our cadre corps today has a serious problem, the gap between the young and old. Nearly every day the death of another of the old veterans is reported. . . . The fact that younger men must be promoted is a problem that was raised long ago. I remember that this document was put together this way: On May 8, while I was at Hangzhou resting, it occurred to me that this was indeed a big problem, and I simply wrote down my view about training young and middle-aged cadres. When I returned I sent a copy to comrade Hu Yaobang, and another to comrade Deng Xiaoping."[15]

On that same day, Deng Xiaoping also addressed the conference, saying,

> The reaction of foreigners to the Sixth Plenum of the Eleventh Central Committee was that we had used peaceful means to solve the problem of succession, to solve the great problem of the membership of the Central Committee. They praised us for solving this problem in so stable and smooth a manner. But, unless we solve the problem of the succession of cadres throughout all of the nation, within the next three to five years, there could be a lot of chaos. . . . To solve this big problem of lowering the average age of our cadres, we old comrades must be enlightened. We must take the lead. Otherwise, the problem cannot be solved. . . . For example, we have already touched on the problem of the system of

lifelong tenure for leadership positions, but we have not fully solved it. The problem of the retirement system has likewise not been fully solved. The establishment of advisory committees is a kind of transitional measure.[16]

Following this conference, as secretary-general of the Central Committee, Hu Yaobang worked hard to promote middle-aged and young cadres throughout the country. On July 20, 1982, meeting with graduating students of the Central Party School training class, he said, "Our party has now sent out a resounding message that we must care about, cultivate, and help middle-aged and younger cadres, that we must support and promote those showing promise. . . . Comrades Deng Xiaoping and Chen Yun have said that our cadres must be more revolutionary, better educated, more specialized, and younger. They have also said that the success of the four modernizations depends on whether or not our cadres are modernized."[17]

Less than a year after this talk, on June 1, 1983, Hu began using the expression "the third echelon." He said, "To provide for the long-term peace and security of the nation, to give the guiding policies of the party and nation continuity, we must begin today to build the third echelon." In November, while visiting Japan, he remarked that beginning in 1984 more than one thousand middle-aged and young people would be placed in leadership positions at departmental and regional levels, to lay a foundation for building a third echelon.

By 1985, Hu had put together the basic conceptual structure for building the third echelon. At the beginning of the year, during a working tour of Jiangxi province, he told cadres,

> Today our cadre ranks may be said to include three generations. The main duty of the first generation is to enjoy old age. The most important task, the first duty, of the second generation is to help the young comrades come up into positions of responsibility. And in the attempt to do this a little better. . . I have composed a few words: may the first echelon enjoy long life and quiet dignity, may the second echelon aid and support the later generations, may the third echelon throw all their energies into the battle. I hope that our three echelons . . . will work closely together, that our party and nation may forever prosper, right into the . . . twenty-second century. This correct guideline on building the "three echelons" may well go down in history as one of the creations of our party.[18]

In February, *Liaowang zhoukan* (Outlook Weekly) followed up with a concrete explanation of this creative idea, pointing out that the three echelons "form a dynamic cohesive structure. Today's second echelon will become tomorrow's first echelon and today's third echelon will become tomorrow's second echelon. With the orderly change of places the tasks of each will likewise change. And behind them will be an even finer preparatory echelon growing up. . . . This should be our procedure and our future."[19]

In September 1985 the Party Congress accepted Hu Yaobang's conception of an echelon structure. Of the 348 Central Committee members and alternates elected by the Twelfth Congress, 64 were new, young representatives. At the same time, Hu Qili, Qiao Shi, Wu Xueqian, Li Peng, and Tian Jiyun became third-echelon leaders appointed to the Politburo. Wang Zhaoguo and Hao Jianxiu were elected to the Secretariat of the Central Committee. A group from the original Communist Youth League system became an important force in positions from the central government down through the local offices (see appendix). Furthermore, some 1.8 million cadres throughout the nation retired, to be replaced by 3.3 million young cadres promoted to high leadership positions.

Since "political power comes from the barrel of a gun," it is also significant that Hu Yaobang's influence in the armed forces increased greatly because of his experience in the Long March and the army, and also because of the implementation of a series of policies in which the eleven military districts were reduced to seven, and the army was reduced in size and modernized, bringing in new personnel. Men who had worked under Hu in the army and army Youth League representatives were promoted to positions in the headquarters of the three armed services. Xu Xin, who had been head of the 22d Regiment of the Third Column of the Shanxi-Chahar-Hebei Field Army (of which Hu Yaobang was political commissar) and who had invented a way of blowing up underground tunnels in the campaign against Shijiazhuang, was now an assistant chief of staff. Two other commanders of famous brigades, Liu Jingsong and Yan Tongmao, were made commander of the Shenyang Military District and assistant commander of the Beijing Military District respectively. Gui Shaobin, head of the political department of the 8th Column when Hu Yaobang was head of the same in the 18th Infantry Corps, and Wei Jinshan, who had been political commissar of the "Linfen Brigade," now became assistant political commissars in the navy. Wang Zibo, who had been a regiment commander of the 13th Column, was now assistant comander of the Nanjing Military District. Li Yaowen, now naval political commissar; Xin Guozhi, assistant political officer of the North China Sea fleet; Wang Songgui, assistant political officer of the Second Artillery Corps; and Ren Shaozu, vice-chairman of the Committee on Science and Technology Industries of the Ministry of Military Defense, were all originally army representatives of the Communist Youth League system.

At the same time, the high command of the armed services also promoted a group of younger officers up from the military ranks, reducing the average age of the officers at the military district level by seven years. The age of officers at the infantry corps level fell from fifty-six in 1982 to forty-seven. At the battalion level many young officers who had received military academy training were promoted.

Hu Yaobang's massive implementation of the policy of cadre and officer "modernization" was of course carried out in accordance with the approved guidelines of the Central Committee, and with the approval of China's real leader, Chairman of the Central Committee Advisory Committee and Chairman of the Central Committee Military Affairs Committee Deng Xiaoping.

On July 21, 1985, meeting with Kimura Mutsuo, speaker of the Japanese House of Councillors, Deng said, "The central task of the Party Congress that will convene in September will be to lower the age of the Central Committee. . . . This Party Congress and the proposed Thirteenth Party Congress that is slated to meet in 1987 will be equally important and authoritative because the problem of lowering the age of our officials has not been solved well by the Twelfth Party Congress. Since Secretary-general Hu Yaobang will be seventy next year, and Zhao Ziyang is sixty-five, they will continue to work hard for a few years making the essential preparations for the succession of younger people. Because there are some who fear the young people can't assume higher responsibilities, let them continue for two or three years." In addition, Deng emphasized that he would step down and let Hu Yaobang and Zhao Ziyang run things. He soon made preparations to retire.

The situation seemed to be very good. The system for the succession of party officials appeared to be moving in the right direction. All of this made Hu Yaobang resolve to solve the problem of the succession system at the Thirteenth Party Congress. On May 24, 1986, meeting with veteran cadres in Sichuan, he gave an even bolder, more creative speech. He said,

At the Thirteenth Party Congress next year, we must be resolved to solve (the problem of lowering the age of cadres). One-third of the older comrades who are members and alternates of the Central Committee will retire, and some 110 to 120 new comrades will join the Central Committee. Of these, 80 to 90 percent will be about fifty years of age. At the same time we should have some Central Committee members who are in the over thirty-five or forty age bracket. The Central Committee needs young people. The older cadres must support the new cadres, must let them be involved in the work. When we were young we could work for two days and two nights straight with no problem. But after you pass sixty you're no good after midnight. It would seem that the Central Committee should also implement a system of retiring at age sixty. At present, forty-year-old Central Committee members seem awfully young. But at the time of Liberation, Chairman Mao Zedong was fifty-six, Zhou Enlai was fifty-one, and Deng Xiaoping was forty-six.[20]

This speech, which that summer was sent to all party organizations in the form of a classified document, aroused an enormous reaction.

At the same time, at the Beidaihe Conference preceding the Sixth Plenum of the Twelfth Central Committee, Hu advised Deng to set an example by taking the lead in retiring from the Politburo while continuing to oversee things as chairman of the Central Committee Advisory Committee. Clearly, Hu's scalpel had already begun to probe into dangerous territory.

Coup D'Etat of the Old Men—China's Tragedy

On December 5, 1986, more than a thousand students of the Chinese National University of Science and Technology of Hefei, Anhui province, held a demonstration opposing the method of "officially appointed candidates," which the people then vote for to be representatives to the National People's Congress (NPC), and calling for the right to hold democratic elections. This ignited a democratic movement among Chinese students that spread throughout the nation and lasted for a month. The students boldly wrote the words "democracy" and "freedom" on their battle flags, while at the same time expressing support for the party's political reforms.

This was the largest student movement since the Tiananmen incident a decade earlier. It moved the whole nation, shook the central government, and ignited a power struggle within the party.

The leaders of the reform faction—Deng Xiaoping, Hu Yaobang, and Zhao Ziyang—split over this issue. Deng retreated from the five cadre changes (the attempt to bring in cadres who were more revolutionary, better educated, more specialized, and younger, and to change the personnel system), from the reforms in the political system, and from the student democratic movement. He went over to those in the party who constituted the conservative faction in their political consciousness (or the original White [Nationalist] Area faction from World War II, which Liu Shaoqi had headed), including Chen Yun, Peng Zhen, Bo Yibo, Yao Yilin, Deng Liqun (originally Liu Shaoqi's secretary), and Hu Qiaomu. He also joined forces with the old army leaders of the Red Area armed forces faction—Nie Rongzhen, Yang Shangkun, Wang Zhen, Song Renqiong, and Xu Qiuli. With the help of these two groups he engineered the January 1987 coup that forced Hu Yaobang, the leader of the active reform group, to resign.

Why call this incident a coup d'etat? On January 16, 1987, an enlarged meeting of the Politburo released the following announcement:

> 1. Unanimous agreement to accept Hu Yaobang's request to resign the position of secretary-general of the Central Committee of the party.
> 2. Unanimous vote to make Zhao Ziyang acting secretary-general of the Central Committee.
> 3. The above two items to be presented to the next plenary session of the Central Committee for ratification.
> 4. To retain Hu Yaobang as a member of the Politburo of the Central Committee, and of the Standing Committee of the Politburo of the Central Committee.

The announcement also said that those attending this meeting included "eighteen members of the Politburo of the Central Committee, and two alternate members; four secretaries of the Secretariat of the Central Committee; seventeen responsible persons of the Central Advisory Commission; two responsible persons of the Central Committee Discipline Inspection Committee; and other relevant comrades." The meeting was called and chaired by the chairman of the Central Committee Military Affairs Committee and chairman of the Central Advisory Commission, Deng Xiaoping. At the same time, Bo Yibo, who was not a member of the Politburo, presented the summary of complaints against Hu Yaobang.

If the above facts are compared with the relevant provisions of the Party Constitution passed by the Twelfth Party Congress, this enlarged meeting of the Politburo qualifies as a coup d'etat. It was illegal for the following reasons: First, according to Section 3, Article 21 of the Party Constitution, it is the secretary-general of the Central Committee who is responsible for calling meetings of the Politburo and its Standing Committee, and of the Secretariat of the Central Committee. It was illegal for Deng Xiaoping as chairman of the Military Affairs Committee and of the Central Advisory Commission to call a so-called enlarged meeting of the Politburo.

Second, Section 3, Article 20 specifies that the secretary-general of the party is elected by a plenary session of the entire Central Committee. Therefore, it is illegal for any organ other than a plenary session of the entire Central Committee to accept the resignation of Hu Yaobang.

Third, Section 3, Article 22 specifies that "The Central Advisory Commission assists and advises the Central Committee on political matters. . . . The vice-chairmen of the Central Advisory Commission may attend plenary sessions of the Politburo in a nonvoting capacity. When the Politburo deems it necessary, members of the Standing Committee of the Central Advisory Commission may attend plenary sessions of the Politburo in a nonvoting capacity." By dragging "seventeen responsible members of the Central Advisory Commission, two responsible members of the Central Committee Discipline Investigation Committee, and other relevant comrades" into this enlarged meeting of the Politburo to act as a pressure group and "majority opinion," Deng Xiaoping was continuing the autocratic methods by which Mao Zedong dealt with his opposition within the party. This was illegal.

Fourth, in accordance with Section 3, Article 22, it was illegal for Bo Yibo, attending the meeting in a nonvoting capacity as vice-chairman of the Central Advisory Commission, to make the only summary presentation of the indictments against Hu Yaobang.

This shows that the power group of old men represented by Deng Xiaoping violated the Party Constitution and the "principle of collective leadership" to pull off the January coup d'etat. They had been carefully planning this coup in secret for quite some time.

Deng Xiaoping's boycott of Hu Yaobang's speech at the enlarged meeting of the Central Committee Military Affairs Committee in December 1986 illustrated Deng's power over the high-ranking military officers. Then, in January, through Yang Shangkun, general secretary of the Military Affairs Committee, Zhuo Lin, director of the General Office of the Military Affairs Committee, and Qin Jiwei, commander of the Beijing Military District, Deng Xiaoping made military arrangements for the coup. Peng Zhen deployed the People's Armed Police, which was under his control.

In the meantime, both the civil and military arms of the old men's forces were advancing on three fronts to whip up public support for a coup. Beginning in late December 1986, Peng Zhen, Bo Yibo, and others held several meetings of party political commissars, criticizing Hu Yaobang for being "too rightist," for "releasing a bourgeois liberal flood," for being "responsible for the student movement incident," and so forth. They accused Hu of "forcing many old comrades to retire," of "promoting a lot of cadres from the Communist Youth League system," of "using the law to punish the children of old comrades who had violated the law." These were Hu's three great crimes. They also proclaimed that they and Deng Xiaoping were in good health and perfectly capable of administering the government. Deng, who was very unhappy with Hu's policy toward Japan, meeting with the new leader of the Japanese Liberal Democratic Party, Takeshita Noboru (who originally was supposed to meet with Hu), said, "The lessons of history have taught us that our leadership must be reorganized. . . . At present the right is the major obstacle. . . . I have offered to resign many times, but everybody disagrees. It seems that I must continue to struggle."

A group of old men averaging eighty years of age, based on their strong common desire to wield power and their stubborn political conservatism, put together the power to overthrow Hu Yaobang and planned this coup d'etat. The six indictments of Hu Yaobang that Deng Xiaoping presented to the expanded session of the Politburo and Bo Yibo's summary speech criticizing Hu were the voice of this group of old men.

At this meeting, Hu showed the courage of a veteran of the Long March. He debated fiercely with Deng and Bo. He refrained from saying anything about many false accusations. He strongly defended China's need to continue to liberalize and reform, saying that intellectuals needed to be treated better, and that the average age of the cadres needed to be lowered. A young fighter in the old Long March and an old fighter in the new Long March, Hu Yaobang was thus overthrown by a group of old men. This was a tragic abortion of all of China's contemporary reforms.

This tragedy illustrates at least the following problems:

1. The power structure of the CCP is that of an autocratic pyramid, in which power is held by a small group of men at the top of the pyramid.

2. The military nature of the political power in the CCP continues to exert a powerful influence. The gun controls the party, the civil bureaucracy, and the people.

3. The CCP system of the peaceful succession of power has collapsed. The policy of buying a peaceful transition by establishing the "Central Advisory Commission" has failed. The policy of five changes in the cadre corps has been tabled, and the drama of power struggle continues to be played out within the halls of the central government.

4. Looking at the past twenty years of Deng Xiaoping's life, from the Antirightist campaign of 1957 to the movement against bourgeois liberalism of 1987, one sees that politically and ideologically he has always been inflexible and repressive. Consequently, as long as the old men headed by him hold power, a thorough revamping of the political system is impossible, the democratization of Chinese society will enter a period of temporary dormancy, and China's intellectuals will continue to "sing songs" within the bird cage of the "four upholds."

5. Chinese foreign policy will undergo some minor adjustments. Unless there is a much greater growth in relations with the United States, relations with Europe and the Soviet Union will become closer. In its relations with Japan, China will make political pronouncements that are rather severe in tone, but economically Japan will become an important trading partner.

6. In economic reforms, the leading edge of the liberalization policy will be blunted. Chen Yun's "birdcage economics" will merge with the policies of the old state economic planning faction headed by Bo Yibo and will gradually gain a greater voice.

7. The coup of the old men will bring about developments in the contradictions between the old and the new in China, between reform and conservatism, between democracy and autocracy, between the privileged bureaucracy of the party and army and the intellectuals and common people. These developments will move in the direction of increasing the opposition. In the next five or six years, China will undergo enormous changes. Because of Hu Yaobang's potential political power and influence, and because his creative efforts to reform China were in tune with the wishes of the people and with the flow of history, it is hard to measure the role they will play in the momentous changes ahead.

13
Personality,
Character, and Interests

The history of modern China has been one of tumult and change. It is in just such times that a number of great leaders have emerged. Looking back over the stories of these heroic ancestors, one thing that particularly strikes the eye is the number of those with Hakka backgrounds who became revolutionary leaders and strongly influenced the progress of modern Chinese history.

The historical record shows that among those with Hakka backgrounds were Taiping leaders Hong Xiuquan, Yang Xiuqing, Feng Yunshan, Wei Changhui, Shi Dakai, and Li Xiucheng; leaders of the 1911 Revolution Sun Yat-sen, Liao Zhongkai, Deng Yanda, Zou Lu, and Qiu Fengjia; and leaders of the Chinese Communist revolution Peng Pai, Zhu De, Ye Ting, Ye Jianying, and Deng Xiaoping. At the same time, under the leadership of these famous revolutionary leaders there were many other Hakka men and women who committed themselves to the revolutionary movements of China and of the world. And now a new star has been added to the list of great Chinese leaders with a Hakka genealogy, that of Hu Yaobang.

The Hakka are one branch of China's main ethnic group, the Han. They originated in the central plains of China. For various reasons, including the invasion of China by other nationalities, civil war, population growth, and lack of a fixed land base, over the last fifteen hundred years the Hakka have undertaken four major migrations: in the fourth century in the Eastern Jin period when they moved south across the Yangzi River; at the end of the Tang and early Song dynasties [tenth century]; at the end of the Ming and early Qing dynasties [seventeenth century]; and finally after the failure of the Taiping uprising, about 1867.

In the early Qing dynasty, in the time of the Kangxi, Yongzheng, and

Qianlong emperors [early to mid-eighteenth century], Liuyang county became a well-known county in which half the population was Hakka. The reason so many Hakka came to settle in this county on the border of Hunan and Jiangxi provinces can be traced back to the hatred that the Ming dynasty Taizu emperor, Zhu Yuanzhang, developed toward the people of the county. According to the *Liuyang Gazetteer*, "In the early years of the Ming dynasty Hongwu reign period [1368–1399], because the people of Liu[yang] gave aid and presents to Chen Youliang [who had set up an independent kingdom that was defeated by Zhu Yuanzhang in 1363], infuriated, the Ming Taizu emperor increased the land tax to 2.14 *dou* (bushels) (from the normal tax of 1.7 *dou* per mu), increasing the county tax to 801,130 *dou* as punishment for three hundred years, bringing hardship and suffering from which the people had no redress."[1]

In the early years of the reign of the Ming dynasty Chongzhen emperor [r. 1628–1644], Feng Zuwang, the magistrate of Liuyang county, petitioned the court as follows: "Liuyang is a very mountainous area bordering on Jiangxi province. The rebellion of Chen Youliang in the Boyang and Dongting Lake area retreated before the [imperial] troops. Every possible mountain slope was cultivated. In time came peace and a new generation. Seeking a happy land, the people gradually moved away to other places. The flight from the poverty and heavy taxes of Liuyang took place slowly. Also, because of the steep mountain peaks and ridges, in all directions there is not a single flat plain as large as 100 mu [18 acres]. Even a village of ten families will be spread out up a narrow, winding mountain valley. Distance brings change. Thus one family has only one barren piece of land, and one clan may span many barren mountains. Because so many troops have been stationed there recently, the people cannot make a living. Families have been split, and more than half have fled."[2]

These disastrously heavy taxes continued through the Kangxi and Yongzhen reigns. The *Liuyang Gazetteer* notes, "In the 56th year of the Kangxi emperor [1717], some 70–80,000 could not pay their tax debts. The officials had resigned, the people had fled, and the towns were deserted. . . . Since the Yongzheng reign [1723–1736] [the tax] has been equivalent to double that of the early Song dynasty, and the harm of these oppressive taxes has gone on since the beginning of the Ming dynasty to now, more than 370 years."[3]

This abnormal situation was not rectified until the Qianlong era [1736–1796]. In accordance with the memorial of Shi Yizhi, then

governor-general of Hubei and Hunan, the Qianlong emperor can-
celled the heavy tax that had been imposed in anger by the Ming Taizu
emperor more than 370 years earlier. "Based on the register of working
males from the 53d year (of the Kangxi reign, 1715), by the beginning
of the 3d year of the Qianlong emperor [1738], the number of people
who had left the area reduced the register of working males by 4,984,
meaning a lost revenue of some 1,078 ounces (*liang*) of silver."[4]

In periods of fighting and turmoil the Hakka, who were good at
taking advantage of opportunities and had a frontier philosophy (of
settling in mountainous areas or in the sparsely populated border areas
between two provinces), would go into areas from which "the officials
had resigned, the people had fled, and the towns were deserted." It was
precisely when "families had split up and more than half had fled" and
the Qianlong emperor had abolished the heavy taxes that the Hakka
migrated into Liuyang county. According to the research of Professor
Luo Xianglin, "The Hakka families of Chen county, Liuyang county,
and Pingjiang county who were mixed in with the original inhabitants
of Hunan and Jiangxi provinces had come in the early Qing dynasty
from Guangdong or Jiangxi provinces."[5] The Hakka who settled in
Chen county, according to the *Chongzheng Tongren xipu* [a Hakka
genealogy], "for the most part immigrated in the early Qing dynasty
Kangxi, Yongzheng, and Qianlong reigns" from Meizhou and Xun-
zhou [Guangdong province].[6] But the Hakka who settled in Liuyang
and Pingjiang counties were all registered as Hakkas or half Hakkas
from Jiangxi province. South township of Liuyang county is a mountainous area close to the Jiangxi border to which large numbers of
Hakka began moving after the third year of the Qianlong reign (1738).
During this period, more than 40,000 Hakka from Guangdong and
Jiangxi moved into Chen, Liuyang, and Pingjiang counties. Hu Yaobang's ancestors, then, were Hakka from Jiangxi province who moved
to Liuyang during the middle of the Qing dynasty and finally settled in
the Zhonghe mountain hamlet.

Hakka Temperament and Character

Carrying with them the culture of Central China and inheriting the
physiology of their ancestors, traveling great distances throughout China, the Hakkas have been a great mobile army, rich in the pioneer
spirit. They have built roads where no roads went before. They have
founded homes in the wilderness. They have gone anywhere that of-

fered hope and promise. Thus, they do not have a narrow concept of territory and are not strongly tied to any one local region. Having a very cosmopolitan outlook, they feel at home anywhere in China. In his student days, Hu Yaobang read *On the Yalu River* and *A Wandering Youth* by Jiang Guangci and thought to himself, "The characters in these stories know how to wander. Why can't I be a revolutionary!"[7] Thus, modeling himself after the early Chinese Communist revolutionary leader Li Lisan, he left home and devoted himself to the revolution. While on the one hand he was influenced by the revolutionary atmosphere of the time, on the other hand this was also the Hakka spirit of "all men are brothers" springing to life and expressing itself under these new historical conditions. In the new historical era of the reforms, Hu has committed himself with pride to the new Long March, looking always forward like a true revolutionary. This too perhaps reflects the pioneering, cosmopolitan temperament of the Hakka people.

With their pioneering mentality, the Hakka would move into new territory and as outsiders had to face the hostility of the native inhabitants. In the process of opening up new living space for themselves, they would have to struggle against both hardships imposed by the natural environment and inevitable conflicts with the local inhabitants. This process forged in the Hakka a strength of character, a determination not to bend or give in to adversity. Hu Yaobang never indulged in servile flattery, never changed his original vision, but held firmly to his ideals. This was a reflection of the resolute character of the Hakka, joined with the true spirit of the professional revolutionary.

The Hakka, when faced with hardship, went out from their ancestral homes to plant their feet and set down roots in a new place using just their bare hands. They had to learn how to adapt to new environment, to deal with new situations, to develop new ideas and new human relationships. They had to readjust and adapt themselves to the "survival of the fittest." It was for this reason that the Hakka developed the qualities of stressing reality, of adaptability, of being flexible. Throughout the long course of the revolution, Mao Zedong, Zhu De, Deng Xiaoping, Wang Jiaxiang, Li Fuchun, Xu Xiangqian, and others saw Hu Yaobang as someone who could flexibly implement party policy and the true intent of the leaders in accordance with the real conditions. This is the reason why Hu was able to work with different factions in the army, the party, and the government.

Hu's flexibility is evident in the way he has responded to the difficulties of official life. For example, in his relationship with Peng Zhen, he showed his mastery of the art of dealing with officialdom. When Hu was first secretary of the Communist Youth League, Peng was one of the top men in the party. Every year at the time of the college graduations in Beijing, there would always be a big ceremony at which leaders of the Central Committee would be invited to speak. Peng was invariably a major figure at these ceremonies. One year, after Zhou Enlai was asked to speak at the ceremony, Peng sought out Song Shuo, head of the University Work Department of the Beijing City Committee, and said, "This year you have invited the premier to speak. If the premier gives a talk, what can I possibly talk about?" When he heard about this, Hu Yaobang talked it over with Song Shuo and, in the name of the Central Committee of the Youth League and the University Work Department, held an unprecedented second meeting of all the graduating students at which Peng Zhen was asked to speak. Peng talked about how he had led the "December 9" movement in a speech that was moving and well received.[8]

This kind of realistic flexibility was precisely the kind of creative adaptation that shows up in the contact of Chinese revolutions with foreign cultures. In creating his Taiping Heavenly Kingdom of peasant egalitarianism, Hong Xiuquan adopted the teachings and sayings of Christianity. Sun Yat-sen adopted the philosophy of land revolution from the Japanese people's rights movement thinkers and from Western constitutional democracy and legal thought and combined them with the anti-Manchu nationalistic thought of the post-Taiping thinkers to create his Three People's Principles and five-power constitution. Taking the principle of seeking truth from facts, of "who cares whether a cat is black or white as long as it catches mice" as their foundation, Hu Yaobang and Deng Xiaoping decisively discarded the Mao Zedong style of socialism and made a breakthrough in Marxism and Leninism to create a Chinese style of socialism. This may indeed be regarded as being very much in tune with the personality, temperament, and special character of the Hakka revolutionaries.

When the Hakka moved out from the North China plain to settle in other areas, the culture of Central China that they took with them became the tie that binds the spirit of the Hakka people. This is why the Hakka place particular emphasis on their family trees, revere their ancestors, and emphasize education. It is also why they build clan temples, which are also the sites of the schools where their children first begin their education. This proud spirit illustrates first of all the advantage that their desire to preserve culture and education gives the Hakka people. Through education and excellence they bring honor to their families. By extension, this helps develop a strong sense of nationalism and a desire to fight to preserve Chinese culture. Hu Yaobang clearly bears the birthmark of the Hakka spirit.

In the epic of his life struggle, Hu's Hakka qualities have been joined with the struggle of the Communist Party in the fight for the ideals of communism and with the fate of the nation to give him the strength to carry on his efforts to build a rich and strong new China. It is these qualities that have molded his determination to push forward even when it means going against the current fad, to stand defiantly at the forefront of history, leading the reforms.

Hu Yaobang's Interests

All those who have met Hu or heard his speeches come away with the impression that he is a good speaker and a heavy smoker (he smokes more than two packs a day). Indeed, Hu likes to give speeches, and he speaks dynamically. He will also frequently stop to smoke a cigarette. To an outsider he looks like a revolutionary who is good at mobilizing people, a good propagandist. But thanks to his free and uninhibited nature and his competitive, curious, and optimistic personality, after many years of training, he is known among party insiders as having many talents and skills, and a broad range of knowledge.

As noted earlier, Hu left school in his second year of junior middle school and committed himself to the revolution. The store of knowledge he commands is basically self-taught. When talking to the children, his wife, Li Zhao, says, ''Your father grew up in humble surroundings and left home when he was very young. His knowledge all comes from learning at work, from arduous practice.''[9] Zhu Zhongli, the wife of Wang Jiaxiang, says, ''Hu Yaobang joined the Red Army when he was very young, and was in school for only a few years. But he is a very conscientious and determined person. No matter whether he was on the battlefield or enduring the hardships of directing the troops, or very busy with a difficult tense task, even when he was attacked by Lin Biao and the 'gang of four,' he was always studying.''[10]

On his reading, we have proof from his own speeches. Addressing cadres of the Chinese Communist Youth League, he said that every one of them should read 200 million characters. At the rate of 10,000 characters a day, 200 million characters would take over fifty years.

Having devoted himself to the Chinese Communist revolution for more than half a century, Hu Yaobang has himself done this, hence his advice. Hu's reading covers a broad range of interests, but it falls mainly within three categories: (1) Marxist-Leninist philosophy, political economics, and political theory; (2) history; and (3) literature. His knowledge and views on the first two categories, through diligent and painstaking reading and thinking, are those of a self-taught scholar well versed in these subjects. In addition, Hu has a special fondness for literature. He has spent much time reading Tang and Song poetry and classical literature. He has also read widely in classical and modern fiction, both Chinese and foreign short stories, novels, and plays. A number of writers, both Chinese and foreign, are among his friends, such as the Japanese writer Yamasaki Fukuji, the Chinese-American Han Suyin, the Chinese-Canadian Chen Ruoxi, and such Chinese writers as Sha Yexin, Bai Hua, Liu Binyan, and Zhou Yang. This is the reason that he has a more thorough and profound understanding than does the average high-level cadre of the writer's and artist's need for creative freedom. His support for creative freedom and his defense and appreciation of writers is confirmed by everyone in the arts and is well known among the public at large.

Hu Yaobang's Chinese brush writing is also very good, with a style that is smoothly flowing and dynamic, strong and forceful. Japanese Prime Minister Nakasone Yasuhiro praised Hu's brushwork as being from the native land of brush calligraphy and sighed that his own writing was not so good. In fact, Hu's writing is comparable to that of a calligrapher even though he has little time to practice. But to achieve this level he had to put in some hard work. In 1965 when he was working in Shaanxi he worked closely with Shu Tong, secretary of the provincial committee, and they became good friends. Shu Tong was a well-qualified, veteran high-level cadre. He had once been head of the Political Department of the Third Field Army and first secretary of Shandong province. In 1960 he made the error of being too adventuristic and was sent to Shaanxi. Shu Tong had the reputation of being the "Red Army's brush, the calligrapher of the Chinese Communists." He was especially well known for his large characters on hanging scrolls. That year, Hu asked Shu Tong if he might become his student. This improved his calligraphy a great deal.

From childhood Hu has been very fond of music. He can read music and sing. He sings not only such stirring songs as "Yellow River Song" and the school song of Yan'an's Resistance University, he also very much appreciates romantic popular songs. He once said that the uncritical rejection of popular songs shows a kind of stupidity, and that we should fight against stupidity. Hu is also a good dancer, and he knows some of the dances of China's minority nationalities. Because he is open-minded (*kaiming*) he even supports disco dancing for Chinese young people.

Hu was also one of the uninhibited friends of Deng Xiaoping's "Bridge Club." In the 1960s he would play bridge with Deng, Wan Li, Wu Han, and others at the Chinese Communist officer's club on Yang-feng Alley in Beijing, often for many hours at a time. In the Cultural Revolution, Hu was severely criticized by Mao Zedong's Red Guards for being one of the top generals of Deng Xiaoping's bridge headquarters. Later, when Hu came back for the second time, because he had a heavy work load he did not continue to play cards. In April 1982 he accompanied Deng Xiaoping on a visit to Korea. In the train on the way, "Deng started talking with him about bridge. Hearing that he no longer played bridge, he said it was a shame. At the time, Deng said that playing bridge was good training for the mind, and that when one was very busy, it was a good way of relaxing. Hearing this, Hu replied that he would later return to the card table."[11]

One of Hu's bridge partners was one of the great *Go* players in the China-Japan tournaments, Nie Weiping. Hu met Nie in the 1960s at the home of Hu Keshi, who was then second secretary of the Central Committee of the Communist Youth League. At the time, Hu Yaobang said to Nie, "I hear you are a very good *Go* player. I like *Go* too, but my level of play isn't very high. You would have to spot me at least four pieces."[12] If Hu Yaobang could play against a national champion taking a handicap of just four pieces, this would indicate that his *Go* game was very good indeed. According to Zhu Zhongli, during the Yan'an period she and Hu "frequently played *Go*, and we took it quite seriously. Once we started a game, neither of us would concede defeat and we would have to play to the very end. Thinking back on it, this is really very interesting. He would never take a move back. Sometimes if he made a wrong move and put a piece down in a place that would influence the whole board he would just exclaim softly, 'Whoops, that's bad. That was the wrong move!'"[13]

Hu Yaobang is also good at Chinese chess. The time of the gambling incident involving Hu Yaobang, Mao Zedong's younger brother Mao Zetan, and the Japanese Dr. Hieda was the highlight of his chess career.

14
Thought

Based on his revolutionary activities and on his words and writings in different historical periods of his long career, the development of Hu Yaobang's thought may be roughly divided into four periods: (1) youth and exploration (1926–1936); (2) acceptance and maturation (1937–1956); (3) adjustment and reexamination (1957–1976); and (4) breakthrough and creativity (1977–).

In reflecting back on the period of his youth, Hu has said that the little mountain village in which he grew up was very isolated. He could not even finish or fully comprehend the Four Books and Five Classics of the Chinese tradition, which left him frustrated in his youthful search for knowledge. When he left his village, after studying at the Liwen Elementary School in Wenjia and the Liuyang County High School, although he quickly became involved in leadership of youth work, he was still just a promising young cadre being trained in concrete, day-to-day work activities under the nurturing of the party.

Beginning in 1937, after finishing the training course at Resistance University in Yan'an, under the careful cultivation of Mao Zedong, Hu accepted materialism and became a member of the Chinese Communist Party and a believer in Mao Zedong Thought. In this second period, Hu gradually matured into a capable, experienced, and intelligent worker, flexibly applying the theories of Mao Zedong and the policy and directives of the party in real-life situations. Thus this may be called his period of acceptance and maturation.

Beginning in 1957, following the Antirightist movement and the failure of the Three Red Banners [of the Great Leap Forward], thanks to his long involvement in the leadership of Communist Youth League and to the influence of Deng Xiaoping, Hu began seriously to test in practice the validity of the directives of Mao Zedong. The momentous rise and spectacular fall of the Cultural Revolution caused him, during his fall from favor, to begin a series of reexaminations and to pull away from the influence of Mao's later thought. This was his period of adjustment and reexamination.

In 1977, when Hu returned for the second time to resume his work, during this great historical juncture when the CCP decided to turn from revolution to reform, his thought took an enormous leap forward, constantly breaking through "restricted zones," constantly creating anew. This may be called the breakthrough and creative period of his thought.

Because during the first two periods Hu Yaobang was not a prominent figure in the Chinese Communist Party, and because there are few extant materials from this period, the present discussion of the outlines of Hu Yaobang's thought will concentrate on the last two periods.

Philosophical Thought

Combining Theory with Reality and Practice. Hu Yaobang's world view is indisputably that of a firmly convinced materialist. A materialist believes that correct theories are things within the realm of spirit that reflect the laws of the development of real things. The correctness of a theory must be tested in practice. Ever since hearing Mao Zedong lecture on his essays "On Practice" and "On Contradiction" at Resistance University, in the practical activity of combining theory and reality, Hu has used these essays as his primary intellectual tools.

Regarding this practice of combining theory and reality, in the introduction to the 1872 German edition of their *Communist Manifesto*, Marx and Engels said, "The practical application of these fundamental principles will depend, as the Manifesto itself states, everywhere and at all times, on the historical conditions existing at the time."[1] Later, Lenin flexibly applied Marxist theory to the realities of capitalist Russian society in his practical revolutionary activities. The reason Mao Zedong was able to lead the Chinese revolution to success was that the leadership of the CCP believed that Mao Zedong Thought represented "a unity of Marxism-Leninism and Chinese revolutionary practice."

At the great convocation commemorating sixtieth anniversary of the founding of the Chinese Communist Party, Hu Yaobang stated,

> Combining the universal principles of Marxism with Chinese reality requires a long, cyclical process of repeated practice, knowledge, more

practice, and more knowledge. In each new historical era, we must liberate thought and continually be in touch with and discover through practice the new situations and problems, so that our own minds will contain a rich and diverse supply of concrete perceptual knowledge. At the same time we must use our brains and work hard to master the knowledge and methods of the social and natural sciences, so that our perceptual knowledge will move on to the next step, which is the creation of systematic forms of rational knowledge and well-structured theory, which we must then constantly test in practice.[2]

Five years after this talk, when visiting Italy, Hu expressed the practice of combining theory and reality even better. He said,

There have been two great victories and several severe setbacks in the history of the Chinese Communist Party. If we look at both the positive and negative sides of this problem we will learn that Marxism must be constantly enriched and developed in practice. It is not a static, unchanging dogma. We must be good at both upholding the fundamental principles and discarding those particular principles that are already out of date or that practice has proven do not fit the real situation, and replacing them with new principles. Marxism is the highest crystalization of the spiritual civilization of all mankind. Today, under new historical conditions, we must push Marxism forward, and we must also constantly absorb and summarize the newest results of the contemporary development of human civilization. Here we recall a passage from *Marxism at the End of the Twentieth Century* written by Enrico Berlinguer in 1983 to commemorate the 100th anniversary of the death of Marx: ''Marx teaches us that the real process of history and society indisputably is influenced by thought and ideology, but in this process, both thought and ideology (including revolutionary ideology, and Marxist ideology) are also limited in their practical applications, and changes in reality may even gradually give them new connotations, new forms, and new content.''[3]

From this we can see that Hu Yaobang's defense of the practice of combining theory and reality is consistent with his creative spirit and has always been so.

Practice is the Only Criterion of Truth. Mao Zedong led the Chinese Communist revolution to victory using primarily armed struggle, but his emphasis on the use of ''class struggle'' to achieve socialist construction and revolution met with repeated failure. The insistence of the ''whatever clique'' that whatever Mao said or wrote was the true way to do things meant that even theories that had been proven false in practice were still the ''absolute truth.'' Clearly, the actions of the ''whatever clique'' could only lead China down the road to total disaster.

Hu Yaobang's belief that practice is the only criterion for testing the truth emerged from a developing process of knowledge and understanding. From his training at Resistance University in 1937 to the early years after Liberation, Hu clearly believed that the thought of Mao Zedong was a correct theory deriving from practice by combining the principles of Marxism and Leninism with the realities of the Chinese revolution. It was because he took this as his premise that he stressed the tie between theory and practice, that one should not become a dogmatist who just talks about empty theory in the abstract. For example, at the first youth conference of 1958, he said:

> Those who do not pay attention to learning theory think that practice is theory. They do not understand that though practice can give rise to theory it cannot take the place of theory. The facts prove that many young people who have studied theory can better synthesize their experience and attain a higher level of self-consciousness that reduces their blindness and helps them do better work. Those who have poor study habits will be unable to apply the methods of combining theory and practice in their studies and consequently will fail to make the effort to grasp the true spirit of a work on theory, with the result that although they may have read some books on theory they cannot concretely apply the theory.[4]

In this quote, the emphasis is on the fact that we must combine theory and reality, but it also teaches the proposition that theory needs practice to enrich it, and that theory must stand the test of truth. But Hu still accepted Mao's theories as the first premise by which the correctness of something was to be determined. Not until after suffering under the Cultural Revolution would Hu replace this idea with the proposition that "practice is the only criterion for testing truth."

Clearly, it was from reflecting upon the "serious mistakes of Mao's later years" that Hu came to realize that "taking class struggle as one's guide" as "the way" to carry out socialist construction and revolution was wrong. He used Lenin's words to express his own view: "Theory must derive its life from practice, must be corrected by practice, must be tested by practice. . . . the more ways the better, and the more common experiences there are the richer it will become, and the more reliable, the faster, will the socialist victory be achieved, and the more easily will practice create—because only practice can create—the best ways and means to struggle."[5]

It was with this knowledge that Hu Yaobang took up the great battle of "practice is the only criterion for testing truth" and struck down the "whatever clique." He had become aware that "there is no fixed model" of socialist construction, that the only way to build a Chinese style of socialism was by having reform and liberalization policies that used more "ways and means."

Concrete Practice that Fully Combines Theory and Reality. On the question of how to tie theory and practice together, Hu believes that knowing and doing must be consistent. During his many years of military and political work in the party and Youth League, Hu has always stressed that political propaganda work must go to the front lines, to the grass-roots organizations, to the platoon level, to the masses. And these were not just nice words; Hu really did practice what he preached.

In 1964, at the Ninth National Congress of the Communist Youth League, he said:

> To develop a lively, energetic spirit, one must study hard and must never be complacent. Study is particularly important for Youth League cadres. We must be good at learning from the party and from the masses, from reality and from books, . . . from anyone who has experience and knowledge. It is only by always concentrating on absorbing new and fresh things, by continually increasing our store of new knowledge, by constantly raising our level of thought, that we can maintain a permanently revolutionary spirit. . . . We must do more grass-roots work and pay close attention to the actual results of our work. Deng Xiaoping has repeatedly pointed out that we cadres of the Youth League must learn to be good at details . . . . He has said that it all boils down to doing careful work, to paying more attention to the fine and intricate details. We must seriously study the policies of the party and emphasize research on the problems of youth. We must understand policies. We must have a clear grasp of the situation.[6]

The methods Hu Yaobang speaks of are indeed the concrete methods of practice that thoroughly tie theory and reality together.

In July 1981, at the convocation commemorating the sixtieth anniversary of the founding of the Chinese Communist Party, Hu Yaobang said that we must "work very hard, must study diligently, must ask specialists to teach us, must be good at listening to different opinions. At the same time, we must go out into the real world, carry out systematic, close investigations and studies, must combine well both direct and indirect experience."[7] Although these two talks were given more than fifteen years apart and Hu Yaobang's position in the government had changed, the basic spirit of how to combine theory with reality had not changed at all.

Perhaps it was the lesson learned from Mao Zedong's errors in later years of idealist practice divorced from reality. When Hu Yaobang rose to the highest position of leadership in the party, he did not lose contact with reality just because his position had changed. He was creative in his concrete work. He made it a habit to reply to one letter from the public every day. He continued to go to the front lines, visiting some 1,500 of China's 2,000 counties. He also went on frequent observation visits abroad, asking specialist professors to give lectures. This has made it possible for him to hear the sounds of reality, always adding new information to his store of knowledge. Among the top leadership of the Chinese Communist Party, Hu is one of the few who really does practice tying theory fully to reality.

The Theory of Combining Two into One. Mao Zedong criticized Engels's three great and coequal laws of dialectical materialism, saying, "Of Engels's three categories, I do not believe that two, the mutual transformation of qualitative and quantitative change (*zhiliang hubian*) and the negation of a negation (*foding zhi foding*), are on the same level as the unity of opposites (*duili tongyi*). This is a three-part pluralism, not monism. The most fundamental is the unity of opposites."[8] Mao's theory not only made the unity of opposites in a contradiction into the only fundamental law of dialectics (one divides into two), it also resulted in the rejection of the three stages of dialectical development, "thesis, antithesis, and synthesis," which is formed by these three coequal laws.

Yang Xianzhen was one of the first within the party to express his opposition to "one divides into two." Yang received inspiration from the "thesis, antithesis, synthesis" proposition of Fang Yizhi, the Ming dynasty philosopher. In November 1963, in a published lecture of one of the rotating training classes of the Party School, Yang asked, "What does one affirmation of one affirmation, one negation of one negation, one affirmation of one negation, and one negation of one affirmation mean?" He here clearly began to suggest the philosophical idea of "two combine into one."

Mao Zedong replied to this criticism with, "One eats one, a big fish eats a little fish, is a synthesis. Past books have never put it this way, including my own writings. Yang Xianzhen has suggested that two combine into one, by which he means that two different things are inseparably tied together. Where in the world is there any tie that cannot be cut? There may be a relationship, but it must always be cut. There is nothing that cannot be divided."[9]

There is clearly a difference between the views of Hu Yaobang and those of Mao Zedong. While accepting part of Mao's views Hu discarded other parts. Looking at Hu's discussions on a whole series of problems, after applying the principle of opposition and unity to analyze things or solve a problem, his ultimate objective was to achieve a unity between the two opposing sides. He placed the emphasis on harmony, on joining. This was very different from Mao's insistence that struggle was absolute, that the revolution was omnipotent, that war was the way to deal with all contradictions. In other words, Hu Yaobang was faithful to Engels's three-stage formula of "thesis, antithesis, and synthesis," and to the three coequal laws of the dialectical method. At the commemorative meeting for the centenary of the death of Marx, Hu said:

> At this point I would especially like to say a few words about the way in which Marx and Engels valued the natural sciences. They carefully studied a great amount of materials on the theory of mathematical and natural science and on technology. They used the results of the natural sciences, especially the three great discoveries of the nineteenth century—the conservation and conversion of energy, biological cells, and biological evolution—as the solid scientific foundation of the Marxist world view. Engels's *Dialectics of Nature* and *Anti-Dühring* are a concise reflection of the results of their studies in this area.[10]

In a talk to the art world in 1982, Hu's topic was "One step up from the method of dividing one into two." The sense of this talk was that two combine into one. He said:

> The question of philosophical knowledge is the same on the artistic battleline as it is in other areas, it has its own laws of development. It goes from disunity to unity, and then to disunity again and then to a new unity. It goes from uncertainty to certainty, and then again to uncertainty and then to even greater certainty. From disunity and inconsistency, in the process of practice, through discussion, knowledge becomes continually deeper, more unified, more consistent, moving forward to disunity yet again, and yet again to inconsistency. It is the cyclical nature of this process that gradually raises knowledge to a new and higher level. This is the law of the development of thought.

He also criticized two lines by Yu Xin in the poem "Lament for Jiang Nan," "The way of heaven and the stars, things end and do not return," as not being dialectical. In Hu Yaobang's view of the dialectical method, the central theme was that two combine into one.[11]

It was also with this understanding that Hu criticized Mao's theory of contradiction for "seriously confusing different types of contradiction, especially the different types within the party, to the point that he even turned a number of problems completely upside down." Hu believes that

> [we] should use totally different methods to solve the contradictions between different opinions that inevitably appear frequently in our work and in our thought. First of all, every major decision should be gone over carefully many times before coming to a final decision. Second, in party meetings, party members should be allowed to express their opinions freely and to criticize anyone, and they should be protected even if they are wrong. Third, the only important thing is that one should really try to think carefully, and then even if some kind of bias appears in someone's work, he should be allowed to change. Fourth, if someone disagrees with a main policy of the Central Committee, as long as he does not violate it and works to uphold it, he should be allowed to reserve his opinion. . . . [If there are antagonistic contradictions within the party, and some people] do not change, then they must be dismissed from the party . . . but this does not mean that such antagonistic contradictions should be treated as a contradiction of us versus the enemy, that such persons are the enemy.[12]

Hu criticized Mao Zedong's handling of contradictions among the people: "From the Antirightist movement until he died, for this period of nearly twenty years, many of the contradictions among the people, even though they were only partial contradictions, were exaggerated and treated as contradictions between us and the enemy."[13] Hu's view of contradictions within the party and between the party and the people in the socialist period are a logical development of his concept of "two combine into one."

In short, many of Hu Yaobang's views and policies derive from his moderate stance of "two combine into one." For example,

- He thinks that the formula for criticism and for self-criticism is unity—criticism—unity.
- His view of wealth is: don't be afraid of wealth, prosperity pro-

gresses in waves. It is not divisive or polarizing.

• In the period of socialism, intellectuals have already become part of the working class.

• His view of social productivity is: the methods of quantitative change—reform—should be used to achieve qualitative revolutionary objectives.

• He approves of using the formula "one nation two systems" in negotiations for the unification of Hong Kong and Taiwan with the mainland. The relationship of Hong Kong and Taiwan with the mainland "is just like that of the three branches of an extended family. Of these three branches, we are the big branch. The second branch is Taiwan, and the third branch is Hong Kong. This extended family is the People's Republic of China. We all belong to this family."[14]

• On the question of China's ethnic nationalities, it is also necessary "to correct the erroneous tendencies of the Great Cultural Revolution and of the Antirightist movement before it. . . . Today, when all of China's ethnic nationalities have already carried out socialism, the relationship among the nationalities is one among the working people. For this reason it is wrong to say that 'the ethnic nationality problem is really a class problem' [Mao Zedong's expression]. This kind of propaganda can only lead to serious misunderstandings concerning the nature of the relationship among China's ethnic nationalities."[15]

• His view of war and peace is: "Europe, including all the nations and peoples of Eastern and Western Europe, do not want a third world war, and we in China, maintaining a foreign policy of peaceful independent sovereignty, have a role to play in maintaining world peace. We should correct the view of ten-odd years ago that war is inevitable."[16]

All of the above points demonstrate Hu Yaobang's theory that "two combine into one."

Philosophy of Foreign Relations

Hu Yaobang's philosophy of foreign relations is a reflection of his resolute pursuit of liberalization and reform in China. Until recently, as secretary-general of the Chinese Communist Party, Hu was the head of the government. An analysis of his philosophy of foreign relations necessarily divides into two levels: state-to-state relationships and party-to-party relationships. In his activities at these two different levels, Hu has both continued and broken through the foreign policy and strategy formulated by Mao Zedong and Zhou Enlai. He has shifted the focus of foreign relations to national interests and domestic needs. He has pursued a balanced foreign policy focused on the interests of the developed nations of the Second World.

In principle, Hu Yaobang has continued to emphasize Mao's theory of the three worlds, of implementing the foreign affairs line of independence, sovereignty, anti-imperialism, and anti-hegemonism. In dealing with state-to-state relations, he has observed Zhou Enlai's five principles: "mutual respect for sovereignty and territorial integrity, mutual nonaggression, mutual noninterference, mutual benefit, and peaceful cooperation."

At the Twelfth Congress of the CCP in 1982, Hu said, "In the thirty-three years since the founding of our People's Republic, we have shown the world that China never attaches itself to any big power or group of powers and never yields to pressure from any big power. China's foreign policy is based on the scientific theories of Marxism-Leninism and Mao Zedong Thought, and it proceeds from the fundamental interests of the people of China and the rest of the world. It follows an overall long-term strategy, and it is definitely not swayed by expediency or by anybody's instigation or provocation."[17]

From the theoretical point of view, Hu has declared that the Soviet Union "has already changed from being a socialist nation into an expansionist hegemonial state." Seen from the perspective of historical experience, "The major capitalist countries of the world, led by the United States, have for a long time regarded us as an enemy, have carried out a blockade and boycott against our nation. . . . Beginning in the 1960s, the Soviet Union abrogated its economic contracts with our country, and our economic relations with the Soviet Union and with certain states of Eastern Europe have been curtailed drastically."[18] In addition, the heavy concentration of Soviet troops along China's borders and the U.S. sale of weapons to Taiwan have served to deepen Hu Yaobang's skepticism and worries about the hegemonism of both the Soviet Union and the United States.

Hu thinks that Mao Zedong's past attempts to assume the leadership of the Third World and his methods of giving gratuitous military and economic assistance and exporting revolution "have a few mistakes and lessons." Consequently, he advocates, "To those poor countries that are facing difficult times and are being invaded and threatened, if possible, we will give military and economic support and assistance. On military assistance, the Central Committee has a general rule to charge only for basic expenses. For economic assistance, the experience of history has shown that the method of giving completely gratis benefits neither side."[19]

Clearly, in accordance with the power and interests of China, Hu could only pursue a flexible foreign policy that is responsive to maintaining the balance of power and stability within the appropriate restraints imposed by the principle of "peaceful coexistence."

In order that China realize the modernization plan of "quadrupling national economic production" by the end of the century and rise up from the Third World to join the nations of the Second World, Hu believes that it should concentrate on developing friendly relations with the economically developed countries of the Second World and seek broadly based cooperation and exchanges in the areas of economics and trade, science and technology, and culture and education. By accomplishing this, China will be recognized as a significant partner on the world stage.

After becoming secretary-general of the Central Committee, in addition to visiting North Korea, Romania, and Yugoslavia, Hu Yaobang also emphasized strengthening friendly relations with non-Communist nations. He placed special emphasis on visiting economically developed Western nations of the Second World. He traveled to Japan in November 1983, to Australia and New Zealand in April 1985, and to England, Germany, France, and Italy in June 1986.

In the area of party-to-party relations, Hu developed closer ties with the Communist parties of the Second World, including those of France, Italy, Australia, and Spain. Under the prevailing conditions, these parties, as they explore the paths to political power, exhibit a creative, independent spirit of reform and are searching for ways to apply Marxism to the realities of their own countries. They share with Hu Yaobang a common language and sense of mission. During his visit to Italy, at a conference of Communist cadres, Hu said:

> The facts prove that there is no one pat formula, that the textbooks give us no ready-made set of replies to the question of how different countries should move toward or build socialism. Ultimately, socialism still emerges from practice. In the West, you have had a new and very complex situation since the Second World War. You have been working hard to explore the roads that lead to socialism. In the East, we are now instituting reforms, improving the socialist system, exploring the way to building a uniquely Chinese form of socialism. . . . The success of our explorations and efforts will help advance all human society and make a contribution to the development of Marxism.[20]

China is rich in natural resources and has an immense market, but it is also a huge political state with a backward economy. In order for China quickly to join the nations of the Second World, and at the same time maintain its independence and dignity, Hu Yaobang's concentration on a balanced foreign policy is essential both in principle and in practice. It is also a realistic line that is in tune with the interests of the state and the Chinese people. Hu Yaobang's revision of Mao Zedong's theory that war is inevitable is a natural reflection of his policies of liberalization and reform. It is also a logical reflection of his policy of strengthening cooperation with all the countries of the Second World.

15
Hu Yaobang:
A Preliminary Assessment

What is a flag?
Flying in the wind, attacking,
A flag should always be the fighting companion of the wind,
The wind, it is the breath of the people.

—Gong Liu[1]

Madame Chennault (Chen Xiangmei) once said that she approves of writing biographies of China's contemporary political leaders, and that pointing out that their strengths and weaknesses is a kind of democratic restriction. I agree. As a fellow Chinese with common feelings, I must consider her my comrade. I can take comfort in the fact that I am the first citizen of the People's Republic of China to have written a biography of a contemporary Chinese leader, Hu Yaobang. This is undoubtedly an historic step forward.

But in writing a biography of Hu Yaobang, it is necessary to analyze the nature of contemporary Chinese society before attempting to give a reasonably appropriate historical assessment of the role he played in the social environment and in movements that surrounded him.

There can be no doubt but that Mao Zedong was once a great leader. He listened to the cries of the peasants for land and defeated the several-million-strong army of Chiang Kai-shek using just rice and a few rifles. On October 1, 1949, he raised the five-star red flag over the whole land. But from that point on, we must ask, what kind of a nation emerged from the repeated revolutions and movements that he and his comrades in the party and army mobilized throughout the young republic?

In the later days of the Cultural Revolution, as Mao was approaching his death, this great man with feet of clay who with Liberation had begun to lose touch with reality and stood high above the people, seemed suddenly to have a vision. Following the transformation to a socialist system of ownership, he rushed forward again to enter the communist society of the Great Leap Forward, the people's communes, and the sweeping Three Banners movement, running straight to the historically unprecedented Cultural Revolution of the proletariat. But his feet touched only a mystical rugged road. Of this republic that he had created with the barrel of a gun, he said, "Lenin said that one might build a bourgeois state without the capitalists, to preserve bourgeois legal rights. This is precisely the kind of nation we ourselves have set up. It is hardly any different from the old society, divided into classes with eight levels of salaries, with pay according to one's work, and exchange for equal value."[2] He also said, "The commodity system and the wage system we have instituted are also unequal. This can only be controlled under a dictatorship of the proletariat. Thus it was very easy for people like Lin Biao to rise up and turn it into a capitalist system."[3]

According to the basic principles of Marxism, a system with a privileged cadre class and eight levels of wages constitutes one form of the relations of production. A privileged class and pay according to one's work represents one form of the relations of distribution. A commodity system and the exchange of things of equal value are reflections of the relations of exchange. An economic base in which the relations of production, the relations of distribution, the relations of exchange, and backward productivity are all "hardly any different from the old society" can only be a capitalist type of economy that is "hardly any different from the old society." Now what kind of socialism can a superstructure that rests upon this kind of a capitalist-type economic base possibly be? And what kind of a dictatorship has this become that men like Lin Biao could come to the top? Whether Mao Zedong or Lin Biao, honest officials or corrupt officials, rise to the top, they have no choice but to play out their roles on the stage of the economic base that has been determined by history. Guns can seize political power and a dictatorship can be benevolent or repressive, but none of them can easily change the basic nature of a nation.

In *Das Kapital*, Marx says, "No matter what social form production takes, labor and the means of production are factors in production. In the event that they are cut off from each other, both of them are still potential factors in production. If anything is to be produced, they must always be brought together. The particular method or form of this union is what distinguishes the social structure of each different economic era."[4]

Following the so-called socialist transformation of ownership in 1955, the union of Chinese labor, peasants, and other workers (including intellectuals) with the means of production, through the particular form of state bureaucratic collective power, became the existing form of capital production. The social structure took the form of state bureaucratic collective capitalism. The workers of China never became the owners of the means of production.

All of this disturbed Mao Zedong, who thought of himself as the revolution, as truth, as the original motive force of the revolution. The landlords, rich peasants, and capitalists had been overthrown, and the intellectuals had been rejected as rightists. Where in the socialist revolution was the bourgeoisie? He made the blind judgment that "They are in the Communist Party itself. They are the capitalist roaders who have taken power within the party." He did not realize that in accordance with the fact that the nation was "hardly different from the old society," it was none other than the top man, the boss of the "bureaucratic class" or "capitalist roaders who have taken power within the party," that is, Mao himself. This impoverished, empty, loyal, great, frightening, murderous "socialism," which the dead Marx would not have accepted, was rejected by the people.

The nature of Chinese society being what it is, those who run down to the Shenzhen special economic zone and say that it is, "except for the five-starred red flag, entirely capitalist," those defenders of the true way who rail against "bourgeois liberalism" when the people and intellectuals courageously break through the old "Marxist-Leninist taboos" in the more relaxed atmosphere of the reforms, these people are no more than dead ghosts mourning over their own lost souls. China is what it is: a Third World nation with a backward economy that has taken the usual path of state bureaucratic capitalism. So for China the question of being "capitalist" or of being "socialist" is not a real issue. The so-called four fundamental principles are no more than four meaningless, useless totems used by the defenders of the true way to frighten people. The important issue is to discard the Mao Zedong style of state bureaucratic capitalism and to take a more humanistic, rational, open, democratic road that will bring prosperity to the people more quickly.

Following the Third Plenum of Eleventh Central Committee, a great social reform that was welcomed heartily by the people spread throughout China, and it was Hu Yaobang who stood at the forefront of this great tide of reform. When we transcend individual emotions and stand back from the misunderstandings of the historical moment to evaluate objectively the achievements of one of the top leaders of the CCP, the important thing is to see whether or not he listened to the people, was faithful to the interests of the nation and the people, and was following the tide of historical development.

When Hu Yaobang joined the revolution back in the days of the Jiangxi Soviet, he once said, "Let me see. There are ninety-nine bad things about joining the Communist Party. Those at the front suffer hardship, those at the back have it easy. Those in the front have to face the spears of the enemy, those at the back just stay out of it. You may have your head cut off or be thrown in prison. You are forced to do very dangerous work. If there aren't enough uniforms you have to give yours to someone else. If there's not enough to eat, you have to let the masses eat first while you go hungry. . . . As for the good things about it, it seems to me there is only one, you give yourself wholeheartedly to serving the people and the people protect and support you."[5]

Having lived through fifty years of political storms and change, the old guard within the party have forced Hu Yaobang to resign because he advocated breaking through the taboos of Marxism-Leninism and moved China one step forward by reforming the political system, because of his "three-don'ts" policy toward intellectuals (don't hit anyone with a stick, don't pull anyone's hair, don't put labels on people) and the three liberalizations (be tolerant, generous, and relaxed), because he advocated implementing a policy of the five changes in the cadre corps of the party, because he expressed sympathy with the democracy movement of the Chinese students. Clearly, Hu remained faithful to his ideals for half a century. This is indeed rare and admirable.

Hu Yaobang and his comrades had begun to right everything that the Mao Zedong era had turned upside down. He had resolutely begun the movement to vindicate those who had been unjustly accused. He had firmly led and developed the great debate over "practice is the only test of truth," had liberated the thinking of the people, had shattered the old idols and forced the "whatever clique" from power. He had actively implemented the production responsibility system in agriculture and returned the land to the peasants, and he had encouraged the impoverished peasants to use every means to fight for prosperity. He had implemented policies of tolerance and liberalization for intellectuals, creating a fluorishing academic and artistic atmosphere unknown since Liberation. He boldly supported the opening to the outside, letting the winds of contemporary civilization blow across the ancient lands of China, bringing economic reform to the cities and reforms to the political system. He has indeed exerted all his energy in bringing China into the modern world. But he has been forced to resign by the old men. That we now will not be able to observe and evaluate the continuing work of Hu Yaobang is most unfortunate for the Chinese nation.

But based just on Hu Yaobang's life and achievements described here, we may say that he is a man of great character, a communist who has taken the ideas, cares, and worries of the people as his own, who has dared to uphold the truth and to right wrongs. He is a great politician who could feel the pulse of the times and follow the course of history. As a leader of reform he has always looked ahead and broken new ground. At a turning point in Chinese history, he has done everything he possibly could do.

This does not mean, of course, that Hu has not made some mistakes. He himself once said that he had been 2 percent wrong. This probably referred to the period of the "Anti-Rightist" movement when he unthinkingly seized a number of rightists in the Communist Youth League organization. It may also refer to his agreement with the criticism of Peng Dehuai at the Lushan Conference in 1959. These were of course mistakes, but they were not severe. Considering the historical conditions of the time, they were understandable.

I would argue that Hu's one big mistake was in the 1960s when he pushed hard at the conference of the Central Committee of the Communist Youth League for studying the works of Mao Zedong and for the movement to learn from Lei Feng. We might ask, if all of China's young people had been like Lei Feng and become "whatever" followers who only "read the works of Chairman Mao, listened to the words of Chairman Mao, and did whatever Chairman Mao told them to do," what hope would there be for China's future?

Today, the historical facts again ruthlessly, unmistakably reveal one point: those who today are obstacles to reform in China, who have struck down Hu Yaobang, are precisely those leftist tyrants who want the people to continue to be like Lei Feng, who would again shackle the people with the thought of Mao Zedong and create surplus value for themselves. This is one of the painful lessons of history.

In 1898, Tan Sitong, from the same county as Hu Yaobang, was executed and made a martyr to the cause of the 1898 Reform Movement. In 1980, Hu Yaobang said with great feeling and intensity, "We are traveling a very uneven narrow mountain path. The wind and the

rain whip fiercely around our heads and beneath our feet lies a treacherous cliff. . . . The road is long, the path is difficult and dangerous. . . . In the great struggle for the four modernizations of our
country let us join hands and hearts and march forward!''[6]

Without any doubt, Hu Yaobang and Tan Sitong shared the same
spirit of devoting their lives to the struggle for the reform of China. The
record of Hu's achievements in reforming China will go down in
history. It is impossible to estimate the effect that the vibrations he has
set in motion will have on the future course of Chinese history. He is a
true son of the people, a flag of hope flying on high, a flag of battle
against the forces of evil and corruption.

Appendix

Members of the government who were formerly leaders in the Communist Youth League under Hu Yaobang, before January 1978

CCP Central Committee and Departments[1]

Hu Yaobang
Hu Qili
CCP Central Committee Secretariat
  Hao Jianxiu (f)
  Wang Zhaoguo
CC General Office
  Wen Jiabao, director
CC Propaganda Department
  Zhu Houze, director
  Zeng Delin, assistant director
CC Organization Department
  Wei Jianxing, director
  Wang Zhaohua, assistant director
CC International Liaison Department
  Zhu Liang, director
  Li Shuzheng, assistant director
CC Organs
  (Wang Zhaoguo, secretary, Party Committee)
All-China Youth Federation
  Liu Yandong (f), chairman
All-China Student Federation
  Liu Nengyuan, chairman
International Youth Committee
  Lu Jinlian
Youth League Central Committee
  Song Defu, first secretary
All-China Women's Federation
  Hu Dehua (f), secretary, Party Organization Committee
People's Daily
  Qian Liren, secretary, Party Committee
Central Party School
  Feng Wenbin, vice-president

State Council

Qiao Shi, vice-premier
Ministry of Foreign Affairs
  Wu Xueqian, minister

Ministry of Culture
 Wang Meng, minister
 Gao Zhan, vice-minister, Standing Committee
Ministry of National Safety
 Jia Chunwang, minister
Ministry of Textile Industry
 Wu Wenying, minister
Ministry of Broadcasting, Film, and Television
 Ai Zhisheng, minister
Political and Legal Commission
 Qiao Shi, secretary
Education Commission
 Yang Haibo, vice-chairman
Family Planning Commission
 Wang Wei, chairman
Physical Education Commission
 Li Menghua, chairman
General Office of Publishing
 Bian Chunguang, director[2]

Provincial, Municipal, Autonomous Region Branches

Beijing
 Xu Weicheng, assistant secretary
 Wang Jialiu (f), Municipal Committee, Standing Committee
 Han Kai, Municipal General Labor Union, chairman
 Guan Shixiong, Municipal CPPCC, vice-chairman
Shanghai
 Jiang Zemin, municipal mayor
Tianjin
 Li Ruihuan, Municipal Committee secretary, mayor
Fujian
 Hu Ping, governor
 Chen Guangyi, first secretary, Provincial Committee
Gansu
 Ma Zuling, Standing Committee, Provincial Committee
Guizhou
 Hu Jintao, secretary, Provincial Committee
 Wang Chaowen, assistant secretary
Hebei
 Jie Feng, governor
 Xing Chongzhi, secretary, Provincial Committee
Hubei
 Qian Lianlu, assistant secretary, Provincial Committee
Inner Mongolia
 Zhang Shuguang, secretary, Provincial Committee

Jiangsu

  Hu Fuming, Standing Committee, Provincial Committee

Jiangxi

  Wan Shaoquan (f), secretary, Provincial Committee

Liaoning

  Li Changchun, governor, assistant secretary

Qinghai

  Huang Jingbo, secretary, Provincial Committee

Shandong

  Liang Buting, secretary, Provincial Committee

Shaanxi

  Bai Jinian, secretary, Provincial Committee

Shanxi

  Li Ligong, secretary, Provincial Committee

  Xu Jianchun (f), vice-chairman, Standing Committee; Standing Committee, National

People's Congress

Notes:

1. Most names in the chart were part of the Communist Youth League when Hu Yaobang was its first secretary. A few were strongly supported and promoted by Hu in his campaign to train and promote the third echelon.

2. After January 16, 1987, when Hu resigned as secretary-general of the party, Zhu Houze, director of the Propaganda Department, and Bian Chunguang, director of the General Office of Publishing, also resigned.

Notes

Note to Epigraph

1. Petöfi Sandor (1823–1849) was a Hungarian poet and revolutionary. This quote comes from a letter he wrote to a friend on July 17, 1947. China's famous writer Lu Xun used this same quote in his collection *Ye cao* (Weeds) in 1926.—ed.

Notes to Chapter 1

1. Wang Ruhuang and Zou Junjie, eds., *Liuyang Gazetteer* (1874), *juan* 2.

2. Strictly speaking, Hu Yaobang's native place is Zhonghe village, Zhonghe brigade, Zhonghe commune (originally called Zhonghe township). Zhonghe village is a small, multisurname mountain village comprising some thirty families. The Hu clan was considered an important village clan with many households and their own clan temple.

3. Quoted in *Baokan wenzhai* (Excerpts from the Press), August 7, 1984.

4. *Dagong bao*, overseas edition, March 26, 1984.

5. Nie Yuanzi was a female philosophy instructor who wrote a big-character poster (*dazi bao*) attacking the Beijing University administration in May 1966 and was praised by Mao Zedong.—trans.

Notes to Chapter 2

1. *Zhongguo laonian* (China's Elderly) (October 1983), pp. 6–7.

2. Ibid., p. 6.

3. Modern schools in Hunan date back to the work of Tan Sitong. In the fall of 1895 he brought together men dedicated to progress and founded the first mathematics society in Liuyang county, the forerunner of new studies in Hunan. In October 1897, to promote the reform movement, Tan Sitong, with the support of Governor Chen Baozhen, shook off the interference of the Hunan conservative clique headed by Ye Dehui and in Changsha founded an Institute of Contemporary Affairs (Shiwu Xuetang) in preparation for training new talent that could master both Chinese and foreign studies. From this point on, new-style schools were set up throughout the province.

4. *Peng Dehuai zhishu* (Peng Dehuai's Own Account) (Beijing: People's Publishing House, 1981), p. 145.

5. *Jiefang jiangling zhuan* (Biographies of PLA Generals), vol. 1 (Beijing: Liberation Army Press, 1984), p. 336.

Notes to Chapter 3

1. *Gongchan guoji youguan Zhongguo geming de wenxianziliao* (Materials of the Communist International Concerning the Chinese Revolution), vol. 2 (Beijing: Chinese Social Science Press, 1981), p. 88.

2. *Selected Works of Mao Zedong*, Chinese edition, vol. 1 (Beijing: People's Publishing House, 1967), p. 103.

3. Central Committee of the Chinese Communist Party, "The New Revolutionary Tide and Achieving Victory First in One or Several Provinces," June 11, 1930. Photocopy of current decisions passed by the Conference of the Politburo.

4. *Baodong zhoukan* (Insurrection Weekly) 13 (May 26, 1931). Published by the Soviet Cultural Society of Liuyang County.

5. Cai Xiaoqian, *Jiangxi Suqu, Hongjun xi cuan huiyi* (Recollections of the Jiangxi Soviet and the Red Army Flight West) (Taipei: Chinese Communist Studies Press, 1978), pp. 89–90.

6. *Hongse Zhonghua* (Red China), July 12, 1933.

7. *Baixing* (The Hundred Names) (Hong Kong) (June 1985).

8. Cai Xiaoqian, *Jiangxi Suqu*, p. 92.

9. *Hongse Zhonghua*, April 7, 1934.

Notes to Chapter 4

1. *Zhongguo Gongnonghongjun Diyi Fangmian Jun changzheng ji* (Record of the Long March of the First Front Army of the Chinese Workers and Peasants Red Army) (Beijing: People's Publishing House, 1955), p. 58.

2. According to the *Zunyi huiyi wenxian* (Zunyi Conference Documents) (Beijing: People's Publishing House, 1985), the Red Army took Zunyi on January 7, 1935; the Zunyi Conference was held from the 15th through the 17th. But according to the author's evidence, Zunyi was taken on January 6, 1935, and the Zunyi Conference was held from the 14th through the 16th.

3. Wu Xiuquan, *Wo de licheng* (My Career) (Beijing: Liberation Army Press, 1984), p. 84.

4. *Zunyi huiyi de guangmang* (The Radiant Splendor of the Zunyi Conference) (Beijing: Liberation Army Press, 1984), p. 233.

5. Guo Hualun, *Zhonggong shilun* (On the History of the CCP), vol. 3 (Taipei: Institute for International Relations, 1983), p. 59.

6. Cai Xiaoqian, *Jiangxi suqu*, p. 376.

7. *Xinghuo liaoyuan* (A Single Spark Can Start a Prairie Fire) (Beijing: Liberation Army Press, 1985) 1:69.

Notes to Chapter 5

1. *Selected Works of Mao Zedong* 1:136.

2. For a translation of whole poem, see Stuart Schram, *Mao Zedong* (Penguin Books, 1972), p. 195—trans.

3. Shen Yikui and Yuan Xuemuo (Qing dynasty), ed., *Shilou Gazetteer, juan* 3, "Customs," and *juan* 2, "Population."

4. *Xinghuo liaoyuan* 4:64.

5. *Zhonggong yanjiu* (Chinese Communist Studies) (Taipei) 15, 8:47.

6. Yang Dezhi, *Hengge mashang* (Riding into Battle) (Beijing: Liberation Army Arts Press, 1984), p. 180.

7. *Zhongguo qingnian yundong shi* (A History of Chinese Youth Movements) (Beijing: China Youth Press, 1984), p. 142.

8. Edgar Snow, *Random Notes on Red China*, Japanese edition (1975), p. 98. See also *Zhongguo Gongchandang zuzhishi ziliao huibian* (A Compilation of Materials on the Organizational History of the CCP) (Beijing: Red Flag Press, 1983).

9. *Zhongguo qingnian yundong shi*, p. 159.

10. Zhang Guotao, *Wo de huiyi* (My Reminiscences), vol. 3 (Hong Kong: Mingbao Yuekan Press, 1974), pp. 1263–67.

11. Bing Kun, ed., *Wang Weizhou zhuan* (Biography of Wang Weizhou) (Beijing: Zhongguo Zhanwang Press, 1984), p. 226.

12. Zhang Guotao, *Wo de huiyi* 3:1271.

13. *People's Daily*, December 26, 1983.

14. Lin Biao, "Conclusions on the Third Term All-School Cadre Meeting of Resistance University," photocopy.

15. Ibid.

16. *Zhonggong yanjiu* (Taipei) 15:47.

17. *Huiyi Wang Jiaxiang* (Remembrances of Wang Jiaxiang) (Beijing: People's Publishing House, 1985), p. 1.

18. See *People's Daily*, May 29, 1984.

19. *Ming bao yuekan* (Ming Bao Monthly) (Hong Kong), enlarged edition (January 1985), p. 4.

20. Ibid.

21. *Huiyi Wang Jiaxiang*, p. 102.

22. *Selected Works of Wang Ming*, vol. 5 (Tokyo: Jigu Press, 1975), p. 246.

Notes to Chapter 6

1. *Selected Works of Mao Zedong* 3:998.

2. *Mao Zedong junshi wenxuan* (Selected Military Writings of Mao Zedong), Japan reprint, classified edition (*neibu*) (1985), pp. 294, 299.

3. *Nie Rongzhen huiyi lu* (Recollections of Nie Rongjen), vol. 3 (Beijing: Liberation Army Press, 1984), pp. 647–63.

4. Ibid.

5. Ibid.

6. *Xinghuo liaoyuan* 9:305–10.

7. Ibid.

8. Ibid.

9. Yang Dezhi, *Hengge mashang*, pp. 327, 352.

10. *Nie Rongjen huiyi lu* 3:647–63, 682.

11. Ibid.

12. Yang Dezhi, *Hengge mashang*, pp. 327, 352.

13. *Nie Rongjen huiyi lu* 3:647–63, 682.

14. *Mao Zedong shuxin xuanji* (Selected Letters of Mao Zedong) (Beijing: People's Publishing House, 1983), p. 312.

15. *Mao Zedong junshi wenxuan*, pp. 507–14.

16. This story comes from Ren Baige, *Zai Xu shuai zhihui xia* (Under the Command of General Xu) (Beijing: Liberation Army Press, 1984), pp. 415–28.

17. *Mao Zedong shuxin xuanji*, p. 312.

18. *Zai Xu shuai zhihui xia*, pp. 415–28.

19. *People's Daily*, overseas edition, November 20, 1985.

20. *Zai Xu shuai zhihui xia*, p. 329.

21. *Jiefang jun bao* (Liberation Army News), September 23, 1985.

22. Ibid.
23. Ibid.
24. Ibid.
25. Ibid.

Notes to Chapter 7

1. *Xi'nanqu jianshui zhanxing tiaoli* (Articles on Rent Reduction in the Southwest District), photocopy.
2. *People's Daily*, June 6, 1979.
3. *Xiang Xibei Xinan jinjun* (March into the Northwest and Southwest) (Chengdu: Sichuan People's Press, 1985), pp. 252–54.
4. Ibid.
5. *Xinwen yanjiu ziliao* (Research Materials on Journalism), vol. 8 (Beijing: Xinhua Press, 1981), p. 27.
6. *Selected Works of Mao Zedong*, Chinese edition, vol. 5 (Beijing: People's Publishing House, 1977), pp. 83–87.
7. *Liaowang* (Outlook) (Beijing) 45 (November 5, 1984): 8.
8. *Selected Works of Mao Zedong* 5:83–87.
9. *Xinwen yanjiu ziliao* 21:3.

Notes to Chapter 8

1. *People's Daily*, October 4, 1955. Gao Gang, who had first pushed the agricultural production cooperative movement in the Northwest, would have been among these radicals, but he was purged by 1954.
2. *Selected Works of Mao Zedong* 5:182.
3. *Zhongguo qingnian* (China Youth) 22 (1955).
4. *People's Daily*, November 22, 1960.
5. *Zhongguo qingnian bao* (China Youth News), August 30, 1985.
6. Cited in Kobayashi Bundan, ed. and trans., *The China Youth Movement* (Meiji Library Press, 1966) (in Japanese).
7. *Collected Documents of the Eighth Congress of the Chinese Communist Party*, photocopy.
8. *Xinwen yanjiu ziliao*, p. 32.
9. *Selected Works of Mao Zedong* 5:430.
10. *People's Daily*, May 16, 1957.
11. The Plum Blossom Laughter (*Mei hua xiao*) column of the Qinghua University Jinggang Shan (Red Guards), eds., *Pipan Liu, Deng xiuzhengzhuyi luxian zhuanji* (Collection of Criticisms of the Liu-Deng Revisionist Line) (1969), pp. 78–84.
12. *Sanzhong Quanhui yilai zhongyao wenxian xuanbian* (Selected Major Documents since the Third Congress), classified edition (*neibu*), vol. 1 (Beijing: People's Publishing House, 1982), p. 381.
13. *Beijing zhichun* (Beijing Spring) 3 (1979).

Notes to Chapter 9

1. *Hong qi* (Red Flag) 9 (1958).
2. Mao Zedong's second talk to the second session of the Eighth Congress of the CCP [May 1958], photocopy.
3. Mao Zedong's talk at the Sixth Plenum of the Eighth Central Committee

[December 1958], photocopy.

4. *Zhongguo qingnian* 18 (1958).

5. Ibid., no. 20.

6. Ibid., no. 21.

7. Ibid.

8. Ibid., no 23.

9. *Chen Yun wenxuan* (Selected Works of Chen Yun), classified edition (*neibu ben*) (Beijing: People's Publishing House, 1981), p. 93. [This letter is translated in *Chinese Economic Studies* 15, 3–4 (Spring-Summer 1982): 127.—ed.]

10. *Peng Dehuai zishu*, pp. 282–86.

11. *Mao Zedong sixiang wansui* (Long Live the Thought of Mao Zedong) (Japanese edition) (Modern Criticism Press, 1974), p. 308.

12. *Zhongguo qingnian* 19 (1959).

13. That is, hadn't the original editor of *People's Daily*, Deng Tuo, just been fired for not exaggerating? Indeed, Wu Lengxi, who took over at *People's Daily* in 1958, was said to have "learned the lessons of Deng Tuo's mistakes with Mao"—that is, he was unlikely to resist Mao's whims. Deng Tuo had written the column "Three-Family Village" in the Beijing Municipal Party's theory journal, *Frontline*, in the early 1960s. This column is generally regarded as a critique of Maoist excesses.—ed.

14. *Zhonggong wenhua dageming ziliao huibian* (Collected Source Materials on the Chinese Communist Great Cultural Revolution) (Hong Kong: Mingbao Monthly Press, 1969), p. 457.

15. *Mingbao yuekan* (Mingbao Monthly) (August 1980).

16. *Zhongguo qingnian* 9 (1963).

17. See *Pipan Liu, Deng*.

18. Yu Qiuli (1914-), from Sichuan, is a Long March veteran who served with Hu Yaobang in the civil war and as a high military planning officer after Liberation. He was criticized, but not purged, in the Cultural Revolution. Liu Lanbo (1908-), from Liaoning province, was active in Yan'an from 1940 and in Beijing ministries after Liberation. He was purged in March 1967.—ed.

Notes to Chapter 10

1. *Zhongguo qingnian bao*, May 4, 1966.

2. *People's Daily*, June 16, 1966.

3. Ibid., overseas edition, May 31, 1986.

4. *Zhonggong dang shi renwu zhuan* (Biographies in Chinese Communist Party History), vol. 14 (Xian: Shaanxi People's Press, 1984), p. 104.

5. Zhu Zhongli, *Canlan hongye* (Magnificent Red Leaves) (Changsha: Hunan People's Press, 1985), pp. 204–205.

6. Ibid.

7. Quoted from *Hong qi* (February 1976).

Notes to Chapter 11

1. *People's Daily*, February 17 and March 14, 1977.

2. *Feiqing yuebao* (Situation on the Mainland Monthly) (Taipei: Institute on International Relations, March 1980), p. 62.

3. "Hu Yaobang's Talk of November 1980 to the Central Committee Politburo," photocopy of a Japanese language edition.

4. *Deng Xiaoping wenxuan* (Selected Works of Deng Xiaoping) (Beijing: People's

Publishing House, 1983), p. 35.

   5. *Feiqing yuebao* (July 1980), p. 86.

   6. *Deng Xiaoping wenxuan*, p. 109.

   7. *Zhengming* (Contention) (Hong Kong) (August 1980), p. 57.

   8. *People's Daily*, December 24, 1978.

   9. *Zhengming* (August 1980), p. 58.

  10. *Mingbao yuekan* (August 1980).

  11. *Zhengming* (August 1980), p. 58.

  12. *Feiqing yuebao* (March 1980), p. 66.

  13. Copy of Deng Xiaoping's original manuscript.

  14. *People's Daily*, March 1, 1980.

  15. *Zhengming* (August 1980), p. 63.

  16. *Beijing zhichun* (January 1979).

  17. "Hu Yaobang's Talk of November 1980 to the Central Committee Politburo."

  18. Central Directive No. 23 of 1981, Japanese translation from *Documents of the Central Committee of the CCP*.

  19. Ibid.

Notes to Chapter 12

   1. Feng Jian et al., *Zhongnanhai de chuntian* (Zhongnanhai Spring) (Beijing: Xinhua Press, 1983), p. 7.

   2. *Baokan wenzhai* (Excerpts from the Press) (Beijing), classified reference, May 8, 1984.

   3. *People's Daily*, May 31, 1980.

   4. Feng Jian et al., *Zhongnanhai de chuntian*, p. 8.

   5. *Da gong bao* (Hong Kong), October 16, 1985.

   6. *Xinhua wenzhai* (Excerpts from New China), September 1984, pp. 168-70.

   7. Ibid.

   8. Ibid.

   9. *People's Daily*, January 7, 1985.

  10. Ibid., overseas edition, November 18, 1986.

  11. "Deng Liqun's Lecture of June 4, 1983 at the Central Party School," photocopy.

  12. "Deng Xiaoping's Talk at the Second Plenum of the Twelfth Central Committee," photocopy.

  13. Central Committee 1983 Document No. 37, photocopy.

  14. *People's Daily*, October 28, 1983.

  15. *Chen Yun wenxuan 1965-1985* (Selected Works of Chen Yun: 1965-1985) (Beijing: People's Publishing House, 1986), p. 267.

  16. *Deng Xiaoping wenxuan*, pp. 339-40.

  17. *Liaowang yuekan* (Outlook Monthly) 8 (1982): 2-3.

  18. *Xinxi huibao* (News Gazette) (classified distribution), January 11, 1985.

  19. *Liaowang zhoukan* (Outlook Weekly) 8 (1985): 4.

  20. *Yomiuri shinbun* (Tokyo), February 1, 1987.

Notes to Chapter 13

   1. Wang Juxing and Zou Junjie, eds., *Liuyang xianzhi, juan* 6, "Food and Commodities."

   2. Ibid.

   3. Ibid.

4. Ibid., *juan* 5.

5. Luo Xianglin [Lo Hsiang-lin], *A Guide to Studies of the Hakka*, Japanese edition (Taiwan Jicun Shanghuishe, 1942), p. 102. Also, the first two sections of this chapter are based on the following works: Dai Guohui [Tai Kuo-hui], *Taiwan and the Taiwanese*, Japanese edition (Yanwen Press, 1979); Dai Guohui, *Taiwan shi yanjiu* (Studies in the History of Taiwan) (Taipei: Yuanliu Press, 1985); Han Suyin, *The Crippled Tree*, Japanese edition (Spring and Autumn Press, 1970).

6. Lai Jixi, gen. ed., *Chongzheng Tongren xipu* (Genealogy of the Hakka) (Hong Kong: n.p., 1924), *juan* 1. The title derives from Hakka lore: They consider themselves true (*zhengtong*) Han Chinese who revere (*chongbai*) the culture of their ancient homeland on the North China plain. Hakka associations around the world call themselves "Chongzheng Associations."

7. *Guangjiao jing* (Wide-angle Lens) (Hong Kong) (May 1980), p. 35.

8. *Mingbao yuekan* (August 1980), p. 12.

9. *People's Daily*, overseas edition, May 31, 1986.

10. Zhu Zhongli, *Canlan hong ye*, p. 205.

11. *Mingbao yuekan* (January 19, 1986).

12. *Bei jiang* (Northern Borders) 1 (1984): 52.

13. Zhu Zhongli, *Canlan hong ye*, p. 108.

Notes to Chapter 14

1. *Selected Works of Marx and Engels*, Chinese edition, vol. 1 (Beijing: People's Publishing House, 1973), p. 228.

2. *People's Daily*, July 2, 1981.

3. Ibid., June 23, 1986.

4. *Zhongguo qingnian* 23 (1958).

5. *People's Daily*, December 26, 1983.

6. Ibid., July 7, 1964.

7. Ibid., July 2, 1981.

8. *Mao Zedong sixiang wansui*, pp. 557–58.

9. Ibid.

10. *People's Daily*, March 14, 1983.

11. *Sanzhong Quanhui yilai*, 1:347–71.

12. *People's Daily*, July 1, 1986.

13. Ibid.

14. *Baixing* (June 1985), pp. 52–53.

15. United Front Work Department of the Central Committee of the CCP, Office for Research on Documents of the Central Committee of the CCP, ed., *Xin shiqi tongyi zhanxian wenxian xuanbian* (Selected Documents on the New Period United Front) (CCP Central Party School, 1985), pp. 93–94.

16. *People's Daily*, June 12, 1986.

17. Ibid., September 8, 1982 [English translation: *The Twelfth National Congress of the CPC*] (Beijing: Foreign Languages Press, 1982), p. 55].

18. *Sanzhong Quanhui yilai* 2:1112–28.

19. Ibid.

20. *People's Daily*, June 23, 1986.

Notes to Chapter 15

1. Gong Liu (1927-), from Jiangxi, is a poet and writer who worked for years in the

PLA Cultural Department. In 1957 he was purged as a "rightist." In 1978 he became editor of *Anhui wenyi*. Among his famous poetry collections is *Liming de cheng* (City of Dawn). See *Zhongguo wenxuejia cidian: Xiandai, diyi fence* (A Dictionary of Chinese Writers: Modern Period, Volume 1) (Sichuan People's Publishing House, 1979), pp. 74–75.

2. Quoted from *Hong qi* 6 (1976), title page.
3. Quoted from ibid. 3 (1975), title page.
4. Karl Marx, *Das Kapital*, Chinese edition, vol. 2 (Beijing: People's Publishing House, 1964), p. 18.
5. *People's Daily*, March 20, 1986.
6. *Sanzhong Quanhui yilai* 1:386–87.

Index

About the Author

Yang Zhongmei was born in Shanghai in 1945. He is a 1967 graduate of the department of humanities, Shanghai East China Teachers' College. In 1981 he went to Tokyo to study at Rikkyo University, where he received his Ph.D. in 1987. There he did research on the history of the Chinese Communist Party and Sino-Japanese relations. His Master's thesis was on "Qu Qiubai and His Thought." Yang's major publications include "A Study of the Gao Gang, Rao Shushi Incident," "A Study of the Zunyi Conference," and "The Fiction of the Writer Zhang Xianliang."